CW01508359

Introducing Practical Discourse Analysis

This introduction to discourse analysis provides students with an accessible, yet comprehensive, overview of the subject and all the skills and knowledge needed to become capable discourse analysts. Through practical coverage and advice, this book introduces discourse analysis as a set of analytical tools and perspectives that can be applied to an assignment, project, or thesis. Across seven chapters the book is divided according to practical themes and topics, allowing students to establish a deeper understanding of discourse analysis. Students will be taught how to identify and categorize established theories and methodologies, including conversation analysis, critical discourse analysis, and more. Through figures, examples, chapter summaries, and more than thirty learning activities, this volume teaches students the foundational skills to approach the analytical process with more confidence and background knowledge, making it suitable for undergraduate and graduate students studying discourse analysis.

CHRISTOPHER J. JENKS is Professor and Chair of Intercultural Communication at Utrecht University. He has also worked in the United States, the United Kingdom, South Korea, Hong Kong, and Denmark, specializing in the way spoken and written discourse performs a range of communication actions and indexes a number of social phenomena. He is author and editor of more than ten books and numerous journals, including *Researching Classroom Discourse: A Student Guide* (Routledge, 2020) and *New Frontiers in Language and Technology* (Cambridge University Press, 2023).

Introducing Practical Discourse Analysis

CHRISTOPHER J. JENKS

Utrecht University, Netherlands

CAMBRIDGE
UNIVERSITY PRESS

Shaftesbury Road, Cambridge CB2 8EA, United Kingdom

One Liberty Plaza, 20th Floor, New York 10006, USA

477 Williamstown Road, Port Melbourne, VIC 3207, Australia

314–321, 3rd Floor, Plot 3, Splendor Forum, Jasola District Centre,
New Delhi – 110025, India

103 Penang Road, #05–06/07, Visioncrest Commercial, Singapore 238467

Cambridge University Press is part of Cambridge University Press & Assessment,
a department of the University of Cambridge.

We share the University's mission to contribute to society through the pursuit of
education, learning and research at the highest international levels of excellence.

www.cambridge.org
Information on this title: www.cambridge.org/highereducation/isbn/9781009250535
DOI: 10.1017/9781009250498

First published 2025

Printed in the United Kingdom by CPI Group Ltd, Croydon CR0 4YY, 2025

A catalogue record for this publication is available from the British Library

Library of Congress Cataloging-in-Publication Data
Names: Jenks, Christopher Joseph, author.
Title: Introducing practical discourse analysis / Christopher J. Jenks.
Description: Cambridge, United Kingdom ; New York, NY : Cambridge
University Press, 2025. | Series: Cambridge introductions to language
and linguistics | Includes bibliographical references and index.
Identifiers: LCCN 2024028769 | ISBN 9781009250535 (hardback) | ISBN
9781009250542 (paperback) | ISBN 9781009250498 (ebook)
Subjects: LCSH: Discourse analysis. | LCGFT: Introductory works.
Classification: LCC P302 .J45 2025 | DDC 401/.41–dc23/eng/20240814
LC record available at https://lccn.loc.gov/2024028769

ISBN 978-1-009-25053-5 Hardback
ISBN 978-1-009-25054-2 Paperback

Additional resources for this publication at www.cambridge.org/jenks

Contents

1 What Is Discourse?

CHAPTER OUTLINE

Learning Outcomes

This chapter has two aims. First, the chapter establishes what it means to do *discourse analysis*. Second, the chapter defines, and identifies examples of, *discourse*.

The contents of the chapter are organized according to the following learning outcomes. After reading this chapter:

1. You will know what discourse analysis is;
2. You will understand that there are many types of discourse;
3. You will understand that discourse is your object of study;
4. You will know how your object of study fits within a research project.

1.1 A Short Guide to This Book

This book is a practical guide to *doing* discourse analysis. The emphasis on the act of doing is important, as discourse analysis is often discussed from a theoretical perspective. This book departs from this tradition by providing accessible and practical overviews and strategies suitable for the novice discourse analyst. Doing discourse analysis requires collecting and analyzing **data**, or what this book refers to as your **object of study**.

Chapters 1–3 are designed to help you identify and analyze your object of study. Chapter 1 helps you identify an object of study by providing examples of discourse. Chapter 2 helps you understand what an analysis is by discussing its internal structure as it would be presented to an audience in written form. Chapter 3 helps you conduct an analysis by reviewing the different analytic perspectives and levels that can be adopted. The structure of an analysis is foundational to understanding how to analyze an object of study, so it is important to read Chapter 2 before Chapter 3.

Chapters 4–6 build on Chapter 3 by showing how context, researcher subjectivities, and theory are central to adding nuance and detail to your analysis. Chapter 7 ends the book by introducing a model for doing discourse analysis which summarizes the themes, issues, concepts, and principles introduced in previous chapters while attending to the issue of research questions.

Summary 1.1
1. This book uses **object of study** as a synonym for **data**.
2. Chapters 1–3 help you identify and analyze your object of study.
3. Chapters 4–6 help you strengthen your analysis.
4. Chapter 7 presents a model for doing discourse analysis.

1.2 Defining Discourse Analysis

Defining discourse analysis is ostensibly simple in concept. The endeavor involves explaining what discourse is and discussing how discourse is analyzed. Take, for example, the definitions taken from two popular introductory books on discourse analysis.

In this book we take a primarily linguistic approach to the analysis of discourse. We examine how humans use language to communicate and, in particular, how addressers construct linguistic messages for addressees and how addressees work on linguistic messages in order to interpret them.

(Brown & Yule, 1983, p. ix).

Discourse analysis is the study of what we humans do with language and how we do it … Discourse analysis is a big field made up of many different relatively small groups, each doing discourse analysis in their own way; each using their own terminology and defending their own theories of language, communication, and society.

(Gee, 2018, p. ix).

Both definitions identify three facets of discourse analysis: humans, language use, and approaches. The first two facets are related to your object of study; that is, humans and language use represent the discourse in discourse analysis. The third facet is related to your analysis. That is, approaches represent the analysis in discourse analysis. Each aspect will be unpacked below for the purpose of defining discourse analysis.

First, discourse analysis entails studying humans. Although this statement may appear self-evident, the "human factor" is incredibly salient to how discourse analysis is put into practice. That is, discourse analysis is more than just describing language. Discourse analysts recognize that humans use language for, and modify their communication according to, a number of social and cultural factors. For example, a school's policy on providing feedback will likely dictate whether and how a teacher corrects students. The human factor additionally represents all aspects of society that influence why and how a particular language feature is used. For instance, a country's popular culture will likely dictate societal preferences for a particular regional accent. Aspects relevant to the human factor are approximate to what Gee (2014) refers to as "big D Discourse."

Learning Activity 1.1 helps you reflect on the human factor in discourse.

Learning Activity 1.1　The Human Factor

In this exercise, the learning objective is to help you become aware of how the human factor influences how we think about and use language. Reflecting on the human factor is an excellent way of identifying potential topics to investigate.

This learning activity is based on an actual class that was taught by the author at a university in Asia. Approximately fifty students were asked in one in-class assignment to list ten words that they associate with "English speaker." Some of the top answers are listed below. Please think of why many of the students provided these answers. Both the student answers, and your responses to them, are likely to offer examples of the human factor.

Top Answers Given

1. Foreigners
2. American
3. British
4. Global
5. White people

What do these five answers say about the students? How does growing up with a particular language, such as English, shape how you think about yourself and engage in communication with others? Are there aspects of your life that influence how you feel about different languages? Your answers to these questions offer some examples of how the human factor influences how we think about and use language.

Second, discourse analysis entails studying language use. This focus should not be confused with the study of language, which is limited to descriptions of linguistic features, such as looking at a series of disparate syntactic structures without considering the human factor. The use in language use denotes a concern for the situational factors (i.e., context) that influence, and are influenced by, communication. Language use is approximate to what Gee (2014) refers to as "little d discourse."

Identifying and understanding these situational factors requires examining the functions of language. For example, "hello" may function as a greeting, an elicitation, or a pre-announcement depending on the communicative situation in which the word is used.

Language use can also be understood by examining its organization. All communicative situations possess an organization with parts that can be examined individually or collectively. For instance, a speech, a mission statement, a work email, and a conversation between friends all possess a narrative organization: a beginning, a middle, and an end. A discourse analyst may wish to examine the entire narrative structure of a mission statement or look at only the beginnings. Furthermore, some aspects of language use possess an organization. For example, topic management and turn-taking, which are present in most conversational exchanges, are two aspects of language use that possess an organization. A discourse analyst may look at the entire turn-taking organization of a business meeting or examine just the organization of individual turns.

Learning Activity 1.2 helps you reflect on the two main ways of studying language use as a discourse analyst: function and organization.

Learning Activity 1.2 Language Use

In this two-part exercise, the learning objective is to help you understand that people do things with language and that there is an organization to how this "doing" is accomplished.

For the first part of this exercise, identify one or two language examples for each of the language functions identified below. One example for each language function is provided to get you started. Do some language examples possess multiple functions? Why can the same words, utterances, or texts perform multiple functions? Can you also think of other language functions not listed below?

Language function	*Example*
1. request	*"please help me"*
2. promise	*"it will not happen again"*
3. apologize	*"my fault"*
4. suggest	*"maybe try looking it up"*
5. question	*"are you hungry"*
6. introduce	*"this is my cousin"*
7. invite	*"tell me more"*
8. inform	*"This is your captain. We are currently flying at 30,000 feet"*
9. refuse	*"next time"*
10. respond	student raises hand (in response to *"any questions"*)

For the second part of this exercise, identify the communicative situations that you are likely to see or hear under the organization column. One example for each organizational feature is provided.

Organizational feature	*Example*
1. introduction	Job seekers introducing themselves during interviews.
2. beginning	Teachers starting their lectures.
3. topic management	Colleagues managing topics in meetings.
4. turn-taking	Friends interrupting each other during a conversation.
5. ending	Customers terminating unsolicited phone calls.

Can you think of any language functions that you are likely to experience in each example provided above?

Third, discourse analysis is made up of different approaches that can be used to study your object of study. The literature may refer to these approaches as theories, frameworks, methods, or methodologies. Approaches are created according to disciplinary traditions and interests, and therefore what analysis means and how it is put into practice will vary from one researcher to another. Collectively, these disciplinary traditions and interests create layers of interpretation that make it difficult to tease out the core principles of discourse analysis. Indeed, entire books and anthologies are devoted to explaining just one approach within discourse analysis.

This book strips away these disciplinary layers by identifying several core principles and practices that will help you get started with discourse analysis. For example, Chapter 3 presents the basic perspectives and levels of analysis that can be used to study your object of study.

The current section has defined discourse analysis as an area of study with three core facets: the human factor, language use, and approaches. Figure 1.1 offers a visual illustration of discourse analysis.

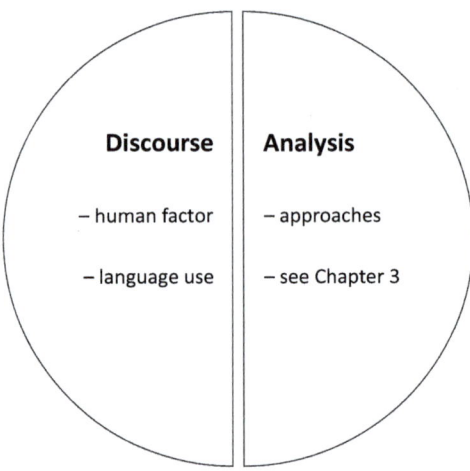

Discourse

– human factor

– language use

Analysis

– approaches

– see Chapter 3

FIGURE 1.1
Three aspects of
discourse analysis

Discourse analysis requires looking at both the human factor and language use, though there is considerable variation in how much attention is placed on each aspect of discourse. How a researcher approaches these two aspects of discourse is related to the analysis in discourse analysis (see Chapter 3).

The next step after defining discourse analysis is to consider examples of discourse. The next section, in providing examples of discourse, reveals possible objects of study for your research.

Summary 1.2

1. Discourse analysis can be broken into three parts: the human factor, language use, and approaches.
2. The discourse in discourse analysis consists of language use and the human factor.

1.3 Types of Discourse

Discourse is meaning. Humans ascribe meaning to all aspects of life from the utterances spoken by an individual during a fleeting moment with a stranger to religious principles that are preserved through texts and stories over many centuries. Furthermore, meaning can be found in more than just spoken words and texts. For example, symbols (e.g., company logos) and objects (e.g., a tall mountain) can possess meaning, creating discourse: a company logo can be associated with a sense of quality, or a tall mountain may be a part of folklore.

Meaning can also be found in belief systems or ideologies. For example, traditions that guide how families prepare and consume meals during important holidays represent meaning created by individuals within and across communities. Although belief systems and ideologies can be expressed in the material world though language and communication (e.g., praying before eating a meal), they get passed down from one generation to another and therefore transcend time and space.

Learning Activity 1.3 Reflecting on Discourse

In this exercise, the learning objective is to establish the ways in which discourse is all around you.

Complete the exercise by answering the questions in the left column. The right column addresses how your answers to these questions are related to, or are example of, discourse. The classroom is used as a point of reference.

The classroom	*Discourse*
1a. Think about a time when you were in a classroom if you are not presently in one now. Are there any implicit or explicit rules that determine how you should behave or communicate with the teacher and your fellow classmates, such as using a particular language, asking to speak, or leaving the classroom during a lecture?	1b. The implicit and explicit rules that you identified represent discourses. These discourses may be located in the material world, such as a sign on the wall reminding students to be quiet upon entering the room. In addition, classroom rules may not be located in the material world, such as the unwritten rule that students must raise their hands before talking.

The classroom	Discourse
2a. We are all made up of different social categories, such as man, woman, mother, sister, Asian, and student, to name a few. What are your social categories? What social categories are relevant and not relevant to your participation in classrooms? Why are some social categories relevant in the classroom while others are not?	2b. Your social categories are not only a part of your identity, but they can also be expressed as or through discourses. Your identity as a student is a discourse that can be expressed as a belief system (e.g., "I think students should respect their teachers.") or through language and communication (e.g., the types of questions that you ask your teacher versus your fellow classmates).
3a. What types of questions do teachers ask students? What types of questions do students ask teachers? Do teachers and students ask different questions? Why would teachers and students ask different questions?	3b. Discourse is all of the language spoken and written in classrooms, including question types. What is said, written, or otherwise communicated is influenced by other discourses, such as classroom rules and identities. For example, a teacher is more likely to ask questions to test understanding rather than to seek unknown information.

The questions in all three rows present opportunities to reflect on the discourses that occupy and shape classrooms. The first row demonstrates how discourse may or may not be located in the material world, persisting over time and space creating a history of experiences and belief systems. The second row shows how discourse is part of who we are, and illustrates how who we are may be tied to expectations to communicate in a particular way. The third row connects discourse with speaking and writing in general, and question asking in particular. Although speaking and writing are discourse examples that can stand alone as objects of study, language is shaped by other discourses, such as social rules and identities.

Discourse is pervasive, influencing how we think about, and manage, the world around us. Reflecting on the many discourses that influence one situation, such as the classroom, will get you closer to understanding what discourse analysis is capable of doing. With that said, stating that "discourse is meaning" or "discourse is pervasive" gives rise to a degree of openness or even ambiguity that is not helpful when it is time to identify a specific object of study. To address the ambiguity that comes with attempting to identify discourse, the following subsections identify seven types of objects of study that are commonly investigated in discourse analysis: (1) grammar; (2) actions and practices; (3) identities; (4) places and spaces; (5) stories; (6) ideologies; and (7) social structures. While not exhaustive, the list offers sufficient examples for readers to get started with discourse analysis (see Figure 1.2).

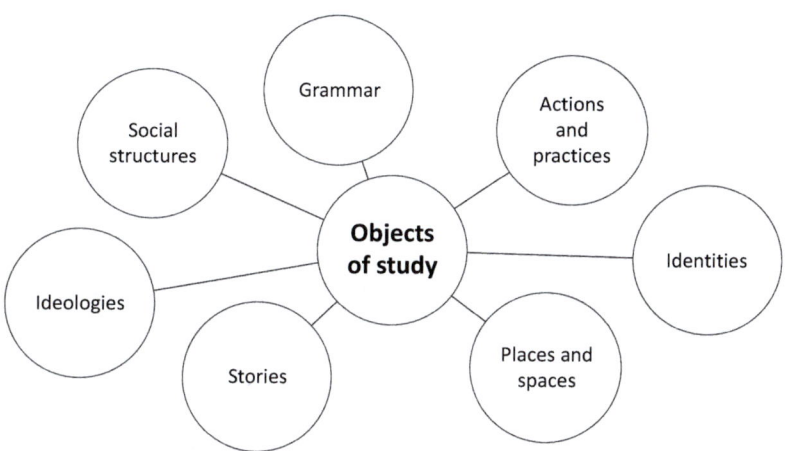

FIGURE 1.2
Objects of study

1.3.1 Discourse as Grammar

Discourse is connected to the grammar of a language. Grammar is a system of rules that outlines how words, sentences, utterances, and phrases should be structured and used. A linguistic approach to grammar is situated primarily at the sentence level, which involves studying grammatical rules separate from other sentences or discourse (i.e., studying language rather than language use). Conversely, discourse analysts are interested in how grammar connects multiple sentences or instances of discourse, creating meaning that is specific to a communicative situation.

To this end, a discourse approach to grammar looks at how grammatical items create meaning above the sentence level and beyond the language being used: these two discourse perspectives to grammar are referred to as texture (for a detailed account of texture, see Hasan, 1989).

For example, a discourse analyst may examine how the conjunction *and* accomplishes different functions (i.e., creates meaning) in texts through connection and repetition.

> **Bible, Genesis 1 (New International Version)**
>
> 3 **And** God said, "Let there be light," **and** there was light.
>
> 4 God saw that the light was good, **and** he separated the light from the darkness.
>
> 5 God called the light "day," **and** the darkness he called "night." **And** there was evening, **and** there was morning – the first day.

The sentence- and clause-initial conjunction *and* possesses in part a narrative function in this excerpt: the conjunction connects different observations to create a sequence or story of events. This narrative and temporal function is different from the *and* found within sentences that connects separate ideas to establish a coherent whole, such as the sentence found in the actual mission statement of drinkware and gear company Stanley 1913:

Founded in 1913 by inventor William Stanley Jr., Stanley has been there for generations of adventures. We're built on invention, innovation **and** inspiration with a timeless spirit that complements your wild imagination.

In the Stanley 1913 example, the conjunction *and* creates meaning within (rather than above) the sentence level by functioning as a device that connects attributes on which the company is built. Discourse analysts are not typically interested in studying grammar within sentences unless its use reveals something about the human factor, language use, or both.

As an object of study, grammar offers exciting possibilities to understand the ways in which grammatical items create meaning above the sentence level (i.e., the aspect of discourse concerned with language use) and beyond the language being used (i.e., the aspect of discourse concerned with the human factor). While there are no set rules that must be followed when selecting a grammatical item as your object of study, there are several steps that can be followed to get you started with the process of studying grammar from a discourse analytic perspective.

First, many discourse analysts identify an object of study as a result of noticing something interesting or peculiar about a grammatical item being used in their day-to-day lives. Try thinking of a human encounter where a grammatical item serves an important role in how you make sense of the situation and the people to which you are communicating. Second, after selecting an object of study, it is important to become familiar with its grammatical rules. This step provides the necessary foundation to explore how a grammatical item does more than create meaning within a single utterance or sentence. Third, you can begin exploring how your object of study creates meaning above the sentence level (language use) and beyond the language being used (the human factor).

Table 1.1 provides additional examples of grammatical items and how you can begin thinking about grammar within, above, and beyond the sentence level.

Table 1.1 Grammar and discourse function		
Grammatical item	**Grammar**	**Discourse function**
we	pronouns substitute nouns or noun phrases	*we* could be used by a customer service worker in response to a customer complaint to deflect the blame from his individual self to the company
this	demonstratives point to, or replace, nouns	*this* could be used to avoid saying a taboo word (substitution), signal a new topic (topic management), or refer back to a previous utterance (reference)
like	prepositions can introduce something, or link to other words or phrases, conveying meaning about direction, location, place, time, or space	*like* could be used to mark something that is about to be uttered as significant, such as "Did you hear what Mary did yesterday, like, OMG."
or	conjunctions connect words or phrases	*or* could be used by an individual asking a question to anticipate a dispreferred response, such as "Are you free to watch a movie with me, or?"

Grammatical rules are commonly understood as fixed with limited possibilities for deviation. Grammar used at the discourse level in comparison is flexible with greater opportunities to flout rules. Everyday communication provides opportunities for language users to deviate from grammatical rules because humans use grammar in ways that differ from what is established in reference books and language classrooms.

Learning Activity 1.4 Reflecting on Discourse as Grammar

In this exercise, the learning objective is to identify additional discourse functions and communicative situations that are related to the grammatical items identified in Table 1.1. In so doing, you will be supporting the observation that grammatical rules are open to negotiation when grammar is used at the discourse level.

1. Can you think of other discourse functions, as well as their communicative situations, for *we*, *this*, *like*, or *or*?

2. Can you think of other communicative situations where you may experience the discourse functions already identified for *we*, *this*, *like*, or *or*?
3. Can you think of examples of when we break grammatical rules during communication?
4. Why are we more likely to break grammatical rules during communication?
5. What specific encounters or situations are more likely to experience greater grammatical rule-breaking?

Studying grammar from a discourse perspective requires understanding the functions of grammar use. To this end, Table 1.2 identifies four functions taken from Halliday & Hasan (1976) that will help you develop some understanding of how to study grammar from a discourse perspective.

Table 1.2 Discourse functions of grammar

Grammar	Discourse
Tense	The extent to which a particular verb tense is likely to appear in a communicative situation, such as how the future modifying "will" would tend to be used in instructions, directives, or proposals: "You will need to take a right after the left" or "This project will investigate …"
Collocation	The likelihood that one word or phrase will co-occur with another word or phrase, such as "do" and "business" or "save" and "money." Collocations reveal a lot about the purpose, culture, and competence of the author responsible for the language.
Substitution	The replacement of one word or phrase for another word or phrase because of given information or knowledge, such as the word "one" in "I love him. He is the one" or "so" in "Think. Doing so is good."
Reference	The act of citing a word that is located within or beyond the place of reference. Reference includes words like "she," "him," "the," "this," and "that." Reference items point back to something (anaphoric), forward (cataphoric), or outside a text (exophoric).

In addition to these four examples, Halliday & Hasan (1976) provide a comprehensive account of grammatical items and discourse functions that can be used to identify an object of study. Readers looking for a more pedagogical account of discourse and grammar should consider reading McCarthy's (1991) seminal book on discourse analysis for language teachers.

1.3.2 Discourse as Actions and Practices

Discourse represents what humans do with language. The observation that language is used to do things should come as no surprise to readers, as humans are social beings that communicate for numerous reasons and purposes. Viewing what humans do with language as a set of actions and practices is one way to understand discourse. For example, there are a number of actions and practices that are associated with being in a relationship with a partner. The practices that are associated with being in a relationship may include working on a family budget, planning a holiday, parenting a child, and discussing future plans. These practices, say, working on a family budget, involve a range of actions, such as agreeing, disagreeing, seeking clarification, asking for help, and expressing confusion.

Actions and practices represent different objects of study (for a similar distinction, see Scollon, 2001). This distinction can be messy, however, as actions and practices occasionally refer to the same thing. For example, asking questions is a practice central to police officers during interrogations, but it is also a generic action that occurs in most situations. Despite this imprecision, the distinction is useful in selecting a specific object of study, as actions and practices provide a simple way of understanding how discourse is used and organized. This point will be returned to later in this subsection. For now, it is important to first address what actions and practices are.

An action refers to what is accomplished in and through language. Discourse analysts possess a broad understanding of language: an action can be accomplished using verbal, non-verbal, textual, pictorial, or other visual resources. Examples of using language to accomplish an action include suggesting, offering, apologizing, declaring, and promising. The precise terminology used to label and categorize actions will vary from one theory or scholar to another. An older, but relatively simple way of understanding actions can be found in Speech Act Theory (Searle, 1976), which presents five categories for understanding what people do with language (for other frameworks used to examine actions, see Waring, 2017). For example, requesting and advising are actions that fall within the category of "directives," which includes any language that is used to get someone to do something. Table 1.3 identifies the five categories used in Speech Act Theory.

Table 1.3 Discourse as actions		
Category	**Description**	**Action examples**
Representative	Establishing the truth of a statement: "I am an excellent student."	asserting, claiming, describing, suggesting
Directive	Encouraging an action: "Read for ten more minutes."	requesting, inviting, commanding, ordering

Table 1.3 (cont.)		
Category	**Description**	**Action examples**
Commissive	Committing to an action: "I will do my homework tonight."	promising, pledging, offering, vowing
Expressive	Expressing a state of being: "I really enjoy discourse analysis."	congratulating, greeting, thanking, apologizing
Declarative	Changing the state of affairs: "You have passed the exam."	declaring, resigning, hiring, sentencing

These five categories provide an excellent starting point in your journey to identify an object of study. For example, your discourse project could investigate how a category of action, such as a directive, is used to participate in different situations, such as ordering food at a restaurant, checking in at a hotel, or running a business meeting. Alternatively, it is possible to investigate how one communicative situation includes a range of actions.

Learning Activity 1.5 Reflecting on Discourse as Actions

In this exercise, the learning objective is to identify the varied actions that you are likely to experience in different communicative situations. Table 1.3 can be used as a reference guide if additional help is needed.

For the first exercise, please identify four communicative situations with which you are familiar. Now identify at least two actions that you are likely to experience in these situations. Four examples have already been provided.

Situation	*Actions*
1a. Job interview	1b. stating (representative), boasting (expressive)
2a. Border control	2b. declaring (declarative), describing (representative)
3a. Argument	3a. promising (commissive), apologizing (expressive)
4a. Asking for directions	4b. thanking (expressive), claiming (representative)

For the second exercise, think about what language would be used for the relationships that you have identified in the first exercise. Four examples have already been provided.

Situation	Action	Language example
1a. Job interview	1b. boasting	1c. "I'm an expert in finance."
2a. Border control	2b. describing	2c. "I'm here as a student."
3a. Argument	3b. promising	3c. "The dishes will be done."
4a. Asking for directions	4b. claiming	4c. "I'm completely lost."

Examining actions reveals a great deal about a communicative situation, including the people that are communicating. For instance, the actions used in a business meeting will likely tell you a lot about the belief systems and identities of the participants: a supervisor may allocate turns and questions more than a subordinate, for example.

A practice also refers to what is accomplished in and through language. However, a practice is a "larger" category, as it is made up of actions. Practices can be communication- or situation-specific, though there are instances where a practice falls into both categories. For instance, storytelling is a type of communication (e.g., recalling a past experience using a narrative structure), but it is also a type of situation (e.g., storytelling to young learners at the beginning of a lesson).

Turn-taking is a common communication-specific practice: it possesses a system of actions, such as nominating a speaker, ending a turn, and interrupting, to name a few. Managing topics is also a communication-specific practice that possesses a system of actions, including proposing new topics, changing topics, and ending topics. Situation-specific practices are ubiquitous. For example, a service encounter is a situation that requires a customer service worker to carry out a range of occupational practices, such as the practice of providing help and the actions of promising, describing, and thanking. Additionally, a lesson delivered by a teacher to a class of students is made up of many situational practices, such as lecturing and testing knowledge, with each practice consisting of different actions, such as stating, declaring, and claiming.

Like actions, the precise terminology used to label and categorize practices varies from one theory or scholar to another. Figure 1.3 identifies some common practices that many readers should have encountered or experienced. Readers should refer to Hart (2020) for additional practice examples and the theories that are associated with them.

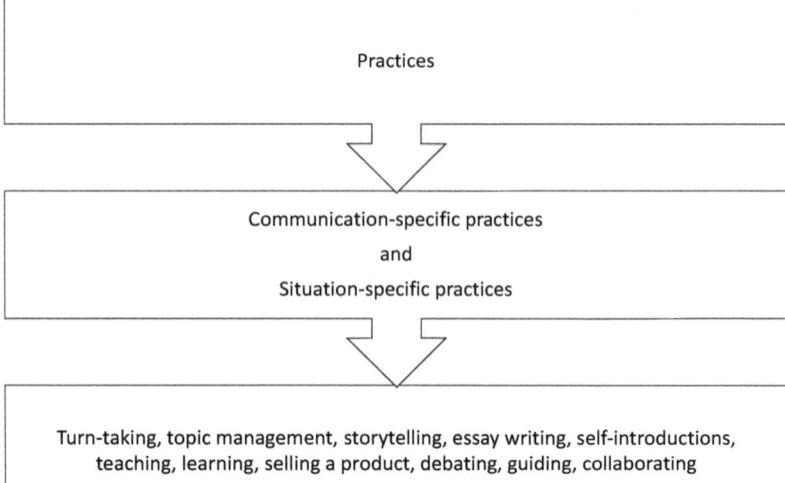

FIGURE 1.3
Discourse as practices

Selecting a practice as your object of study requires familiarizing yourself with the different actions that are related to it. To this end, Table 1.4 lists possible actions for the practices identified in Figure 1.3.

Table 1.4 Practices and actions	
Examples of practices and actions	
Turn-taking nominating a speaker, ending a turn, interjecting, asking to speak	**Classroom teaching** describing, requesting, congratulating, questioning, nominating a speaker
Storytelling describing characters, recalling dialogues, setting the scene, sequencing the story	**Classroom learning** listening, explaining, questioning, thanking, asking to speak
Topic management proposing a new topic, changing topics, ending a topic, referring back to a topic	**Reading the news** describing, greeting, apologizing, referencing, quoting
Essay writing referencing, following guidelines, organizing paragraphs, establishing a thesis	**Selling a car** promising, describing, declaring, requesting, congratulating
Self-introductions providing your name or age, describing your background, revealing your identities	**Debating politics** disagreeing, agreeing, venting, provoking, pestering

A few observations should be made when thinking about practices as an object of study. Practices that are situation-specific, such as classroom learning, may consist of practices that are communication-specific, such as turn-taking or topic management. Furthermore, social and cultural norms, such as traditions or rules, will influence what practices and actions are used in any particular situation; these social and cultural issues are central interests for discourse analysts.

Learning Activity 1.6 Reflecting on Discourse as Practices

In this exercise, the learning objective is to build on the examples identified in Table 1.4. To this end, please identify additional examples of practices along with two or three related actions.

In the next exercise, please use the examples in either Table 1.4 or the ones that you have just identified to answer the following questions.

1. Can you identify actions that are used in only one practice? What do your results tell you about practices?
2. Can you identify reasons why some actions may be used in many practices? What do your results tell you about actions and practices?
3. Can you identify how or why some practices may differ across different modes of communication, such as texting and speaking? For example, will turn-taking be managed the same way in speaking and texting environments?
4. Can you identify how or why some practices may be carried out differently because of situational or cultural reasons? For example, do turn-taking practices vary according to cultural or language backgrounds?

Like all objects of study, the analysis of actions and practices can be studied from two perspectives: the human factor and language use (see Figure 1.1).

Analyzing the human factor in actions and practices involves more than just describing the language used to carry out an action or a practice. The human factor in actions and practices is related to the social and cultural reasons why individuals, communities, or institutions do things with language in particular ways. For example, there may be cultural reasons why the action of congratulating varies from one region to another while engaging in the practice of raising a child. Similarly, there may be social or institutional reasons why the action of questioning varies in frequency according to how big a classroom is when engaging in the practice of lecturing.

Examining actions and practices from a language use perspective requires a focus on the descriptions and interpretations of communication. Although there are several methodological tools that can be used to do this (see Table 1.5), the task of examining actions and practices from a language use perspective can be accomplished in two basic ways. First, you could look at the function of an action or a practice. For example, how is the action of commissives used to fulfill an important function in a mission statement? Do mission statements include pledges, and if so, what do they say about writing such documents? Second, you could examine the organization of an action or a practice. For instance, what is the linguistic structure and order of the practice of writing a mission statement? Do mission statements have a narrative structure (beginning, middle, and end), and if so, what does this organization tell us about the company and author?

Some further reading is necessary to understand the precise ways in which actions and practices can be analyzed. This is because theories and methodologies have unique and detailed guidelines regarding what are and what are not acceptable ways of analyzing actions and practices. Table 1.5 offers some direction regarding this matter by identifying four common approaches to studying actions and practices (for a different way of characterizing the approaches identified in Table 1.5, see Table 3.5 in Chapter 3). The third column of Table 1.5 consists of keywords that can be used in an academic database to locate example studies.

Table 1.5 Approaches to actions and practices

Approach	Example question	Keywords	Reference
Conversation analysis	How do people do things in and through conversational turn-taking?	*sequence organization, turn-taking, turns, turn design, repair, conversations*	Liddicoat (2007)
Systemic functional linguistics	How is the grammar of a language used to do things?	*speech acts, ideational function, interpersonal function, textual*	Halliday (1994)
Multimodality	How do people do things with visual and spatial language?	*semiotics, medium, modes, resources, intermodal*	Kress & Van Leeuwen (2001)
Genre analysis	How are the different parts of written and spoken genre used to do things with language?	*moves, steps, audience, subject, discourse community, tenor, field*	Swales (1990)

It is important to note again that there are many other iterations of, and alternatives to, these four approaches. One such approach is mediated discourse analysis, which offers a number of useful tools to examine the connections between the human factor and language use (Norris & Jones, 2005). Specifically, mediated discourse analysis is primarily concerned with actions, making connections between what is communicated by people and the situation in which this communication occurs.

1.3.3 Discourse as Identities

Identities can be loosely defined as your understanding of who you are. Discourse allows us to express this understanding. Discourse is also central to how we establish membership to social groups, which plays an important role in how identities are formed. For example, identities can form as a result of being a subscriber to, and commenting on, a YouTube channel or growing up in a country and learning the local language(s) and practicing the national traditions.

As an object of study, it is convenient to think of an identity as a category. We all belong to many identity categories, such as father, student, brother, American, manager, and Korean. Identity categories develop over time and can indeed change from one stage of life or social encounter to another. Sometimes identity categories exist in or as binaries, such as teacher–student, father–mother, and old–young. As oppositional categories, these binaries can reveal a tremendous amount of information about how identities are formed and communicated. However, binaries can be inherently problematic, as many individuals do not fit neatly within categories of two. The trans- prefix is often used to denote a fluid movement between categories, such as transgender or transnational. Figure 1.4 presents some of the more common identities categories that are investigated.

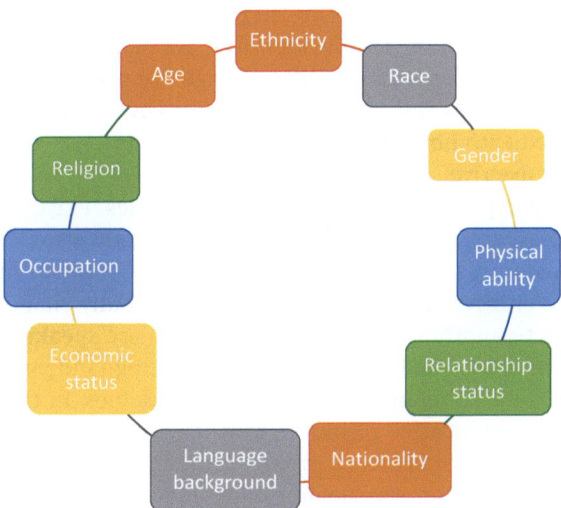

FIGURE 1.4
Identity wheel

Learning Activity 1.7 Reflecting on Your Identity Categories

In this exercise, the learning objective is to identify and reflect on your identity categories.

1. What identity categories are relevant to you?
2. Do you possess more than one identity in any category identified in Figure 1.4?
3. Have any of your identity categories changed over time? Identity categories possess different degrees of saliency (Stryker & Serpe,

1982). That is, some identity categories lie dormant most of the time while other are central to how you live your life.
4. What identity categories possess the most saliency in your life?
5. What human factors influence why some identity categories are more salient than others?

Thinking of identities as categories is helpful in answering *what* questions. What identities are relevant to an individual and what factors influence this self-identification process? However, discourse analysts are not typically interested in answering *what* questions, choosing rather to address *how* questions. How, then, do discourse analysts approach the study of identities? (For a seminal overview of discourse and identity, see Benwell & Stokoe, 2006.)

Discourse analysts possess two, often overlapping, perspectives on identities: the human factor and language use. It is possible to come across different yet similar terms in the literature, such as "performance and history" (Benwell & Stokoe, 2006, p. 29) and "micro and macro" (K. T. Anderson, 2009), but the underlying ideas are all roughly the same. One perspective is committed to looking at how identities are made relevant while people are communicating – this is the language use perspective. The other perspective also looks at the language produced by people, but it is primarily concerned with how societal forces shape identities – this is the human factor perspective.

The language use perspective maintains that identities exist in and through social encounters. That is, what you think about yourself stems from, and is constantly being negotiated as a result of, your social encounters. As such, identities are highly malleable, potentially changing from one situation to another depending on who you are speaking to, the situation in which you find yourself communicating, and your current psychological state, to name a few influential variables. In this sense, identities are communicative resources that are used to accomplish an action or complete a practice. In other words, the actions and practices of individuals will often reveal something about their identities. For example, an individual who possesses multiple ethnic identities, such as Chinese and American, may choose to only talk about one ethnic identity in order to achieve a particular communicative goal, such as seeking approval or showing empathy.

The human factor perspective contends that identities are formed as a result of social norms and cultural expectations. That is, what you think about yourself is heavily influenced by forces outside your immediate life as an individual, such as generational traditions, religious teachings, and community rules. As such, identities are partly "products" of society. The human factor perspective does not reject the ability of individuals to change their identities in and through language – that is, individuals possess some agency over their identities. However, there are many societal forces (e.g., institutional, cultural, governmental, historical, linguistic, and economic forces) that leave an imprint on how individuals make sense of and use their identities. For example, a child born into an English-speaking family in the United States will be socialized into particular linguistic and cultural identities at a very young age; these early experiences and encounters will leave a lasting imprint for this individual.

Although both perspectives represent distinct ways of conceptualizing and investigating identities, in practice, all discourse analysis research can be placed somewhere in between the two. That is, all discourse analysts are concerned with the mediation between the human factor and language use.

The basic difference between both perspectives can be expressed in two questions, which are illustrated in Figure 1.5. The arrows in the figure represent the direction discourse analysts follow when analyzing identities: top to bottom or bottom to top.

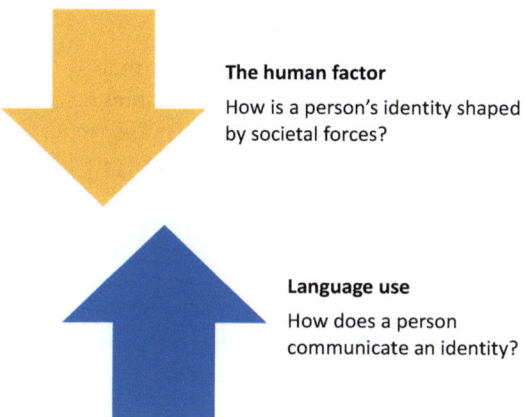

The human factor
How is a person's identity shaped by societal forces?

Language use
How does a person communicate an identity?

FIGURE 1.5
Identities

The human factor perspective points downward, as researchers will often begin with an interest in a social or cultural issue and then make connections to some aspect of language. For example, a discourse analyst may be initially concerned with how discrimination shapes workplace identities, and subsequently find language examples that highlight this connection.

The language use perspective points upward, as researchers will begin with an interest in some aspect of language, such as an action or practice, and only make connections to the human factor when it is relevant in the communication being investigated. For instance, a discourse analyst may be interested in how strangers make declarative statements while talking about the weather, but may discover that the individuals are reluctant to reveal their identities in such encounters because it is not culturally acceptable to do so.

Learning Activity 1.8 Reflecting on Discourse as Identities

In this exercise, the learning objective is to reflect on how language is used to construct identities, and how this self-identification process may be shaped by the human factor.

For the first exercise, please think about how you communicate your identities using different actions or practices: first identify two or three identities; then ask yourself what language is associated with these identities. Two examples are provided for your reference.

Identity	Actions/Practices
Teacher	Policing the language practices of students Requesting students to use your first name in class Assigning homework for the following day
Parent	Supporting a child emotionally Raising a child to be bilingual Providing food and shelter for a child

For the second exercise, please think about how the human factor shapes identities. You can use the six societal variables briefly mentioned prior to this exercise: *institutional*, *cultural*, *governmental*, *historical*, *linguistic*, and *economic*. Two identity examples are provided to get you started.

Societal variable	Identity	Example
institutional	teacher	A teacher's identity may be shaped by how a school enforces language policies in the classroom.
cultural	teacher	A teacher's identity may be shaped by how society views the teaching profession.
governmental	teacher	A teacher's identity may be shaped by what qualifications are needed to become a teacher.
historical	parent	A parent's identity may be shaped by past parental relationships, which influence future parenting styles.
linguistic	parent	A parent's identity may be shaped by how society places value on a particular language.
economic	parent	A parent's identity may be shaped by income levels, which will influence educational aspirations.

The learning activity that you have just completed is a reminder that our identities do not exist independently of other social processes; identities are a part of what we do and how we communicate, such as using language to carry out a job responsibility; there are also social expectations tied to identities, such as what it means to be a father or mother. In other words, our identities are connected to the occupations, relationships, and situations in which we find ourselves participating and communicating. For instance, being a teacher is more than simply declaring that you are one: "I am a teacher." Teachers develop their professional identities over time and across different communicative situations.

Understanding the multifaceted and dynamic nature of identities requires adopting an approach (or approaches) capable of unlocking the connection between the human factor and language. Table 1.6 identifies four approaches suitable for this endeavor.

Table 1.6 Approaches to identities

Approach	Example question	Keywords	Reference
Membership categorization	How do people communicate identities into being?	*identity categories, identity devices, category-bound activities*	Fitzgerald & Housley (2015)
Analysis positioning theory	How do people position identities in relation to values and beliefs?	*group attributes, rights, duties, actions, social acts*	K.T. Anderson (2009)
Socio-cognitive approach	How are identities an expression of knowledge shared within society?	*socially shared knowledge, discourse production, recontextualization*	Hart (2014)
Narrative analysis	How are storytelling practices used to construct identities?	*plots, themes, topical cohesiveness, cognitive structure, setting*	Bamberg & Georgakopoulou (2008)

Although these four approaches draw from different theories, there are notable similarities. For example, membership categorization analysis and positioning theory are both interested in how individuals use language (e.g., actions and practices) to express identities. Additionally, narrative analysis and socio-cognitive theory both consider the role society has in the construction of identities. Conversely, discourse analysts commonly use more than one approach in order to offer a more nuanced understanding of identities. For instance, it is not uncommon for discourse analysts to use membership categorization analysis to understand how identities are constructed with narratives. The references identified in Table 1.6 will help you determine what approach (or approaches) to use.

1.3.4 Discourse as Places and Spaces

Discourse can be found in the physical and digital world. For example, the language that makes up discourse can be found in or on road signs, billboards, discussion forums, public art, shopping malls, company logos, menus located outside restaurants, and online advertisements. These examples are discourse places: they are physical or digital areas with distinct physical or digital boundaries. For example, a train station possesses a recognizable structure with physical boundaries (e.g., a building) that tells individuals when they are entering or leaving the transportation area. A physical classroom is a discourse place, as it possesses a recognizable structure with boundaries (e.g., a room) that tells individuals where the business of teaching and learning is supposed to occur. Both examples demonstrate that what is recognizable as a discourse place comes from the cultural and social norms and expectations of societies. That is, societies possess unique cultural and social norms and expectations regarding not only what discourse places are (e.g., shape, organization, and appearance), but also how to behave and communicate in and with such areas and objects.

What we, as individuals, do in or with discourse places is a matter of space. For instance, how individuals move from one part of a train station to another, and the actions and practices involved in purchasing tickets, seeking information, or asking for help, represent discourse spaces. A discourse space is the meaning created by individuals within, or in response to, a discourse place. For example, the actions and practices of two students playing poker during a lecture demonstrate that they are not treating the classroom as a place for teaching and learning. Rather, the students create a space of entertainment (or a space of rebellion) within the classroom. In this sense, discourse spaces represent how individuals interpret discourse places. Like discourse places, discourse spaces represent the shared knowledge of societies expressed in and through language.

Figure 1.6 establishes that discourse place and discourse space both communicate meaning. However, a discourse space is the meaning

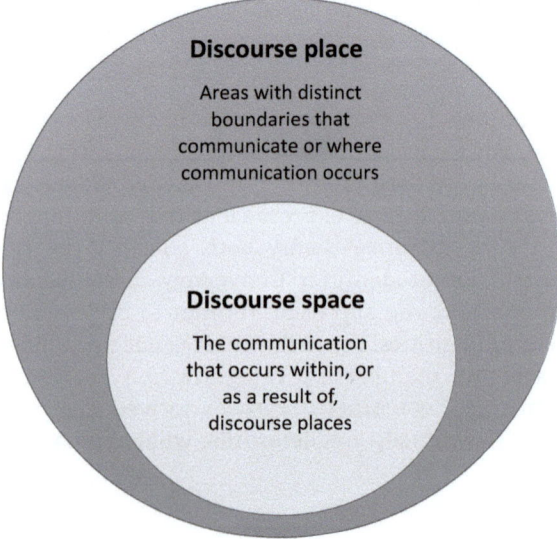

FIGURE 1.6
Discourse as places and spaces

created when individuals communicate in or with discourses places. Discourse places communicate meaning, but are inanimate, and often fixed, physical or digital structures or objects.

The relationship between discourse place and discourse space can be expressed in how individuals derive meaning from, and make sense of, their environments. For instance, restaurants have established norms regarding how to secure a table, order food from a menu, consume a meal, and settle a bill. While norms are relatively fixed, the meaning within places is constantly being negotiated and co-constructed. This process of negotiation and co-construction is based on discourse.

Learning Activity 1.9 Reflecting on Places and Spaces

In this exercise, the learning objective is to explore the relationship between discourse places and discourse spaces.

1. Please identify several discourse places. Remember, discourse places can be a location (e.g., train station), an object (e.g., exit sign in a building), or an area (e.g., a homepage of a website) with distinct boundaries.
2. Now think of how individuals interact in, or communicate with, the places that you have just identified. These examples represent discourse spaces.

Four example combinations are provided for your reference.

Place	Spaces
1a. city park	1b. kids playing, having a picnic, walking a dog, exercising
2a. meeting room	2b. interviewing, presenting a sales report, seeking guidance
3a. traffic sign	3b. directing traffic, communicating rules, accelerating
4a. discussion forum	4b. sharing information, asking questions, socializing, debating

3. What happens when spaces are constructed outside "designated" places? For example, is it acceptable to have a picnic outside a park?

Your answers to the third question will demonstrate that place boundaries are important insofar as they "contain" and communicate expectations regarding acceptable behavior or communication.

4. How do places communicate meaning? Road signs, for example, explicitly communicate laws and rules. Menus communicate what foods are available to order. Can you think of other ways places communicate, both implicitly and explicitly, meaning?

Discourse analysts interested in how meaning is communicated in the physical or digital world will often begin their research with a location, an object, or an area. In other words, when selecting an object of study, it is best to first identify a place that may be of interest to you, such as a textile market in a tourist destination. You can then begin reflecting on the spaces that may occur or unfold in your selected place. For example, what spaces of negotiation are created by tourists when interacting with textile vendors? In this example, the meaning that you are investigating comes from the spaces created by tourists interacting in a place. In other discourse projects, it is common for researchers to examine discourse places with no attention to the individuals that may be occupying a designated place. For example, how do storefront signs in an ethnic enclave located in an urban area communicate language ideologies (Lee, 2014). In this example, the meaning that is being investigated comes from how you, the researcher, understand a discourse place. In other words, a discourse project that examines places and spaces need not include research participants – unless the opinions of such individuals must be taken into consideration (e.g., asking shopkeepers about their signs).

Studies of places and spaces are inherently multimodal. Places occupy the physical or digital world, containing, as well as communicating through, not only words and texts, but also images, signs, moving objects, and graphics, to name a few. Similarly, the language used to understand such places – that is, the spaces created in or as a result of places – is based on multimodal resources and multisensory experiences (e.g., tastes, sights, sounds, and smells).

An interdisciplinary approach – one that attends to how people interact and communicate in diverse geographical environments and landscapes – is needed to study the multimodal and multisensory dimensions of places and spaces. To this end, Table 1.7 identifies four interdisciplinary approaches.

Table 1.7 Approaches to places and spaces

Approach	Example question	Keywords	Reference
Geosemiotics	How is meaning constructed through language in the material world?	*semiotics, inscription, emplacement, indexicality*	Scollon & Scollon (2003)
Multimodal discourse analysis	How is meaning constructed within and across modes of communication?	*production, distribution, design, articulation, strata*	Kress & van Leeuwen (2001)
Cultural geography	How is place a medium through which culture and identity are constructed?	*cultural traces, scales, representations, borders*	B. Anderson (2016)
Visual anthropology	How are human experiences and language represented in the visual medium?	*engagement, sensations, visual technology, senses*	Pink (2006)

In addition to these four approaches, readers should consider familiarizing themselves with the literature on ethnographic methods, which provides useful examples for collecting and analyzing data in diverse geographical environments (for an older but seminal book that discusses ethnography, photography, and visual anthropology, see Collier & Collier, 1986).

1.3.5 Discourse as Stories

Discourse is located in stories, which represent an important part of human sociality. Much of what humans know and understand about themselves and the world around them can be, and is, expressed in stories. A story is defined as an account of some aspect of life, such as an experience, encounter, or emotional state. Stories possess a structure, such as beginning–middle–end, introduction–climax–conclusion, and setup–confrontation–resolution. In this sense, there are different story genres.

Discourse analysts are interested in how such structures are organized; however, researchers are also concerned with how stories allow individuals to accomplish different actions and practices, such as expressing a feeling, sharing an experience, teaching literacy to children, resisting or sustaining power hierarchies, or passing down cultural values to younger generations. Discourse analysts are also interested in how stories are used in specific situations, such as telling a story to a child before bedtime, sharing an experience during a meal, or recounting a challenging work experience during a job interview.

Before outlining how discourse analysts investigate stories, it must be noted that the term **narrative** is often used as a synonym for story. Readers interested in pursuing stories as an object of study will find that the literature frequently uses narrative (see Benson, 2014). For this reason, it is important to use both terms when searching for relevant studies in scholarly databases. In this introductory overview, however, the term story will be used, as it provides a more straightforward way of considering how discourse analysis contributes to the study of storytelling.

In fact, as an expression of an act, the term storytelling is an excellent starting point for introducing how discourse analysts approach stories. Three perspectives of storytelling are relevant to this discussion: the language of storytelling, storytelling as a situated practice, and storytelling as an artifact of society.

First, discourse analysts look at the language used to convey a story (e.g., narrative structure and word choice), or they may be interested in how the language used to convey a story accomplishes an action or practice (e.g., to establish rapport or teach a class). These two empirical concerns can be categorized under what this chapter refers to as language use.

Second, discourse analysts also see the act of storytelling as a situated practice. That is, storytelling is a situated practice that has immediate relevance to the storyteller and audience (e.g., their communicative goals). For example, telling a story about an early childhood experience may be an important part of how an individual wishes to convey a particular identity. This empirical concern also falls under the category of language use.

Third, discourse analysts see storytelling as an artifact of society. That is, the language used in, and the act of, storytelling are connected to a host of societal issues, such as historical events, power dynamics, racial hierarchies, economic policies, and cultural traditions, to name a few. For example, telling a story about a cultural practice may be the only way that a marginalized community can protect their endangered language. This empirical concern can be categorized under what this chapter refers to as the human factor.

Figure 1.7 summarizes this discussion of storytelling foci. The top two slices of the pie chart indicate studies of storytelling that are from the language use perspective. The bottom slice indicates the study of storytelling from the human factor perspective.

FIGURE 1.7
Perspectives of
storytelling

While it is acceptable to investigate one slice of storytelling, it is more common for researchers to examine at least two perspectives. For example, an investigation looking at the language of storytelling, such as the use of metaphors and analogies, may consider how stories are used as a situated practice, such as teaching a group of learners about the importance of word choice. Similarly, an investigation looking at storytelling as a situated practice may consider how stories are connected to a deeper societal issue, such as retelling religious scriptures for monastic ceremonies.

Learning Activity 1.10 Reflecting on Storytelling

In this exercise, the learning objective is to reflect on the language used to construct stories, and what the practice of storytelling tells us about different communicative and social issues.

1. Please think of several aspects of your life that are important to you. Several examples are provided.

1a. my language	1b. my parents' education	1c. my nationality
1d. my ambitions	1e. my hobbies	1f. my relationships

2. Select one of your answers from the first question and use it to form a short, written story. An example is provided for your reference.
   2a. "I spoke Korean almost exclusively with family and friends when I was a young child. After moving back and forth between different countries, we eventually settled in the USA. I remember the social and communicative challenges of living in an English-dominant country. Now, however, I prefer to use English and it feels foreign to speak any other language."
3. Think of the language that you – the narrator – rely on to retell your story. Stories are often made up of language that describes time and space. What language do you use to describe time and space? Several examples are provided to get you started.
   3a. time: "when I was a young child" "Now, however, I prefer to use English"
   3b. space: "moving back and forth" "living in an English-dominant country"
4. What societal issues are addressed in your story? These issues are often located in the characters, settings, or storyline. Some example questions and answers are provided:
   4a. Who is involved? The narrator, as a child and as an adult; family and friends.
   4b. What are the societal issues? Identities; language policy; bilingualism.
   4c. What is the story about? Using a new language in a new environment is difficult.
   4d. What identities are relevant to the story? *Korean speaker; English speaker; foreigner.*
   4e. Where did the story take place? *Different countries; USA.*

The learning activity that you have just completed offers a glimpse into what discourse analysts examine when stories are their objects of study. Using discourse analysis to examine storytelling means viewing stories as **discursive histories**: stories transform past events or experiences from the then-and-there to the here-and-now. In this sense, storytelling transcends time and space. Accordingly, a discourse study may include the language used to express specific moments in time, describe spatial environments, or both. Like discourse as place and space, stories represent the knowledge shared within and across societies. Therefore, it is also possible to adopt discourse analysis to consider the ways in which stories are cognitive representations of past events or experiences.

Stories can be examined in numerous ways and are topics of investigation in many fields of study. Readers have a range of theoretical constructs and methodological principles from which to draw. Table 1.8 identifies four publications that offer some understanding of this breadth and depth.

Table 1.8 Approaches to storytelling			
Approach	**Example question**	**Keywords**	**Reference**
Multilingual autobiography	How are personal narratives shaped and expressed to construct a multilingual reality?	*subject reality, life reality, text reality, linguistic choice*	Pavlenko (2007)
Narrative frames	How can storytelling templates be used to teach, as well as elicit, past events or experiences?	*scaffolding stories, narrative data, story design, frames*	Barkhuizen (2014)
Narrative inquiry	How can the lives and experiences of research participants be used to understand language and social issues?	*language biography, autoethnography, diary studies, life histories*	Benson (2014)
Narrative analysis	What are the different theoretical and methodological approaches used in narrative analysis?	*time–space, positioning, self/other, narrative interaction, narrating, social practice*	De Fina & Georgakopoulou (2019)

Table 1.8 possesses two important points of consideration. First, unlike other objects of study discussed in this chapter, the four publications in Table 1.8 are not based on "approaches," but are rather discussions and conceptualizations of stories. Second, some of the approaches identified in previous sections of this chapter, such as the approaches for actions and practices, can be used to study stories. For instance, it is possible to use membership categorization analysis to investigate stories from a language use perspective, uncovering how identities are constructed in word choice and through storytelling (Day & Kjærbeck, 2019).

1.3.6 Discourse as Ideologies

Discourse is embedded within, and used to express, ideologies. An ideology is a conceptual system regarding some aspect of life, such as law, language, politics, and education. That is, ideologies are conceptual systems of thinking and knowing. Although ideologies are stored as mental representations, they are articulated in and through language.

Ideologies come from, but at the same time shape, our participation in societies. For instance, a political ideology (e.g., democracy) stems from the experiences that we share with each other, but this conceptual system also influences our attitudes to or perceptions of the people with whom we interact (Wodak, 1989). As such, ideologies do not exist within a vacuum, but are rather artifacts of knowledge shared within and across communities. Ideologies are critically important objects of study for the Humanities and Social Sciences, as they are foundational to how individuals make sense of themselves and their social milieu.

An ideology is not simply a belief, nor are all beliefs ideologies. According to van Dijk (2006), ideologies organize behaviors, communication styles, attitudes, and opinions. In other words, beliefs are just one of several consequences of possessing an ideology. For example, a language ideology is a system of many beliefs, such as "there is only one way to speak English," "British English sounds better than American English," "You have an accent," and "double negatives are ungrammatical." Ideologies also influence how we behave, communicate, and feel. A language ideology may, for example, compel individuals to eradicate a particular pronunciation feature or even feel bad about their variety of English. Accordingly, ideologies are inherently powerful in that they compel individuals to think, feel, or behave in a certain way. Indeed, much has been said by discourse analysts about how the power structures within societies, such as racial hierarchies, come from the ideologies of individuals and institutions in positions of privilege and control (van Dijk, 2009). Ideologies, and the power embedded within them, are central to how many discourse analysts understand the ways in which societies are structured (e.g., marriage; see Section 1.3.7 on social structures).

Figure 1.8 provides a visual illustration of the relationship between ideology and its related constructs.

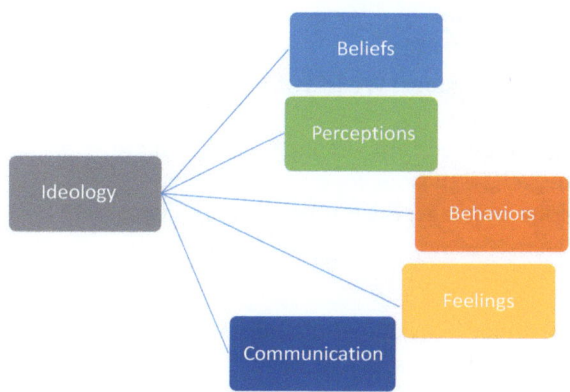

FIGURE 1.8
Ideology and its components

The constructs related to ideology in Figure 1.8 represent some of the ways in which individuals make sense of themselves and the world around them. Other relevant constructs include "values" and "tastes."

For example, a cultural value that champions equal pay between women and men is a part of a gender ideology (Lazar, 2005). The precise names given to these constructs are less important than remembering that an ideology is a conceptual system that organizes how individuals think and behave within and across social groups.

Learning Activity 1.11 Reflecting on Ideologies

In this exercise, the learning objective is to explore your ideologies and how they may shape the ways in which you communicate or use language.

1. Please identify two or three ideologies that you possess. Remember that ideologies and beliefs are not necessarily the same thing. Four examples are provided for your reference.

1a. language ideology	1b. political ideology
1c. racial ideology	1d. gender ideology

2. Now think of one or two beliefs that you possess in relation to each ideology identified previously. Examples are provided for your reference.
   2a. language ideology/belief: "English is a language of imperialism."
   2b. political ideology/belief: "Capitalism breeds corruption."
   2c. racial ideology/belief: "I do not see color."
   2d. gender ideology/belief: "Women do not possess adequate legal protection."
3. Finally, for each ideology, think of how you express your beliefs through an action or practice. Examples are provided for your reference.
   3a. language ideology/language: Trying to maintain a heritage language
   3b. political ideology/language: Wearing a t-shirt that expresses your love for socialism
   3c. racial ideology/language: Supporting policies that are insensitive to racial issues
   3d. gender ideology language: Encouraging a politician to write new laws

As an object of study, an ideology allows discourse analysts to examine how individuals within a particular social group (e.g., university students or immigrants) position themselves in relation to a societal issue, such as educational policies, international relations, and government systems. The types of ideology that can be studied include, but are not limited to, language ideologies, political ideologies, racial ideologies, and gender ideologies. Although many other ideologies exist (e.g., legal, ethical, educational, religious, epistemological), the four identified in Table 1.9 offer an excellent starting point for readers wishing to explore what can be done with discourse analysis. The table also includes references that showcase how discourse analysis can be used to study a particular ideology.

Table 1.9 Types of ideology		
Ideology	**Example question**	**Reference**
Language ideologies	How are values and opinions about language used to construct ideologies?	Kroskrity (2018)
Political ideologies	How is a political ideology expressed in, and used to prop up, a governmental policy?	Bhatia & Jenks (2018)
Racial ideologies	How is race a lens through which ideologies are shaped and disseminated?	Jenks & Lee (2020)
Gender ideologies	How are ideologies shaped by, and based on notions of, gender?	Żuk & Żuk (2020)

Using discourse analysis to investigate ideologies requires observing what individuals or institutions do or say: the purpose here is to examine if particular behaviors, actions, or practices reveal something about their ways of thinking and knowing. For example, a political bumper sticker found on the back of a car may reveal something about the driver's ideological position. Discourse analysts can also elicit an ideological position by asking individuals or institutions to discuss their conceptual systems in interviews or focus group discussions. Ideologies can additionally be studied by observing public video or audio recordings of people discussing their conceptual systems. Such recordings can often be found on video-sharing websites, but ethical guidelines must be followed carefully when using such data.

Discourse analysts rely on a wide range of theories and approaches to study ideologies. Table 1.10 identifies some of the more common approaches adopted by discourse analysts.

Table 1.10 Approaches to ideology			
Approach	**Example question**	**Keywords**	**Reference**
Marxism	How are ideologies created through, and representative of, economic systems?	*superstructure, class, production, Gramsci, cultural hegemony*	Herzog (2018)
Frankfurt School	How are ideologies created through, and representative of, powerful institutions?	*popular culture, mass media, social institutions, state apparatus, Althusser*	Forchtner (2011)

Table 1.10 (cont.)			
Approach	**Example question**	**Keywords**	**Reference**
Discourse analytical	How are ideologies reproduced in and through discourse strategies and structures?	*discourse processing, structures, strategies, social practices, cognition*	van Dijk (2006)
Heteroglossia	How is one ideology constructed and disseminated in the presence of existing ideologies?	*dialogic, polyphony, multiple voices, Bakhtin, utterance*	Jaworski (2014)

Like all objects of study, ideologies can be studied by looking at their discourse from a language use perspective, human factor perspective, or both. For the language use perspective, a common way of investigating ideologies is to understand how words are used to express a particular conceptual system. For instance, the belief that neoliberalism is inherently good is often expressed using keywords or tropes such as "individualism," "pull yourself up by the bootstraps," "free enterprise system," and "global markets." Examining types and ways of expression will promote a better understanding of not only the individuals articulating such thoughts, but also the very ideologies that shape their communication and behaviors.

For the human factor perspective, a common way of analyzing ideologies is to uncover how the language used for a particular conceptual system reproduces or reinforces a societal issue. For instance, an individual expressing the belief that neoliberalism is inherently good can be examined by looking at how political systems encourage their citizens – through rhetorical strategies such as metaphors or tropes – to see competing economic systems as bad or evil, such as socialism.

Of course, language use and the human factor can both be examined, though research using discourse analysis tends to favor the human factor by looking at the societal issues associated with, and that are a part of, conceptual systems. Furthermore, many analysts researching ideologies use critical discourse analysis as a theoretical framework (see Section 1.3.7). This approach entails looking beyond the language use perspective by attending to the societal issues, such as power dynamics, that compel individuals to communicate or behave in a particular way.

1.3.7 Discourse as Social Structures

Discourse is central to how social structures are formed, which are concepts developed within societies that influence how we think, behave, and communicate. Examples of social structures include, but are not limited to, family, religion, political party, sport, socioeconomic status, and ethnicity. Social structures contain relational identities, such as mother, classmate, sports club member, political activist, jurist, bank customer, and Asian.

Formal laws and informal rules typically govern social structures, creating norms and expectations regarding how to think, behave, and communicate in relation to a particular social structure. For example, the family is a social structure with a number of unspoken rules, including notions of the correct ways to socialize children, communicate with older family members, and manage financial obligations. Often social structures are tied to formal rules as well, such as family laws regarding child education, tax incentives, and marriage. As these examples demonstrate, social structures influence each other (e.g., family and law).

Social structures are shaped by ideologies; therefore, the power that is embedded within ideologies transfers to social structures, influencing the morals and values of individuals and institutions. Furthermore, social structures and ideologies are interdependent. On the one hand, ideologies are created as a result of social structures. For instance, the family is a social structure bound to cultural norms that influence how individuals establish related conceptual systems, such as religious or gender ideologies. On the other hand, social structures are human concepts, and are therefore inherently ideological and power-laden: the power dynamics between different family members, for instance, will often influence how individuals think about, and communicate with, each other.

Figure 1.9 provides a visual illustration of the relationship between social structure, ideology, and society.

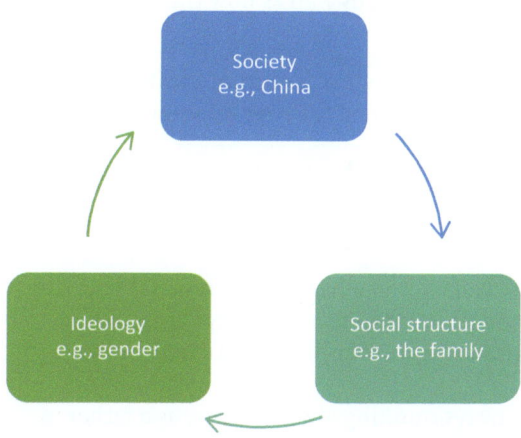

FIGURE 1.9
Social structure

A common way of depicting the constructs identified in Figure 1.9 is to use a vertical hierarchy where society sits at the top, influencing in a downward trajectory first social structures and then ideologies. Although established social structures may govern ideologies in a top-down fashion, a cyclical illustration is a reminder that societies (and thus social structures) do not exist without humans. More importantly, social structures, and indeed notions of society, are constantly being negotiated following a bottom-up trajectory as a result of changing and evolving ideologies.

This discussion of hierarchies and cycles is important to how discourse analysts understand and investigate social structures, which can be expressed in the following question. Do individuals think, behave, and communicate freely or are they constantly being influenced by social structures? The short and simple answer is both. Humans possess some individual control over how they think, behave, and communicate. However, individuals are born into a world with established social structures, which leave a lasting imprint on the ways in which humans think, behave, and communicate. A more theoretically motivated and complex answer to this question requires introducing an important concept: **agency**.

The term agency refers to the control or power that humans possess at the individual level in choosing how to think, behave, and communicate. In many domains of life, humans possess a great deal of agency. For example, adults typically have a great deal of control over what types of sport they wish to watch or play. In other situations, agency is greatly influenced by social structures. For instance, socioeconomic status and class systems have a remarkable amount of control over how individuals manage their lives.

Learning Activity 1.12 Reflecting on Social Structures

In this exercise, the learning objective is to explore the relationship between social structures and agency, as well as how this association manifests in our lives.

1. Please identify two or three social structures that are important to your life. Four examples are provided for your reference.

1a. the family	1b. religion
1c. ethnic group	1d. education

2. Now think of how much agency you have for each social structure. How do your social structures influence your ways of thinking, behaving, and communicating? Examples are provided for your reference.
   - 2a. the family: I am always thinking about my role as a father in this world.
   - 2b. religion: I am not part of a religious group, but I often use language taken from the Bible.
   - 2c. ethnic group: My ethnicity is fixed, but it does not define my communication style.
   - 2d. education: My education has influenced my social network and where I have lived.

3. Finally, reflect on how your social structures may differ if you were raised in a different region or country. What do these differences tell you about social structures and agency?

Discourse analytic approaches to social structures are partly based on how much agency is given to the individual (i.e., the research participant). Some approaches assume that social structures have little influence over how individuals communicate. Conversely, other approaches assume that social structures have a lot of influence over how individuals communicate. Selecting an approach to investigate social structures may be as easy as determining what your position is regarding the issue of agency.

Table 1.11 identifies four approaches to social structures with diverse analytic interests. While these approaches vary in what types of discourse are typically investigated, they all assume that social structures are important in how agentive individuals communicate and use language.

Table 1.11 Approaches to social structures			
Approach	**Example question**	**Keywords**	**Reference**
Critical discourse analysis	How is the power embedded within social structures reflected in the language used by individuals?	*recontextualization, scales, social institutions, hegemony, power*	Fairclough (2010)
Communities of practice	How are communities expressed in and through language and communication?	*learning, meaning, practice, identity, legitimate participation*	Wenger (1998)
Context models	How does language use mediate social structures and agency?	*mental models, subjective representation, social cognition, culture*	van Dijk (2009)
Sociology of knowledge	How is the knowledge shared across communities expressed in social structures?	*symbolic interactionism, knowledge, Berger and Luckmann, consciousness*	Keller (2011)

Although social structures are objects of study, they can be used to understand other objects of study, such as ideologies and identities. For instance, it is possible to use the family as a social structure to explain how individuals construct particular ideologies and identities.

To this end, using a social structure to explain why individuals think, behave, or communicate in a particular way requires drawing from the knowledge shared between you and the research participants. It is possible to draw from this information, as a social structure is made up of cultural knowledge that you, the researcher, share with your research participants. For example, you may be familiar with the way a research participant expresses an identity or ideology because you have experience with a particular social structure such as being a mother or father while also investigating mothers or fathers talking about their belief systems. The understanding that you share with research participants is commonly referred to as **membership knowledge**, which will be discussed later with other related terms in Chapter 5.

Discourse analysts use social structures to explain discourse phenomena because it is necessary at times to understand the intentions and motivations of research participants. Often in discourse analysis research these intentions and motivations are not explicitly revealed in your data, thus requiring you to use the shared knowledge embedded within a social structure to explain why an individual may be communicating in a particular way.

Summary 1.3

1. Discourse is your object of study.
2. Discourse is meaning.
3. Discourse is both material and immaterial, and spans time and space.
4. Discourse can be expressed though language and behavior.
5. Discourse can express thoughts.

1.4 Your Object of Study and Its Role in Doing Discourse Analysis

Now that you have an understanding of what discourse is, it is possible to begin thinking about what your object of study may be. However, before committing to an object of study, it is necessary to reflect on what it means to select and analyze an object of study. For example, objects of study possess different time commitments (see Chapter 2) and theoretical knowledge requirements (see Chapter 6), making it necessary to think about the issue of feasibility and theory when selecting an object of study. For this reason, it is advisable to identify several potential objects of study now and return to them after reading subsequent chapters, especially Chapters 2, 3, and 6. For now, the principles presented below will help you begin this selection process.

1. An object of study must be collected and analyzed in an ethical way: consider any steps that must be taken to obtain ethical clearance for, or any potential copyright issues involved in, your object of study.
2. An object of study should be collected and analyzed in an efficient way: consider how much time you have, and how much time is required, to collect and analyze your object of study.
3. An object of study must be prepared for an analysis (see Chapter 2): consider any transcription, digital, or data management work that will be needed to analyze your object of study.

4. An object of study must be presented in a clear and logical way (see Chapter 2): consider how to structure and order your analysis of an object of study.
5. An object of study can be analyzed according to different perspectives and levels (see Chapter 3): consider what you would like to say about your object of study.
6. An object of study possesses a communicative context (see Chapter 4): consider what you know about the context of your object of study.
7. An object of study reflects personal or professional subjectivities (see Chapter 5): consider how your subjectivities shape your understanding of an object of study.
8. An object of study can be analyzed by drawing from a range of theories (see Chapter 6): consider what theories are needed to understand your object of study.
9. An object of study is discourse: consider what aspect of the human factor or language use you will analyze in relation to your object of study.
10. An object of study must reflect your analytic goals (see Chapter 7): consider how your object of study helps you answer your research question.

| Summary 1.4 | 1. The analysis in discourse analysis is the approach used to examine an object of study. |
| | 2. Different perspectives and levels of analysis exist. |

Learning Accomplishments

The chapter has established what it means to *do* discourse analysis and has identified examples of discourse. This section identifies how each learning outcome has been addressed in this chapter.

1. You will know what discourse analysis is.

Definitions of discourse analysis were provided. It was stated that discourse analysis can be understood by looking first at discourse, and then analysis. The discourse in discourse analysis can be thought of as possessing two components: language use and the human factor. The analysis in discourse analysis represents the different approaches that can be used to study your object of study.

2. You will understand that there are many types of discourse.

It was established that discourse is all around us. Discourse is the meaning that is derived from, and associated with, all domains and aspects of human communication. Discourse is both material and immaterial. Discourses span time and space, and can be stored as memories.

3. You will understand that discourse is your object of study.

Discourse examples were discussed as objects of study. Seven types of object of study were presented: (1) grammar; (2) actions and practices; (3) identities; (4) places and spaces; (5) stories; (6) ideologies; and (7) social structures.

4. You will know how your object of study fits within a research project.

Discourse analysis is data-driven, meaning your objects of study must shape how you plan and conduct your research project.

Key Themes

This Book

1. This book uses "object of study" as a synonym for *data*.
2. Chapters 1–3 help you identify and analyze your object of study.
3. Chapters 4–6 help you build up your analysis of your object of study.
4. Chapter 7 helps you make sense of all the steps to doing discourse analysis.

Definitions of Discourse Analysis

1. Discourse analysis can be broken into three parts: the human factor, language use, and approaches.
2. The discourse in discourse analysis consists of language use and the human factor.

Discourse

1. Discourse is your object of study.
2. Discourse is meaning.
3. Discourse is both material and immaterial.
4. Discourse spans time and space.
5. Discourse can be expressed though language and behavior.
6. Discourse can express thoughts.

Analysis

1. The analysis in discourse analysis is the approach used to examine an object of study.
2. Different perspectives and levels of analysis exist (see Chapter 3).

Reading List

Baker & Ellece (2011) The book offers a one-stop resource for readers looking to reference or learn key constructs in discourse analysis. In this dictionary-style publication, the authors identify many terms, thinkers, and texts that are important to discourse analysis.

Brown & Yule (1983) In this classic book, the authors identify many grammatical and linguistic features that can be analyzed. The book focuses on the minute details of discourse, making it a good introductory book for readers interested in describing language use.

Waring (2017) The author provides an overview of how different discourse examples, such as structure, social action, identity, and ideology, can be analyzed. Many data examples and tasks are provided throughout the book, giving readers opportunities to practice their analytic skills.

2 What Is an Analysis?

Learning Outcomes

This chapter offers an overview of what an analysis is. The aim of the chapter is to introduce the *structure* of an analysis and the principles that shape how to group and sequence data excerpts.

The contents of the chapter are organized according to the following learning outcomes. After reading this chapter:

1. You will know the structure of an analysis;
2. You will understand what data excerpts are and how to introduce them in your analysis;
3. You will be able to create and present your object of study as smaller data excerpts;
4. You will know how to sequence your analysis.

2.1 The Structure of an Analysis

Selecting an object of study is a consequential part of doing discourse analysis. After selecting an object of study, a researcher must consider a number of planning and analytic issues. These issues are reviewed in subsequent sections, so it would be helpful to identify at least one provisional object of study that you can reflect on while reading this chapter. Of course, it is possible and natural to change your object of study after considering its planning and analytic implications.

Selecting and analyzing an object of study is like a student giving a classroom presentation. The real challenge in planning a classroom presentation is not in selecting a topic, but rather lies in tailoring the talk according to who the audience is, how the teacher will assess the assignment, and how much time is given, to name a few points of consideration. For example, a student that has decided to present on World War II cannot and should not attempt to cover as many facts about the war as possible, nor should the presentation include random and disparate information. The student must plan how each slide will address the points of consideration identified above, as well as, and more importantly, the objective of the presentation.

Similarly, a student doing discourse analysis will begin with selecting an object of study, but what is ultimately analyzed and presented in the project must reflect the intended audience; submission expectations, such as word count, writing conventions, and style; as well as, and more importantly, a research question (for more information about research questions, see Chapter 7). Research questions will help you address numerous analytic issues. How many examples are needed to conduct a convincing analysis? How much detail is needed in an analysis? What type of background information is needed before presenting an analysis? Answering such questions requires knowing what an analysis is.

An analysis is an observation of an object of study. Analytic observations help you answer a research question, reveal something interesting about an object of study, or establish an important fact or phenomenon.

Learning Activity 2.1 Reflecting on What to Do with an Object of Study

In this exercise, the learning objective is to reflect on what a researcher may do after selecting an object of study.

Imagine that you are a criminal lawyer compiling a case against a chemical company accused of dumping waste into public waters. The illegal act of dumping chemicals represents your object of study. Like all objects of study, however, you must be selective and decide on what pieces of evidence are the strongest. The court will only allow you to present two items. The five pieces of evidence below make up your object of study. Therefore, please select two from the five examples; after, please justify your choices; it is also helpful to think of why you did not select the other three examples.

1. company letter to a local politician requesting a change in environmental laws
2. CCTV video of a company truck driving in the direction of a lake
3. company barrel found floating in a local lake
4. test results that show lake water contains chemicals produced by the company
5. anonymous testimonial from a former employee who was fired

Each piece of evidence offers a different perspective to the object of study, and provides a unique argument for the case. Thinking about the reasons that guided your choices will help you understand what a discourse analyst must do after selecting an object of study. Like this hypothetical situation, you will need to be selective in a discourse analysis project, and have reasons for selecting particular aspects of an object of study. In short, an object of study is never just presented in discourse analysis, but rather goes through a process of planning and reflection.

An analysis is structured, like the criminal case presented in the exercise, according to aspects of an object of study. An aspect of an object of study that is presented for analysis is commonly referred to as a **data excerpt** (or **data extract**). Take, for example, a newspaper article as an object of study. A newspaper article will not be presented in its entirety in discourse analysis. Rather, fragments of your object of study, or data excerpts from the newspaper article (e.g., words, phrases, punctuation markers, grammatical constructions, references, hyperlinks, images, or videos) will be used to present your entire analysis. How you structure or present the analysis of many data excerpts will be based on what the research question is, how much writing is required, and who the audience is, to name a few. Figure 2.1 illustrates how a discourse analyst may present the observations of data excerpts in relation to the object of study.

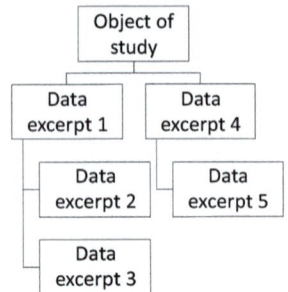

FIGURE 2.1
Object of study and data excerpts

The structure of this example analysis is based on five data excerpts. The example is presented in this way to illustrate that a discourse analyst will have reasons for grouping (see Section 2.5) and sequencing (see Section 2.3) aspects of an object of study in a particular way.

An analysis, and thus its structure (e.g., grouping and sequencing), is based largely on a research question or objective (again, for more information about research questions, see Chapter 7). Therefore, it is helpful to understand how a research question can influence the structure of an analysis.

Learning Activity 2.2 Reflecting on How to Build an Analysis with a Research Question

In this exercise, the learning objective is to reflect on how a researcher may use a research question to structure an analysis.

A research question should include an object of study. Furthermore, a research question should include the analytic focus, or more specifically, the aspect of the object of study that will be examined. The structure of an analysis should be based on these two components of a research question (i.e., the object of study and the analytic focus):

Research question	How do newspaper articles politicize natural disasters?
Object of study	newspaper articles
Focus	politicization of natural disasters

With this example research question, the researcher will need to collect examples of newspaper articles that politicize natural disasters. The researcher will then need to build a collection of data excerpts that offer specific examples of politicization, such as the use of metaphors, adjectives, or verbs. These examples are central to answering the research question, as the analysis of each data excerpt will demonstrate how language is used to politicize natural disasters. The number of data excerpts to use, how to group and sequence them, and what information to include in the analysis will depend on a range of planning and analytic issues, including methodological principles (see Chapter 3).

Please use this discussion to write your own research question. What is your object of study? What is your focus? Is your focus related to the human factor or language use? How will your examples help you answer your research question? How many data excerpts do you think are necessary to provide a strong argument for, or answer to, your research question?

The analysis of an individual data excerpt also possesses a structure, which consists of three major parts.

2.1.1 The Three-Part Structure of an Analysis

An analysis possesses an internal structure with three parts: introduction, data, and analysis. Figure 2.2 offers an illustration of this internal structure.

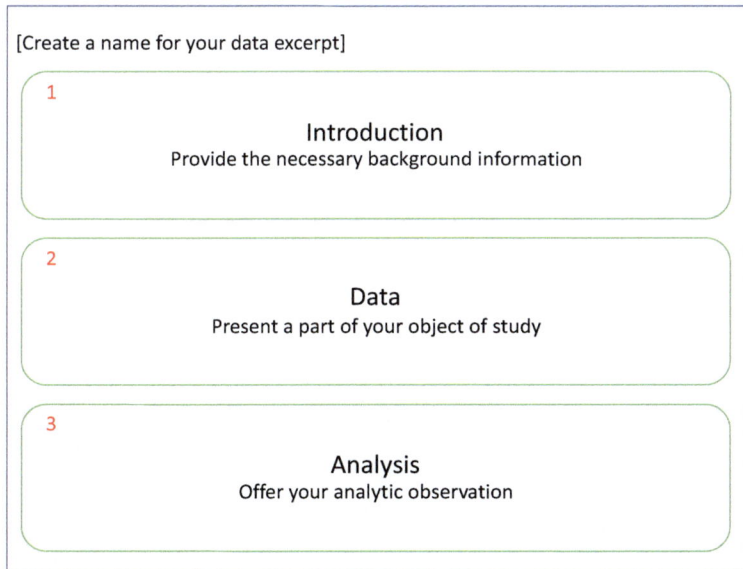

FIGURE 2.2
The three-part structure of an analysis

Note the name section immediately above the introduction. Although data excerpts are not required to have names, they can make it easier for readers to understand and follow your analyses, especially if you are presenting several or many data excerpts. Names can also be used to create a logical order or even a narrative structure that helps you answer your research question.

An analysis should be organized in the order presented in Figure 2.2. That is, it is not advisable to present data before telling the reader what they are or what they should be looking at, as readers need background information in order to understand your analysis fully. Introductions are especially helpful when you are presenting multiple data examples in one analysis, which is common in discourse analysis. Including multiple data examples in one analysis is commonly referred to as presenting a collection. Building and presenting collections is a complex task that will be addressed later in the chapter (Section 2.5).

Part one of the three-part structure is discussed later in Section 2.2: what goes into an introduction. Part two is addressed immediately following this section (see Section 2.1.2): how to present data excerpts according to your medium of data. Part three is addressed in subsequent chapters: what goes into an analysis. Figure 2.3 offers an example of an analysis that is organized according to the three-part structure.

77

Excerpt 3 – Country of origin

In the next data excerpt, the interactants are discussing their backgrounds. Winnie and Roci are talking in the example below. The interactants do not know each other and are in the process of getting acquainted.

```
1       Winnie:   =he- e- [is- actually
2       Roci:             [actually. from hawaii
3                 (1.2)
4       Winnie:   his he a half↓ asian↑
```

The exchange between Winnie and Roci begins with overlapping talk, as indicated by the open brackets in lines 1 and 2. After a brief pause in line 3, Winnie begins to talk again by confirming that a co-participant is half Asian.

Vol. 12, Issue 3, pp. 67-107   © 2023

FIGURE 2.3
An analysis with a three-part structure

The example illustrates several organizational issues that are helpful in planning an analysis. First, the name "Excerpt 3 – Country of origin" clearly signals to the reader when the data excerpt begins: bold font is used in this case, but it is important to refer to any style guidelines that you may be expected to follow for your discourse project. Second, note that there is line spacing between each section of the three-part structure from the name of the data excerpt to the beginning of the analytic observation. This line spacing is called "white space," and it helps the reader follow your analytic observations. Analytic observations with little to no white space are difficult to follow. It is customary to add white space before and after data excerpts, so that the reader can easily identify the beginning of the analysis – this is especially important when using text-based objects of study. Third, note that the data excerpt is presented in a different font: Courier New is used in this case, but the font of your data excerpts will again depend on any style guidelines that you may be expected to follow. How a data excerpt is presented alongside an analytic observation will depend on the medium of data.

2.1.2 The Medium of Data

Data excerpts come in many shapes and sizes. The aim of this section is to provide some examples of what this plurality of data excerpts looks like. The examples presented below are illustrative, and should not be used as a reference for what a good analysis entails (again, the analysis in discourse analysis is discussed in subsequent chapters). More specifically, the data excerpts presented in this section are examples of what the three-part structure looks like according to different medium types. Four medium types are introduced: writing, speaking, images, and multimodal.

2.1.2.1 Writing

Data excerpts within the category of writing include, but of course are not limited to, news stories, academic journal articles, corporate statements, customer reviews, state laws, food labels, social media posts, employee handbooks, blogs, and forum discussions.

Data excerpts that are completely or partially composed of some piece of writing are commonly used in the discourse analysis literature, so many examples can be found for additional support. Data excerpts with writing are easy to manage and present, but there are several planning issues that should be addressed.

Many data excerpts that are composed largely of writing look very similar to data excerpts with speaking. Take, for example, the data excerpt of a news article in Figure 2.4.

Excerpt xx – [name of your data excerpt]

[this is where you place your introduction]

Many years ago, there was a war in a region that should remain unnamed. It is a region that many in the West fear, but for no good reason. Throughout the years there have been many subsequent wars. The region is a topic of great political debate and discussion, leading many to believe that the fear lies not in the region itself, but rather the discourse of political figures and individuals in positions of power. (Jenkings, 7 February 2017, *The Washington News*)

[this is where you place your analysis]

FIGURE 2.4
News article data excerpt

Note that the data excerpt in Figure 2.4 is presented in a different font type and size. Again, this stylistic decision is based on the need to make it easy for the reader to locate where your data is in relation to the analysis. Also note that the data excerpt includes a citation. If the data excerpt that you are using is from a public source, such as a newspaper, journal, website, or blog, then it is customary to include an "in-text" citation. This in-text citation should of course be included in the reference list at the end of your discourse project.

It is also common to use several writing data excerpts for one analytic observation. This practice is based on a collection approach to doing discourse analysis. Figure 2.5 offers an example of what a collection of data excerpts for one analytic observation may look like.

Heading xx [name of your collection]

[this is where you place your introduction]

Data excerpt 1 [name of your data excerpt]
Many years ago, there was a war in a region that should remain unnamed. It is a region that many in the West fear, but for no good reason. Throughout the years there have been many subsequent wars. The region is a topic of great political debate and discussion, leading many to believe that the fear lies not in the region itself, but rather the discourse of political figures and individuals in positions of power. (Jenkings, 7 February 2017, *The Washington News*)

Data excerpt 2 [name of your data excerpt]
This is not a criticism. Political parties come from a history of cultural tribalism. It does not take much looking around to see how the fabric of society is deteriorating as a result of government politics. (Bobbi, 7 November 2019, *The Weekly Gazette*)

Data excerpt 3 [name of your data excerpt]
National polls tell a different story. The public has spoken. It is time for a change. The election of Gary Johnson as the next president makes a momentous time in U.S. history. Let us see what the future holds for our communities. (Freeman, 13 April 2019, *Political Words Weekly*)

[this is where you place your analysis]

FIGURE 2.5
Collection of news articles

Note how the collection of data excerpts in Figure 2.5 includes, or falls under, a heading. It is customary to give your collection a name (especially if you have multiple collections). Collections are typically included as subheadings within a larger analysis section. Also of importance is the introduction and analysis. Collections will often have one introduction and one set of analytic observations. You will still name, or at least number, each data excerpt because doing so will make it easy for you and the reader to refer back to specific points in your analytic observations.

2.1.2.2 Speaking

Data excerpts within the category of speaking include, but of course are not limited to, conversations, speeches, presentations, academic lectures, classroom discussions, tutoring sessions, public service announcements, movie clips, arguments, debates, and YouTube videos.

Data excerpts that are completely or partially made up of someone speaking are commonly used within the discourse analysis literature, so many examples can be found for additional help. Data excerpts with speaking examples take more time to prepare because of the need to produce a transcript, which is a text-based representation of spoken communication. Additional support for the work involved in preparing transcripts can be found in Jenks (2011).

Rather than attend to the technical aspects of transcription work, this section presents the different ways speaking can be presented within the three-part structure.

The most common way of presenting speaking in a data excerpt is to use columns to demarcate the different types of information that should be included in a transcript. The most common types of information included in a transcript are:

(1) when the person is speaking;
(2) who is speaking; and
(3) what is being said or done.

Some variation exists in how the column layout is presented because discourse analysts will apply their own preferences or use specialized transcription software. With that said, many data excerpts with speaking examples will look very similar to the one presented in Figure 2.6.

77

Excerpt xx – [name of your data excerpt]

[this is where you place your introduction]

```
1       Winnie:   =he- e- [is- actually
2       Roci:             [actually. from hawaii
3                 (1.2)
4       Winnie:   his he a half↓ asian↑
```

[this is where you place your analysis]

Vol. 12, Issue 3, pp. 67-107   © 2023

FIGURE 2.6
Standard data excerpt with speaking I

Note again the white space in the data excerpt. White space can be found between each column of information from left to right: (1) when the person is speaking, (2) who is speaking, and (3) what is being said or done. Also note the utterance in line 1 by Winnie: transcripts of spoken communication must accurately represent the recorded speech even if it is somewhat ungrammatical or peculiar (Jenks, 2011). Similarly, the punctuation marks and symbols used in the third column do not follow writing conventions, but rather the symbols represent aspects of speech used in different transcription systems (Jenks, 2013).

The variation in the column layout that you may encounter is often based on stylistic choices. For example, rather than line numbers, some discourse analysts prefer to use time stamps. Instead of spelling out who is speaking, some discourse analysts use abbreviations. Figure 2.7 demonstrates what this variation may look like.

77

Excerpt xx – [name of your data excerpt]

[this is where you place your introduction]

```
00:01   Winnie:   =he- e- [is- actually

00:04   Roci:                [actually. from hawaii

00:07             (1.2)

00:08   Winnie:   his he a half↓ asian↑
```

[this is where you place your analysis]

FIGURE 2.7
Standard data excerpt with speaking II

Vol. 12, Issue 3, pp. 67-107   © 2023

The final data excerpt presented in this section offers an example of how speaking can be represented in a table, using individual boxes for the different types of information found in a transcript. Figure 2.8 offers an example of the table format.

77

Excerpt xx – [name of your data excerpt]

[this is where you place your introduction]

00:01	Winnie: =he- e- [is- actually
00:04	Roci: [actually. from hawaii
00:07	(1.2)
00:08	Winnie: his he a half↓ asian↑

[this is where you place your analysis]

FIGURE 2.8
Nonstandard data excerpt with speaking

Vol. 12, Issue 3, pp. 67-107   © 2023

While the information included in each column remains the same, the table is preferred by some discourse analysts because the lines cutting through the white space are thought to present a more legible transcript of spoken communication. Again, these differences in presentation are often based on stylistic preferences, so it is important to select a layout that you think best captures your object of study.

2.1.2.3 Images

Data excerpts within the category of images include, but of course are not limited to, screenshots of websites, including social media platforms, stills or frames taken from videos, such as a YouTube clip, drawings, and scanned documents. Furthermore, any picture taken from a camera or mobile phone can be potentially used as a data excerpt.

Data excerpts that are only made up of images will often have some embedded language, such as a directive on a traffic sign or food items on a menu. This section is concerned with these image-centric data excerpts.

However, images are also used alongside data excerpts with other medium types, such as transcripts of spoken communication. In these situations, images offer visual representations of something that was written, said, or done, such as a frame taken from a video of a father and daughter discussing food options on a menu. Data excerpts that include images and other medium types are multimodal, and will be discussed in Subsection 2.1.2.4.

Data excerpts with images are relatively easy to prepare and manage, though there are special considerations regarding file type and size that will influence how you organize your analytic observations. More importantly, images containing sensitive or personal information will need to be vetted by an ethics advisor or committee. It is important to refer to institutional regulations that may dictate what file types to use and the ethical procedures to follow in preparing images for research purposes, as guidelines vary from one institution to another.

Image-centric data excerpts contain all the information that you need to present your analytic observations. These types of data excerpts must also be presented using the three-part structure, as Figure 2.9 illustrates.

The image of Figure 2.9 is placed between the introduction and analysis. Some white space is included before and after the image. The image itself contains some language: in this case, Swedish.

Images used in data excerpts can be manipulated to fit a particular empirical goal. For example, it is customary to annotate images with symbols or text to highlight a part of the picture or a particular analytic observation. In the first image, for instance, a proficiency in Swedish may be needed to follow an analytic observation. In such cases, it is

Excerpt xx – [name of your data excerpt]

[this is where you place your introduction]

FIGURE 2.9
Standard image data
excerpt

[this is where you place your analysis]

Excerpt xx – [name of your data excerpt]

[this is where you place your introduction]

FIGURE 2.10
Annotated image data
excerpt

[this is where you place your analysis]

common practice to include a translation within, or immediately out-side, the image. Figure 2.10 provides an example of this annotation.

The translation at the bottom of the image can be placed in other locations within the data excerpt so long as the text is legible. It is also common practice to include such translations in the introduction or analysis. Deciding on where to place an annotation is based on a range of issues from the practical, such as an image's color and composition, to the methodological, such as the need to focus on a particular aspect or part of the data excerpt.

Screenshots are also frequently used as data excerpts. Such images include anything that is visible on your computer screen, though screenshots are often of social media platforms or websites. Screenshots of social media platforms and websites are frequently used in the discourse literature, as they are accessible and cover a range of language and social phenomena. Data excerpts with screenshots follow the same planning guidelines as stated previously, though again care must be taken when using images that contain sensitive or personal information. Furthermore, permission to use screenshots may be needed even if they are taken from public spaces.

Figure 2.11 provides an example of a social media data excerpt included in a three-part structure. The image is placed again between the introduction and analysis with white space before and after the data excerpt.

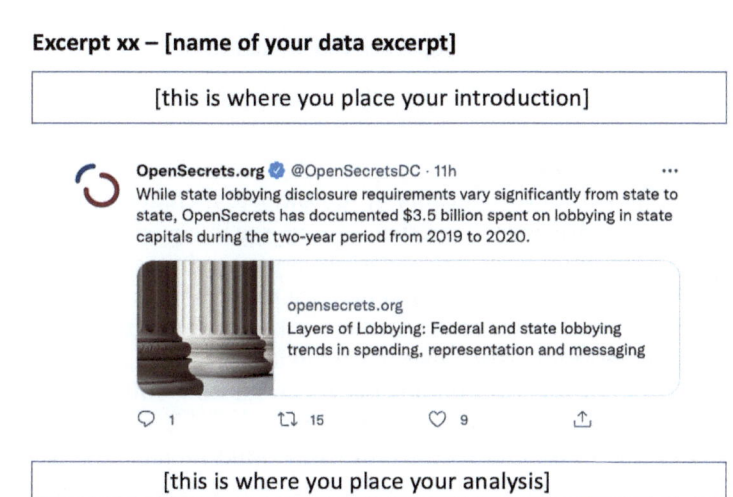

Excerpt xx – [name of your data excerpt]

[this is where you place your introduction]

OpenSecrets.org @OpenSecretsDC · 11h
While state lobbying disclosure requirements vary significantly from state to state, OpenSecrets has documented $3.5 billion spent on lobbying in state capitals during the two-year period from 2019 to 2020.

opensecrets.org
Layers of Lobbying: Federal and state lobbying trends in spending, representation and messaging

1   15   9

[this is where you place your analysis]

FIGURE 2.11
Screenshot data excerpt

Screenshots of social media platforms, such as the one in Figure 2.11, are often multimodal, including text, pictures, symbols, and links, to name a few. Often all of this information is not needed for an analytic observation. In such cases, it is customary to include an annotation to highlight what you would like the reader to consider.

For example, in Figure 2.12, a phrase has been selected to highlight what the reader should carefully consider. The annotation shape used is a bi-directional arrow, which is red in this example.

The annotation shape is placed under two words that represent the researcher's analytic interest. Although it is possible to highlight this type of information in the introduction, placing the annotation within the data excerpt helps the reader locate where the research interest is situated within the larger screenshot. It is also possible to highlight such information in both the introduction and data excerpt.

Excerpt xx – [name of your data excerpt]

[this is where you place your introduction]

[this is where you place your analysis]

FIGURE 2.12
Annotated screenshot
data excerpt

2.1.2.4 Multimodal

Data excerpts within the category of multimodal include any combination of the three previous categories: writing, speaking, and images. One of the most common multimodal data excerpts combines speaking and images. For example, it is common practice to include an image with a transcript of spoken communication when the object of study is a video-recorded conversation. Discourse analysts will typically use images with transcripts of spoken communication to reveal how embodied movements are intricately coordinated with talk.

Other examples of, and reasons for using, multimodal data excerpts include, but of course are not limited to, using scanned images of documents to show what individuals are looking at or talking about, juxtaposing an example of texting with a transcript of speaking to demonstrate how the medium of communication influences language use, and adding a company logo to an excerpt taken from a mission statement to illustrate the significance of visual communication in official institutional language.

Although most images used in discourse projects are inherently multimodal, this section uses the term multimodal to refer specifically to instances when it is necessary to combine two excerpt types within the same analytic observation.

Multimodal data excerpts typically fall within one of two layout types: adjacent and embedded. An adjacent multimodal data excerpt presents two or more categories horizontally or vertically in a side-by-side or top-to-bottom fashion. An embedded multimodal data excerpt transposes one category into another, forming a new multimodal example.

Figure 2.13 provides an example of an adjacent multimodal data excerpt.

Excerpt xx – [name of your data excerpt]

[this is where you place your introduction]

[this is where you place your analysis]

FIGURE 2.13
Adjacent multimodal data excerpt

In Figure 2.13, the image and transcript of spoken communication are presented vertically within a single box. Time stamps are used in this example, which are meant to be read from top to bottom. The images provide a visual illustration of what is being said, helping the reader appreciate the argumentative situation the two political pundits find themselves communicating. Again, note that there is sufficient white space throughout the data excerpt and a three-part structure. The two categories of data excerpt are not, however, transposed or embedded. To this end, Figure 2.14 provides an example of an embedded multimodal data excerpt.

Excerpt xx – [name of your data excerpt]

[this is where you place your introduction]

[this is where you place your analysis]

FIGURE 2.14
Embedded multimodal data excerpt

In Figure 2.14, the transcript of spoken communication is embedded within the image, creating a cartoon strip experience that should be familiar to many. The transcript of spoken communication is numbered and should be read from left to right. Embedded multimodal transcripts can be used to limit the amount of space used on a page, but they take much longer to prepare and present in a legible way. Numerous examples of embedded multimodal data excerpts can be found in the discourse literature if additional illustrations are needed.

Summary 2.1	1. An analytic observation is based on a data excerpt and possesses an internal structure.
	2. A data excerpt is a part or segment of an object of study.
	3. Data excerpts help readers make sense of your object of study.
	4. An analysis consists of an introduction, a data excerpt, and an analytic observation.
	5. The length and content of three-part structures vary considerably.

2.2 The Introduction of an Analysis

Data excerpts contain a great deal of linguistic and communicative information, which can be interpreted in multiple ways. Data excerpts can be exceptionally long, spanning several pages; while others are rich in cultural or political meaning, leading readers to interpret data excerpts according to their own subjectivities. Although there is nothing inherently wrong with long or culturally sensitive data excerpts, it is important to keep readers "on track" with your specific analytic observations. Introductions to data excerpts help you achieve this information management task.

Like all aspects of a discourse project, introductions to data excerpts can be written in a number of ways, reflecting specific disciplinary traditions and research interests. With that said, there are three facets of an introduction that can be addressed irrespective of theoretical beliefs: new information, specific information, analyst information.

1. **New information**: it is customary to provide general information about your object of study, including who the research participants are, somewhere in your discourse project (e.g., the theory or methodology section). Often this general information does not reflect the specificities of a particular data excerpt. Introductions to data excerpts allow you to add new information that the reader may not know but needs in order to understand your analytic observation. This new information can be related to research participants not introduced earlier, the situation that makes up the communication that is being analyzed, or any other background information that will help the reader better understand your data excerpt.

2. **Specific information**: it is not uncommon to point the reader's attention to a specific part or location of a data excerpt, such as an inconspicuous object within a larger image. Specific information may also include explanations of, or translations for, language included in a data excerpt that may be incomprehensible to the reader. It is also necessary to point to specific information in a data excerpt to prepare the reader for something important in an analytic observation. Pointing to specific information in a data excerpt is a strategy that seasoned discourse analysts adopt to ensure that the reader does not miss or overlook important information.

3. **Analyst information**: it is customary to point the reader's attention to transcription and representational decisions made while transforming an object of study into smaller data excerpts. For example, transforming a recording of a spoken conversation into a text-based data excerpt requires using special symbols from a transcription system (for an introductory account of transcription issues, see Jenks, 2011). Including references to, or discussing, such information in an introduction is necessary for the reader to understand a data excerpt fully. An introduction may also include analyst information because it is necessary to discuss how a particular data excerpt fits within a larger collection of excerpts (e.g., explaining how a particular data excerpt fits within a longer recording of people talking.)

Summary 2.2
1. Three approaches can be used to introduce data excerpts.
2. The first approach to introducing data excerpts is referred to as new information.
3. The second approach to introducing data excerpts is referred to as specific information.
4. The third approach to introducing data excerpts is referred to as analyst information.

2.3 The Sequence of an Analysis

Data excerpts need to be presented in an order that reflects an underlying structure. This structure could be temporal, empirical, or narrative. Sequencing is necessary, as most discourse projects are based on the analysis of several or more data excerpts. The need to sequence data excerpts is also a reminder that a discourse project must not simply provide disparate analytic observations of data excerpts, but rather tell a story, create a narrative, or establish an argument. Sequencing data excerpts will help transform an analysis from a collection of disparate analytic observations into a coherent theme that reflects an internal structure. These sequencing structures are discussed below as three, sometimes overlapping, options.

1. **Temporal structure**: one of the more common ways of sequencing your data excerpts is to follow a timeline. For example, if your object of study is a two-hour recording of a classroom lecture, then your data excerpts could be selected and sequenced according to different moments in time from the beginning to the end of the lesson. A temporal structure is useful when the timing of your data excerpts is central to your analytic observations. For instance, it may be necessary to show how language is central to the way an event or encounter unfolds.

2. **Empirical structure**: data excerpts must be selected and sequenced according to an argumentative point. That is, what is your line of argument and how are your data excerpts aligned accordingly? A line of argument could be anything related to a point that you would like to establish in your analytic observations, such as demonstrating that students use a range of nonverbal resources to display engagement, showing that metaphors are used in news articles to review contentious government policies, or arguing that agreements and disagreements are constructed in different ways, to name a few. Put simply, an empirical structure should reflect your research question(s) (see Chapter 7).

3. **Narrative structure**: data excerpts can be selected and sequenced according to an aspect of a story that you would like the reader to know. This aspect of the story could be based on an experience told by a research participant or reflect a particular narrative that you would like the reader to follow in your analytic observations. For instance, a narrative structure could entail sequencing data excerpts according to key figures within, or particular events that make up, a story.

In all discourse projects, it is necessary to select data excerpts that offer the strongest or clearest examples of your argument while considering the extent to which they are representative of your object of study (see Section 2.4). This may entail following one sequencing structure identified above, grouping data excerpts into collections to establish different but related observations, beginning your analysis with the most convincing examples, or using any combination of options identified in this section.

Summary 2.3

1. Three approaches can be used to sequence data excerpts.
2. The first approach to sequencing data excerpts is referred to as temporal structure.
3. The second approach to sequencing data excerpts is referred to as empirical structure.
4. The third approach to sequencing data excerpts is referred to as narrative structure.

2.4 Building a Corpus

It has been established thus far in this chapter that it is necessary to introduce and sequence data excerpts. However, it is not possible to introduce and sequence data excerpts before building a corpus.

A corpus is an aggregation of data excerpts. It includes or represents all the data excerpts that you have collected, and will likely use, for your discourse project. When building a corpus, one of the first issues to address is size. How much data should I collect? The size of your corpus will depend on a number of theoretical and methodological factors, including whether your analysis will adopt statistical calculations or rely mostly on qualitative approaches. For quantitative approaches that make use of statistical calculations or methods from corpus linguistics that can scan through millions of words in a matter of seconds (see O'Keeffe & McCarthy, 2010), bigger corpora are typically considered better than smaller ones. However, qualitative approaches, such as the ones discussed in this book, adopt a somewhat different and nuanced position when it comes to corpus size.

A qualitative understanding of corpus size is based on two interrelated research issues: time and empirical objectives. Data excerpts that are based on highly nuanced information, such as transcripts of spoken communication and multimodal depictions of multi-party talk, will take a long time to prepare, analyze, and present. Time and effort alone will lead to smaller corpora than those based on, for example, text-based data excerpts that do not require much transcription work. For example, it is not uncommon for a one-minute stretch of spoken communication to take approximately one hour to transcribe in detail. Accordingly, if your empirical objective is to analyze the complex details of language use, then it is important to consider the logistical challenges in transcribing and representing such data (see Jenks, 2013).

For a discourse project that is to be completed in three or four months (i.e., the length of a typical academic semester), a corpus of spoken or multimodal communication would typically involve no more than one to four hours of data. The exception to this approximate calculation is if an existing corpus is used in a discourse project. Existing corpora can be found with prepared data excerpts, allowing you to spend more time with analytic observations (so long as permission has been given to use the data).

Great variation exists in what is deemed an adequate corpus size and how much time a researcher has to complete a discourse project. For instance, a corpus of pictures taken of city billboards could range from a few images to thousands, representing the differences in time that a researcher has to collect and analyze data. It is best to consult a mentor, supervisor, or more seasoned discourse analyst for advice on corpus size.

The issue of representativeness must also be considered when building a corpus. Representativeness is the extent to which a corpus accurately depicts its related object of study. That is, is your corpus an accurate representation of what you are investigating, such as the people, the interaction, or the culture?

Representativeness is related to range and balance. With objects of study that represent cultural phenomena or communities, such as political discourse or national identities, it is especially important to select data excerpts that cover a range of examples. Range, however, must be considered alongside balance: that is, it is necessary to strike the right balance of representativeness. For example, if you are investigating the language of a contentious political issue, say abortion laws in the United States, then it may be important to include data excerpts of politicians from different ideological positions discussing their views. With this example, balance would be including data excerpts that, for instance, have an equal number of Democrats and Republicans discussing their views on abortion. Similarly, if you are interested in how "Americans" talk, then it is important to reflect on the extent to which your corpus includes people from a range of age, gender, ethnicity, and other demographic categories. Balancing this range would require considering the defining characteristics of your corpus. For example, will your corpus represent a specific community or demographic, such as Asian Americans or adolescent boys; or will the focus be a larger group, such as Asians or adult English speakers? Finally, representativeness will influence corpus size: a corpus that is representative of its related objects of study will typically require locating more data excerpts in order to achieve range and balance.

After building a corpus, it may be necessary to group your data excerpts into smaller collections of phenomena. Managing these collections requires attending to several empirical issues.

Summary 2.4

1. A corpus is an aggregation of data excerpts.
2. An entire corpus need not be used for a discourse project.
3. A corpus should accurately reflect its related object of study.

2.5 Managing Collections

A collection is a group of data excerpts. Collections are used to establish distinct analytic observations. For most discourse projects, collections will be taken from a larger corpus of data. In other words, most discourse projects are based on collections.

For instance, say you have a corpus of 100 news articles discussing global warming. While looking through this corpus and writing down some initial observations, you may have noticed that there are three distinct and interesting themes: transportation, food consumption, and economic prosperity. This initial noticing may have led you to establish three collections of 20 data excerpts each: one collection of global warming and transportation with 20 examples, one collection of global warming and food consumption with 20 examples, and one collection of global warming and economic prosperity with 20 examples. Although there were 100 examples at the start, only 60 will be used for the analysis. This practice of only using a portion of a corpus is again typical of most discourse projects. That is to say, it is customary to complete a discourse project that is based on a corpus from which only a much smaller percentage of data excerpts are selected for the report. Simply put, you should not feel obliged to include all the data that you have collected for your corpus.

This example of news articles reveals an important part of planning a good analysis. Analytic observations are based on, and begin with, an initial "reading" or "noticing" period, which involves scanning through an entire corpus to determine if there are noteworthy issues, recurring themes, or interesting phenomena worth investigating further. Scanning through a corpus for potential issues, themes, or phenomena to analyze is a necessary step before adopting a more concerted search for data excerpts to use in a discourse project. How you select data excerpts from a larger corpus, and the number of examples used for each collection, will depend on your empirical goals, including research questions, as well as the issue of representativeness. Like building a corpus, smaller collections must accurately represent your object of study. In the example of three collections of news articles, each collection must reflect the overall language used to discuss a specific issue. For instance, in the global warming and transportation collection, it is important to reflect on the extent to which the twenty data excerpts that were selected are representative of the language used to discuss global warming and transportation within the larger corpus.

Summary 2.5
1. A collection is a group of data excerpts.
2. Collections are used to establish distinct analytic observations.
3. Most discourse projects are based on collections.

Learning Accomplishments

The chapter has introduced the structure of an analysis and the principles that shape how to group and sequence data excerpts. This section identifies how each learning outcome has been addressed in the chapter.

1. You will know the structure of an analysis.

The three-part structure was discussed as an ideal model for presenting analytic observations.

2. You will understand what data excerpts are and how to introduce them in your analysis.

A data excerpt was defined as a smaller representation of an object of study, and one that is needed to present a series of analytic observations. Three approaches to introducing data excerpts were reviewed.

3. You will be able to create and present your object of study as smaller data excerpts.

How a data excerpt is presented will depend partly on its medium of communication. This relationship was established by offering many examples of data excerpts from text-based communication to multi-modal objects.

4. You will know how to structure your analysis.

Three approaches to sequencing data excerpts were reviewed. These sequencings were discussed in relation to building a corpus and managing collections of data.

Key Themes

Analytic Observations

1. An analytic observation is based on a data excerpt.
2. An analytic observation possesses an internal structure.

Data Excerpts

1. A data excerpt is a part or segment of an object of study.
2. Data excerpts help readers make sense of your object of study.

Three-Part Structure to an Analysis

1. An analysis consists of an introduction, a data excerpt, and an analytic observation.
2. The length and content of three-part structures vary considerably.

Introducing Data Excerpts

1. Three approaches can be used to introduce data excerpts.
2. The first approach to introducing data excerpts is referred to as new information.
3. The second approach to introducing data excerpts is referred to as specific information.
4. The third approach to introducing data excerpts is referred to as analyst information.

Sequencing Data Excerpts

1. Three approaches can be used to sequence data excerpts.
2. The first approach to sequencing data excerpts is referred to as temporal structure.
3. The second approach to sequencing data excerpts is referred to as empirical structure.
4. The third approach to sequencing data excerpts is referred to as narrative structure.

Building a Corpus

1. A corpus is an aggregation of data excerpts.
2. An entire corpus need not be used for a discourse project.
3. A corpus should accurately reflect its related object of study.

Managing Collections

1. A collection is a group of data excerpts.
2. Collections are used to establish distinct analytic observations.
3. Most discourse projects are based on collections.

Reading List

Mondada (2018) The author discusses the principles of transcribing multimodal data from a conversation analytic perspective. Although the discussion is based on conversation analytic principles, the review of gesture, gaze, and other embodied movements can be applied to all discourse analysis approaches.

O'Halloran (2004) In this edited collection of multimodal studies inspired by systemic functional linguistics, the author examine a range of objects of study from material objects in space to print media. The book offers excellent examples of how to organize analytic observations using different media types.

O'Keeffe & McCarthy (2010) Although much of the book is devoted to analyzing language from a corpus linguistics perspective, the six chapters in the second section of the handbook review issues pertaining to building and designing a corpus. These six chapters are written for a corpus linguistics audience, but the discussion can help all discourse analysts build a corpus. Similarly, the book offers useful examples of how to plan and organize analytic observations.

3 What Are the Perspectives and Levels of an Analysis?

Learning Outcomes

This chapter provides a practical overview of the *analysis* in discourse analysis. The aim of the chapter is to establish how to analyze your selected object of study.

The contents of the chapter are organized according to the following learning outcomes.

After reading this chapter:

1. You will understand that discourse can be analyzed from different, sometimes overlapping, perspectives: language use, the human factor, and the connections between these two vantage points;
2. You will understand that there are different levels of discourse analysis: summation, description, interpretation, evaluation, and transformation;
3. You will understand that the analytic process is multifaceted; it can combine different perspectives and levels of analysis.

3.1 Making Sense of the Analytic Process

The analytic process is what defines your job as a discourse analyst. Your job as an analyst is to *demonstrate* how discourse *operates* within a particular situation. What does this entail?

First, it is important to address what is meant by operates. You know from Chapter 1 that discourse can include anything from how words are used by an individual to accomplish a social action to historical events that shape how language is presently used by speech communities. In this sense, discourse operates within a range of situational phenomena (see Chapter 4). What you decide on investigating within this range of possibilities is your object of study.

Second, it is important to establish what is meant by demonstrate. Demonstrating how discourse operates within a particular situation is another way of saying that you must write something noteworthy about your object of study. Herein lies the crux of doing discourse analysis: a noteworthy analytic observation requires you to apply perspectives and levels of analysis to your object of study. These perspectives and levels are the topic of the present chapter.

Learning Activity 3.1 Getting Started

The analytic process is multifaceted. It is based on the analytic perspectives and levels introduced in this chapter, as well as the theories and methodological issues presented in subsequent chapters.

This seemingly difficult analytic process requires some simplification. To this end, reflect on how the object of study below can be analyzed. In other words, what can you say about the X exchange?

Object of Study 3.1 X Exchange

You are scrolling through your X feed. You come across the following exchange between two users of different political orientations:

X Liz @elizabethjjkk3968 Nov 1
health care must be free in America

X Rebeca @soundreason Nov 2
socialism is evil and so are you

X Liz @elizabethjjkk3968 Nov 2
#crazyrightwinger

As a novice discourse analyst, you may be wondering what you could possibly say about this discourse example without knowing much about the theories and tools discussed in this book. A useful way of approaching the analysis of this X exchange, and indeed all objects of study, is to first ask yourself the following two questions:

1   What do you see?
2   What do you want to say?

First, all objects of study can be *seen* from different perspectives: language use, the human factor, and the connections between these two vantage points (see Figure 1.1 in Chapter 1).

Return to the X example and ask yourself again what you see. Do you see two X users arguing in the heat of the moment? This type of seeing relates to the language used by the X users, such as the specific interactional features used to provide a counter argument.

Alternatively, do you see a communicative exchange that is indicative of the problems that exist in societies? This type of seeing relates to the human factors that shape the ways in which language is used, such as how a history of tribalism may encourage confrontational language. Thus, the first question (What do you see?) is concerned with establishing an analytic perspective for your object of study: language use or the human factor.

Second, all objects of study can be *written about* in several ways using different *levels* of analysis: summation, description, interpretation, evaluation, and transformation. Return to the X example and ask yourself what you want to say about what you see.

Do you want to write about the complex nature of the language used during the X exchange? This level of writing is often associated with *descriptions*, uncovering for example the turn-taking patterns of the political argument or the metaphors used to refute a point. Do you want to write about the hidden belief systems that shape how and why individuals argue on X? This level of writing is often associated with *interpretations*, using theories to explain the X exchange as a representation of the larger social discord that exists in society or perhaps discussing the possible reasons why online platforms encourage deviant behavior.

Thus, the second question (What do you want to say?) is concerned with determining what level of analysis you wish to apply to your object of study: summation, description, interpretation, evaluation, and transformation.

It is important to remember that researchers may not agree on what they are seeing in an object of study (see Chapter 5), and this should not be viewed as problematic in qualitative discourse analytic research (see Chapter 7).

While progressing through the more complex topics discussed in subsequent chapters, you may find it useful to return to this section, and summary Figure 3.1, to remind yourself of the basic aims of a discourse analyst. What do you see? What do you want to say? Figure 3.1 illustrates the analytic process according to these two questions.

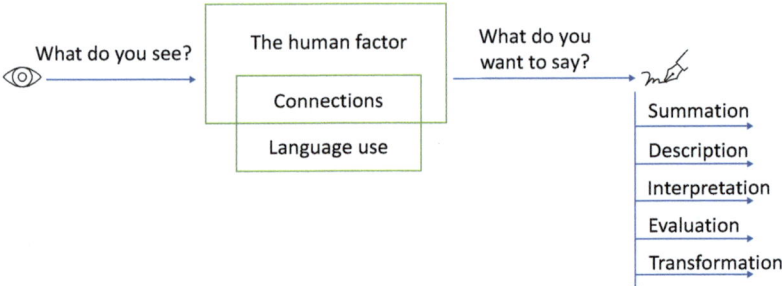

FIGURE 3.1
The analytic process

This illustration represents one way of approaching the analytic process which asks you to consider what is important or interesting about your object of study first, and then think about the tools that inform your analyses. It is possible to begin the analytic process the other way around where your methodology tells you what you are supposed to see. This methodology-first approach is not addressed here, as it requires learning advanced theories that complicate the pedagogical objectives of this chapter.

To this end, the rest of the chapter is devoted to unpacking the different elements of Figure 3.1. The connections between language use and the human factor will not be discussed as a separate section, as most analytic approaches make some type of connection between these two perspectives. Similarly, although the five analysis types are presented in different sections, they can be combined to answer the same research question. Some analysis types also share similar principles and objectives.

3.2 Perspective: Language Use

The language use perspective, which was discussed in Chapter 1 as the discourse in discourse analysis, is often associated with looking at the minute or smaller details of an object of study. A focus on the minute or smaller details of an object of study does not mean that your research is less significant or is devoid of societal implications. A good way of thinking about analytic perspectives is to imagine that you are using a telescope to view your object of study. A language use perspective requires zooming in to your object of study. A human factor perspective requires zooming out from your object of study.

Table 3.1 helps illustrate this analogy by providing discourse perspective examples associated with different objects of study.

Table 3.1 Language use examples		
Object of study	**Language use**	**The human factor**
Billboard ad	color scheme, text type, images	the company's marketing goal
Newspaper article	topic, pronouns, rhetorical devices	the newspaper's political agenda
Presidential speech	voice, amplitude, narrative	the country's economy
Job interview	language of interview, questions-answers	the interviewee's ethnic identity

The discourse examples in the middle column are associated with the language use perspective, as they are features that you see or hear best when zooming in to your object of study. For example, if your telescope is pointed at a billboard, then what you will see are the words, images, and colors of the advertisement. Conversely, the human factor features require you to zoom out with your telescope and consider, for example, the social structures (see Chapter 1) that potentially shape the language of your object of study. For example, the company's reasons for designing the billboard in a particular way are human factors that, while feeding into the language of an object of study (i.e., what the advertisement looks like), exist outside the physical space in which the billboard is displayed.

Learning Activity 3.2 Reflecting on Language Use and the Human Factor

Each object of study in Table 3.1 includes two or three language use examples. However, when identifying your own object of study, there will be a plethora of language use features that you can potentially investigate. Although there is no definitive list of language use examples that you can refer to after selecting an object of study, you can practice identifying discourse perspectives by applying the telescope analogy to other situations.

1. Create your own table by identifying two or more objects of study. Refer to Chapter 1 for ideas if you need inspiration.
2. Are your language use examples similar or different across all of your objects of study? How does your object of study influence the type of language use features that you can investigate?
3. Why have you selected your human factor examples? In what ways do they exist outside the language being used? How do these examples shape your language use features?
4. Do you have any examples in your table that appear to be related to both language use and the human factor (i.e., meso)? This is not unusual if so. And in such cases, the issue of what level your feature belongs to is connected to more complex methodological issues discussed later in this book.

For now, go back to the job interview example in Table 3.1. Identity is treated as a human factor example, as it is something that develops and evolves over time and space, such as identities of gender or nationality. More importantly, identity is treated as a human factor example because while you may be able to see and hear the ethnicity of the interviewee (let's say she is an Asian American), it is only a language use feature if the interactants make it part of the interview process (e.g., by talking about it).

Again, the language use perspective is about zooming in to your object of study. For example, if your object of study is a video recording of a teacher and student discussing the results of an English language test, then your language use perspective would begin with the words, texts, sounds, or images that you see, read, or hear while watching the data: the eye gaze established by the two interactants, the words used by the student, the texts referred to by the teacher, and the gestures made to convey meaning are some of the many language use features that could be examined.

Figure 3.2 provides a visual illustration of where a language use perspective begins in the analytic process. Note that there are no arrows cutting through the different perspectives, indicating an initial focus on language use.

Seeing discourse as language use does not mean you are blind to the human factor. A language use perspective will account for the human factor when it demonstrably shapes, for example, the communication between the teacher and student (also refer back to the interview example above). For instance, the institutional roles established in the classroom over time, the school's policy on providing feedback, or the country's position as it pertains to the importance of learning English may all influence language use.

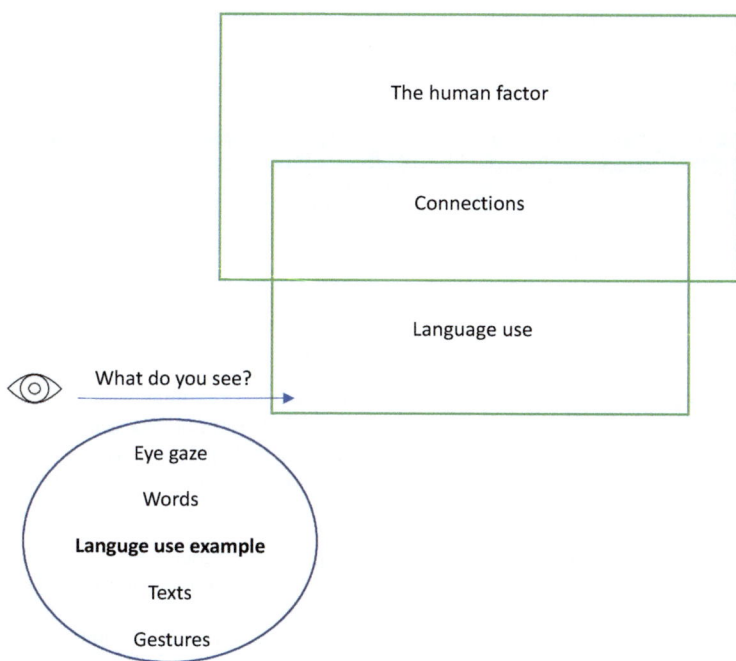

FIGURE 3.2
Seeing discourse as
language use

In this sense, language use perspectives are *inductive* (or bottom-up):
such perspectives begin by zooming in, but will zoom out to look at the
human factor if meso connections can be made (see Figure 3.3).

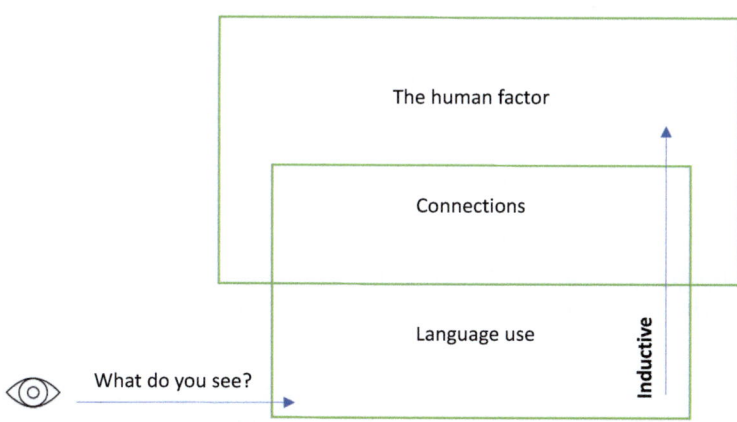

FIGURE 3.3
Language use as an
inductive approach

Making language use and human factor connections begins with
what you have as an object of study. For example, are you looking at an
object of study located in a physical space, such as a roadside billboard
or a public health notice at the entrance of a shopping mall? With language use, your analysis of this example will begin with the texts and
images of billboards or public health notices. Through your analysis of
these texts and images, however, you may discover that several human

factors are shaping why the billboard or public notice is constructed and presented in a particular way. Table 3.2 provides additional examples of connecting language use with the human factor.

Table 3.2 Examples of language use to human factor connections		
Language use	**The human factor**	**Connection**
Turn-taking	power	Looking at the turn-taking practices in a classroom, and discovering through your analysis that teachers restrict opportunities for students to participate.
Pronouns	identity	Looking at the use of pronouns in immigrant communities, and discovering through your analysis that "I" and "we" are used to express different national identities.
Narratives	gender	Looking at how students retell past experiences of learning, and discovering through your analysis that boys and girls sequence their stories differently.
Word choice	racism	Looking at the words used in job advertisements, and discovering through your analysis that linguistic terms, such as native speaker versus non-native speaker, provide opportunities for discrimination.

Seeing discourse as language use reflects a concern for the "here-and-now" of your object of study. How does a conversation between a father and daughter unfold sequentially and interactionally? What textual features are used in an earnings report to shareholders? What gestures are used to display engagement and participation in classrooms? These questions are language use in orientation, reflecting the here-and-now of different objects of study.

Summary 3.2 ends this section with five points that summarize the main principles of seeing discourse as language use.

Summary 3.2

1. Language use features are not small in terms of empirical significance.
2. Seeing discourse as language use requires you to zoom in with your telescope.
3. Language use features are often immediately visible or hearable.
4. Making meso connections is often accomplished inductively.
5. Seeing discourse as language use does not mean ignoring the human factor.

3.3 Perspective: The Human Factor

The human factor, as discussed in Chapter 1, refers to all the social and cultural variables that may influence language use. These variables are often described as being "larger" than language use, as they operate above, or outside, communication. This notion of "larger," however, does not mean that the human factor is more important empirically and socially. Again, the telescope analogy is a simple way of thinking about the analytic process: zooming in with your telescope reveals the here-and-now or the language use of your object of study. The human factor, conversely, requires you to zoom out and consider the variables that are located outside language use.

Table 3.3 helps illustrate this analogy by providing examples of the human factor and their relevance to different objects of study.

Table 3.3 The human factor examples		
Object of study	**The human factor**	**Language use**
Traffic stops	history of racial discrimination, police training, state laws	accusatory words
Street crossings	city planning documents, pedestrians' phone habits	eye gaze
Service encounters	store policy on payment methods, queueing practices of country	physical proximity
Wall graffiti	neighborhood cultures, rival artists, accessibility to the wall	naming practices

The discourse examples in the middle column are related to the human factor, as they are features that exist independently (and outside) of your object of study. For example, if your telescope is zoomed in to a collection of wall graffiti, then what you may see are the naming practices of different artists (i.e., language use). Conversely, zooming out may reveal the culture of a particular neighborhood, which is related to the human factor: cultural traditions will influence how graffiti artists express themselves in other situations. Furthermore, the ways in which a police officer is trained to stop drivers that break the law are related to the human factor, as such training occurs before (and outside) the traffic stops that you have collected for your own discourse project. For some, but certainly not all, objects of study, understanding how the human factor shapes the language use requires specialist knowledge, such as the case of reading city planning documents and understanding how government officials want pedestrians to cross busy streets in a particular way. Investigating the human factor may also require asking for information from individuals that are not part of your object of study, such as the case of how a store owner asks her employees to handle money during service encounters.

Learning Activity 3.3 Reflecting on the Human Factor and Language Use

Each object of study in Table 3.3 includes two or three language use examples. However, when identifying your own object of study, there will be a plethora of language use features that you can potentially investigate. Although there is no definitive list of language use examples that you can refer to after selecting an object of study, you can practice identifying different discourse perspectives by applying the telescope analogy to other situations.

1. Create your own table by identifying two or more objects of study. Go back to Chapter 1 for ideas if you need inspiration.
2. Are your examples of the human factor similar or different across your objects of study? How does your object of study influence what aspect of the human factor that you will investigate?
3. Why have you selected your language use examples? How do your examples of the human factor shape these language use features?
4. Do you have any examples in your table that appear to be related to both language use and the human factor? This is not unusual if so. And in such cases, understanding what perspective you are adopting requires a more complex methodological discussion, which occurs later in this book in Chapter 5 (e.g., membership knowledge).

For now, go back to the wall graffiti example in Table 3.3. Accessibility to the wall is treated as an example of the human factor: while the wall is something that you can see by zooming in (e.g., a handrail or a narrow ledge), it is treated as an example of the human factor because the ease or difficulty with which an artist can gain access to a wall is based on a life history that exists outside its physical location.

The human factor is about zooming out. So, for example, if your object of study is an offensive meme about the race of a presidential candidate posted on a social media platform, then the human factor perspective would begin with the social structures that help explain why such images are posted online. You could, for instance, look at the political climate and culture of the time when the meme was posted. The categories of class that are relevant to the politics of the meme and a country's history with racial discrimination are some of the many examples that are relevant to the human factor.

Figure 3.4 provides a visual illustration of where the human factor perspective begins in the analytic process. Note that there are no arrows cutting through the different perspectives, indicating an initial focus on the human factor.

Seeing discourse from the perspective of the human factor does not mean that you ignore what people are saying, writing, or doing. In fact,

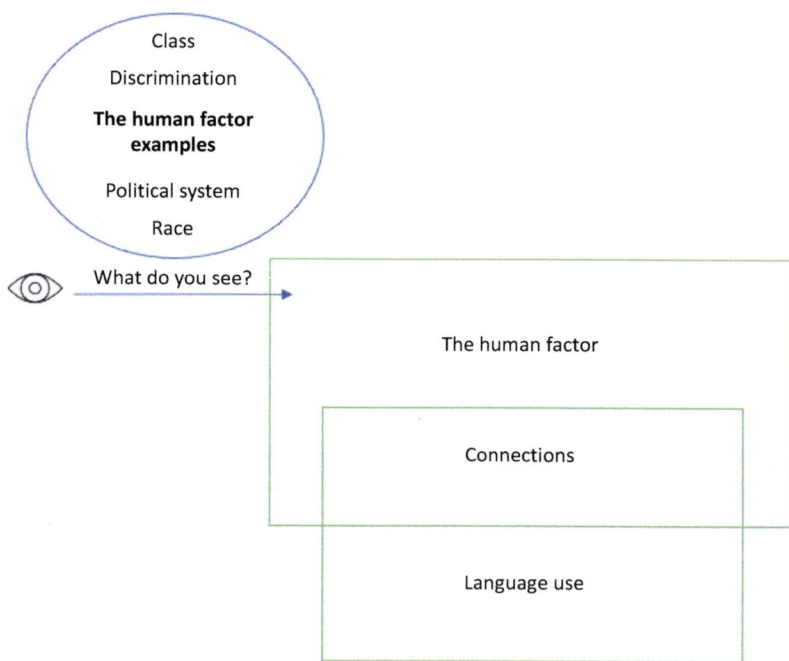

FIGURE 3.4
Seeing discourse as the human factor

observations based on the human factor should be based on language use: this is because the validity, truthfulness, or reasonableness of any analytic observation made of human factors are based on some aspect of language use. That is, in what ways does an observation of human factors manifest in the language used in an object of study? For instance, how can you show in your analysis that city planning documents (the human factor) influence the practice of crossing busy roads (language use)?

In this sense, the human factor is a *deductive* (or top-down) perspective; it often begins by zooming out, but must ultimately zoom in and observe language use.

However, connecting the human factor with language use does not require beginning with a particular perspective. A researcher that is ultimately interested in making analytic observations about the human factor may begin with language use, for example. However, for many discourse analysts that are primarily interested in the human factor, the analytic process begins by zooming out, and following a deductive trajectory as illustrated in Figure 3.5. Table 3.4 provides additional examples of connecting the human factor with language use.

Seeing discourse as the human factor reflects an interest in issues that transcend the "here-and-now" of an object of study. How do cultural expectations of parental responsibility shape the sequential and interactional organization of a conversation between family members? In what ways do regulatory laws influence the language used in a company's earnings report? How does a school's policy on student participation encourage the use of gestures? These questions are reflective of an interest in the human factor.

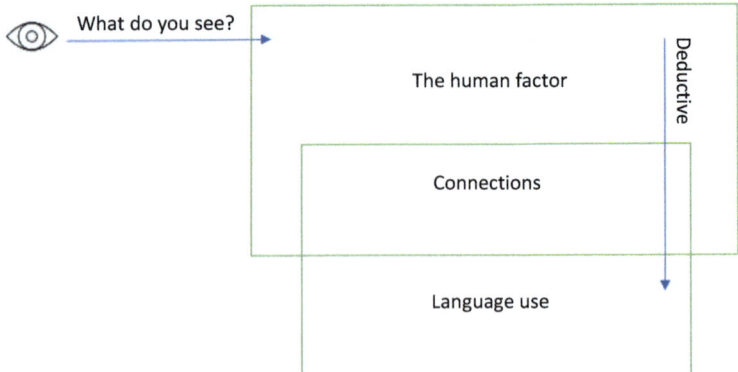

FIGURE 3.5
The human factor as a
deductive approach

Table 3.4 Examples of human factor to language use connections		
Society example	**Language example**	**Connection**
Power	*turn-taking*	Understanding that teachers possess more power than students in the classroom, and exploring how it manifests in turn-taking practices.
Identity	*pronouns*	Understanding that identities are intimately connecting to language use, and exploring how this relation manifests in the use of pronouns.
Gender	*narratives*	Understanding that people may have different life experiences because of their gender, and exploring how such differences manifest in narratives.
Racism	*word choice*	Understanding that racism is expressed at multiple levels of communication, and exploring how this phenomenon manifests at the lexical level.

Summary 3.3 ends this section with five points that summarize the main principles of the human factor perspective.

Summary 3.3

1. The human factor is not larger in terms of empirical significance.
2. Seeing discourse as the human factor requires zooming out with your telescope.
3. The human factor exists independently and outside language use.
4. Making meso connections is often, but not always, accomplished deductively.
5. Seeing discourse as the human factor does not mean ignoring language use.

3.4 Level: Summation

Determining what perspective of discourse that you would like to investigate in your object of study is an important step in the analytic process. However, for most readers, the analytic process must continue beyond this step, as there is an expectation to share your observations in writing. To this end, the next step in the analytic process is establishing what you want to say about what you see. This is done through some level of analysis.

The most basic level of analysis that you can write up is a summation. Although a summary analysis identifies the main points, features, or issues in an object of study, it does so by providing the same information that can be gleaned from watching, listening, reading, or otherwise observing your object of study.

Learning Activity 3.4 Providing a Summary Analysis

Summations require paying special attention to an object of study, but this does not mean that summaries are good analytic observations. Summations do not provide new analytic insights for the reader.

1. Read the interview excerpt provided in Object of Study 3.2. Now write down the main points of the interview and set these notes aside.
2. Consider if the summary in Example Analysis 3.1 adds new information for the reader. Is there any information in the summary that does not already exist in the interview data? Remember, summaries do not provide new information.
3. Now compare your notes from step 1 with the summary provided in Example Analysis 3.1. Are you providing new information? If so, then you are likely adding a perspective that reads more into the data than what is offered in a summary analysis.

Object of Study 3.2 Teacher Interviews

The following excerpt comes from an Asian American teacher reporting on her experiences working at a school:

"… the hiring manager made comments about how I had a 'great English native speaker voice' … When I next met the hiring manager to review the job requirements and lesson plans, they instructed me to tell students that I was a White female from California and showed me (what looked to be a stock photo of) a picture of a blonde female with blue eyes that they would be sending to all of my students. Their justification was that it fit with the company's mission statement of employing only 'English native speakers.'"

Example Analysis 3.1 Summation

The teacher, who was recently hired to work for a school that provides online language instruction, was asked to withhold information about her Asian American identity. The employer asked the teacher to tell her students that she is a White teacher with blonde hair and blue eyes.

A summary is an adequate first step in writing down your analytic observations. That is, summaries begin the process of formalizing your written observations. However, summaries must *not* represent your final analysis: doing good discourse analysis requires using a theory or methodological principle to provide a specialized or technical account of your object of study. Conversely, anyone reading the teacher interview data above will come to the same conclusion as the observation provided in the sample summary analysis. Again, the summary repeats the information already presented in the interview data, providing no new information for the reader.

Learning Activity 3.5 Practicing a Summary Analysis

Find (or reflect on) a recent email or text message exchange that you had with a friend or family member.

1. Identify the main points, features, or issues in your conversation. What is the topic of discussion? Is the exchange short or long? Is the language serious, playful, or simply mundane? Write your summary analysis in 3–5 sentences.
2. Examine your summary analysis. Would readers come to the same conclusion had they read your email or text message exchange? If so, then you have provided a summary analysis.
3. Have you included information that only you and your friend or family member would know, such as an inside joke or a shared experience? This type of information is specialist or technical in nature, as it requires the unique perspective of the researcher or "insider" information (see Chapter 5). Such information is not part of a summary analysis.

Summary 3.4

1. Summations require paying special attention to an object of study.
2. Summations are good analytic observations.
3. Summations do not provide new analytic insights for the reader.

3.5 Level: Description

The most common level of analysis that you can write up is a description. This level of analysis describes the structure of your object of study. The structure of an object of study possesses many discourse features, though it is not your job as a descriptive analyst to describe all of them. Rather, descriptions tell readers what you are seeing, and what you think is interesting, while looking through your analytic telescope (to refresh your memory of this analogy, see Section 3.2). Thus, descriptions are concerned primarily with language use.

Describing a structural component requires detailing its *form* and *function*. That is, descriptions describe what form a discourse feature takes, and what function it serves for the people producing or consuming the language. For example, if your object of study is a family having a conversation, then you could describe the form and function of a particular conversational feature, such as turn-taking practices. You may wish to examine, for instance, whether the family members take short or long turns (form), and how each turn type provides opportunities to talk about different topics (function). A description would not, however, *interpret* how turn-taking practices are connected to the human factors that exist beyond the time and space in which the family conversation took place (see interpretation in Section 3.6).

Unlike summations, descriptions are based on theories and methodological principles, and thus offer analytic observations that can only be fully understood with technical knowledge. For example, grasping the basic thesis expressed in a business report does not require much technical knowledge, but understanding how rhetorical devices are used in such documents to distort the truth does.

Learning Activity 3.6 Providing a Descriptive Analysis

A description provides a technical observation. Specifically, descriptions uncover the form and function of your object of study. Descriptions are concerned largely with language use.

1. Reacquaint yourself with the interview data in Object of Study 3.3. Are there any words or phrases that interest you? Can you say anything about their form and function?
2. Carefully read Example Analysis 3.2, which describes reported speech. Can you identify when the analysis describes the form of the reported speech? Can you identify when the analysis describes the function of the reported speech?
3. Form descriptions are based on the "shape" of a discourse feature. Aspects of shape that you could describe include, but are not limited to, size (e.g., the time it takes to complete a turn or the length of a sentence), linguistic makeup (e.g., the syntactic or

prosodic features of an utterance), and location (e.g., when a topic sentence is introduced in a paragraph or the sequential placement of a question). What aspects of shape are described in Example Analysis 3.2?

4. Function descriptions often use verbs to demonstrate how a language use feature functions within a particular situation. Example verb descriptions include, but are not limited to, "conjunctions *tie* disparate clauses together," "the turn *creates* an opportunity for the man to dispute the claim," and "the image *provides* a space for reflection and reconciliation." What verb is used in Example Analysis 3.2 to establish the function of reported speech?

5. Compare the description (in Example Analysis 3.2) with the summary (in Example Analysis 3.1). What are the similarities and the differences between the two analyses?

Object of Study 3.3 Teacher Interviews

The following excerpt comes from an Asian American teacher reporting on her experiences working at a school:

"… the hiring manager made comments about how I had a 'great English native speaker voice' … When I next met the hiring manager to review the job requirements and lesson plans, they instructed me to tell students that I was a White female from California and showed me (what looked to be a stock photo of) a picture of a blonde female with blue eyes that they would be sending to all of my students. Their justification was that it fit with the company's mission statement of employing only 'English native speakers.'"

Example Analysis 3.2 Description

The teacher uses reported speech in her reflection. Reported speech conveys "what a current speaker, or someone else, said on a former occasion" (Holt, 2007, p. 47). The first instance of reported speech occurs in the beginning of the excerpt ("great English native speaker voice"); the second instance occurs at the end ("English native speakers"). Both instances are short and framed around one key term: English native speaker. Both instances of reported speech mark a "shift in footing" (Goffman 1981, p. 227), which allows the teacher to distance herself from a term ("native speaker") that is fraught with contention.

For the novice discourse analyst, providing technical descriptions requires drawing from theories or methodological principles established in past research. For example, the in-text citations included in the example above provide a specific and nuanced way of understanding reported speech. Referencing previous research (1) establishes the theoretical or methodological principle on which your analysis is based, (2) validates your claims, (3) demonstrates how your descriptions add to existing research, and (4) helps you create analytic observations that are not merely summaries.

All technical descriptions are based on a theoretical foundation or methodological principle. Many books are devoted to describing such theories and methodologies, and must be referred to when developing an advanced understanding of technical descriptions. For this introduction, it is helpful to simply identify several common approaches to descriptions. To this end, Table 3.5 lists four common approaches to description with examples of what can be described; also included are example research questions and book introductions.

Table 3.5 Description approaches			
Approach	**Description**	**Research question**	**Reference**
Conversation analysis	*turn-taking, turn design, sequential organization, conversational topics, repair*	How do strangers initiate small talk?	Liddicoat (2007)
Systemic functional linguistics	*tenor, propositional content, rhetorical structure, actor, mood*	What ideational strategies are used in public service announcements?	Halliday (1994)
Multimodality	*visual grammar, strata, interpretation, framing, semiotic modes*	How are female bodies discursively organized in diet products advertised on social media?	Kress & Van Leeuwen (2001)
Genre analysis	*register, tenor, lexico-grammatical, pathos, moves*	What type of hedges are used in the findings section of academic articles?	Swales (1990)

Although these four approaches collectively represent a wide range of empirical possibilities, many other descriptive tools exist: several handbooks on discourse analysis offer a good starting point in exploring the general differences between descriptive approaches, such as the volume by Hyland & Paltridge (2011).

On a final note, it is necessary to point out that technical descriptions, including those associated with the approaches identified in Table 3.5, can, and often do, form the basis of interpretations. That is, descriptive approaches can also be used as a starting point to make interpretative observations beyond the form and function of an object of study, which is the topic of the Section 3.6.

Summary 3.5

1. Descriptions provide technical observations.
2. Descriptions uncover the forms and functions of objects of study.
3. Descriptions are concerned primarily with language use.

3.6 Level: Interpretation

An interpretation establishes connections between language use and the human factor. Such connections are made by *assigning meaning* to your object of study. In other words, an interpretation takes some aspect of the here-and-now (i.e., what you see by zooming in with your telescope), and assigns meaning to it based on an exogenous theory. Theories used in interpretations are exogenous, as they are not concerned with the internal structure of an object of study (i.e., forms and functions); rather, exogenous theories are concerned with social, cultural, political, or historical issues. Interpretations use these theories to show how a language use feature *indexes* (see Chapter 4) a particular social, cultural, political, or historical issue. Thus, interpretations are concerned primarily with the human factor.

Establishing a connection between language use and the human factor can begin with the former. For example, an interpretation can first look at how a family manages turn-taking practices (language use), and then extend this understanding to a discussion of how conversational turns are influenced by issues that transcend the time and space in which the conversation took place (the human factor), such as how cultural norms influence family communication practices. However, interpretations commonly begin with an interest in, for example, cultural norms; this interest in the human factor is then used as a basis to assign meaning to how families converse.

Although interpretations are often motivated by human factors, it is necessary to establish how such exogenous theories are relevant to language use. That is, interpretations are not blunt deductive tools that are forced onto language use. How a researcher assigns meaning to an object of study is determined by, and varies according to, the theory used in an interpretation. For an excellent overview of theories used to assign meaning in interpretations, see McGee & Warms (2013).

Interpretations make use of theories from a wide range of disciplines within the Humanities and Social Sciences, including perhaps most notably Sociology, Literature, and Anthropology. As such, the theories used to construct interpretations are not concerned with studying language use in isolation of social structures. In other words, interpretations are used to situate your object of study within a larger discussion of a social, cultural, or political issue.

Learning Activity 3.7 Providing an Interpretive Analysis

An interpretation establishes a connection between language use and the human factor. This connection is accomplished by using an exogenous theory to assign meaning to your object of study. The primary goal of an interpretation is to help readers understand the social, cultural, or political significance of your object of study.

1. Reacquaint yourself with the interview data in Object of Study 3.4. What human factors could be discussed in this data (e.g., discrimination or racism)?
2. Carefully read Example Analysis 3.3, which interprets the teacher's experience through the lenses of White normativity. Assigning meaning to an object of study is a practice that will be scrutinized by the reader(s) of your research. Referencing theorists and scholarship can help convince your reader(s) that what you are interpretating is indeed valid. Are you convinced with the meaning that is assigned to this object of study?
3. White normativity is an exogenous theory. That is, the theory is relevant to the data excerpt, but was not created to understand this specific object of study. What other situations are influenced by White normativity?
4. Where is the language use–human factor connection? That is, what language use feature is being analyzed through the lens of White normativity? Is there a specific word or phrase that is referenced in the analysis?

Object of Study 3.4 Teacher Interviews

The following excerpt comes from an Asian American teacher reporting on her experiences working at a school:

"… the hiring manager made comments about how I had a 'great English native speaker voice' … When I next met the hiring manager to review the job requirements and lesson plans, they instructed me to tell students that I was a White female from California and showed me (what looked to be a stock photo of) a picture of a blonde female with blue eyes that they would be sending to all of my students. Their justification was that it fit with the company's mission statement of employing only 'English native speakers.'"

Example Analysis 3.3 Interpretation

The teacher's experience demonstrates that having a "great English voice" is contingent on having white skin, blonde hair, and blue eyes. This conflation of language and race does not exist in a vacuum: it can be partly traced to Hollywood films that transmit images and sounds of English speakers as racially homogenous (Yang & Ryser, 2008). Such images are the outcome of White normativity, which is a larger belief system that sees Whiteness as a baseline for measuring whether someone or something is authentic, normal, or ideal (Jenks, 2017).

Like technical descriptions, interpretations require drawing from past research using in-text citations. This practice helps establish your language use–human factor connection and allows readers to validate your analysis. Exogenous theories can be used to talk about, and focus on, specific language use features; interpretations are also used to talk more generally about an object of study. Example Analysis 3.3 begins with specific aspects of what the teacher has said, though the analysis moves on to a more general discussion about how the entire interview excerpt should be interpreted.

As mentioned above, exogenous theories are used to assign meaning to an object of study. Such theories come from nearly all disciplines concerned with humans and human communication, making it nearly impossible to compile a list of ideas that can be used for your research. However, it is helpful to identify several common theories used in interpretations. To this end, Table 3.6 lists four common interpretation theories with their simplified principles and references.

Table 3.6 Interpretative theories		
Theory	**Interpretation**	**Reference**
Heteroglossia	Any given language possesses multiple "voices" expressed through distinct languages. The theory is used to analyze many discourse issues, including cultural hybridity, identities, and ideologies.	Bakhtin (1981)
Mimicry	Communities living in (formerly) colonized regions subscribe to the ideologies of the colonizer. The theory is often used to explore the complex relationships that exist in postcolonial regions and the discourses that are associated with them.	Bhabha (2004)
Scales	The human experience is based on a process of comparisons, categorizations, and connections. The theory is used to show that discourse, such as an individual's understanding of an ethnic group, stems from, and changes according to, unique situations.	Lempert & Summerson Carr (2016)
Authenticity	Languages are bound to notions of authenticity. For example, the question of who qualifies as an authentic speaker of English may be bound to racial and linguistic categories. The theory is used to examine how individuals discursively construct language ideologies.	Coupland (2003)

It was noted at the end of the Section 3.5 that technical descriptions can be used to establish interpretations. Similarly, interpretations are like evaluations in that both types of analysis assign meaning to objects of study. However, evaluations use exogenous theories to provide a more explicit, and sometimes critical, assessment of objects of study, such as labeling the actions of a political party as bad, evil, or corrupt.

Summary 3.6
1. Interpretations establish language use–human factor connections.
2. Interpretations use exogenous theories to assign meaning to objects of study.
3. Interpretations help readers understand the significance of objects of study.

3.7 Level: Evaluation

An evaluation makes an *explicit assessment* of an object of study. Like interpretations, evaluations create language use–human factor connections by showing how a particular discourse feature *indexes* (see Chapter 4) a social, cultural, political, or historical issue. Unlike interpretations, however, evaluations assess objects of study according to ideological positions, such as the belief that education is built on structural inequalities or the view that plant-based diets are better for the environment. Evaluations are concerned primarily with human factors: they are conducted to participate actively in the validation of an ideology.

Explicitly assessing an object of study requires establishing an ideological position. For example, a discourse analyst may believe that patriarchy oppresses women in society (the human factor). This ideological position is then used to show that family conversations are problematic in that they exacerbate structural inequalities through turn-taking practices. The object of study – in this case, family conversations – must of course support the predefined ideological position. For instance, it may be revealed through your analysis of family conversations that turns are not equally allocated to women, giving you the empirical basis from which to make an explicit assessment (and thus validate your ideological position). Researchers that practice evaluations look for objects of study that can be used to support their ideological positions.

Evaluations are unique in that they explicitly assess objects of study. In the example above, the explicit assessment is that family conversations are problematic because they participate in the oppression of women. Explicit assessments may entail anything from arguing that neoliberalism is evil because it exploits humans to contending that a particular non-profit organization is virtuous for attempting to eradicate world hunger.

Learning Activity 3.8 Providing an Evaluative Analysis

An evaluation makes an explicit assessment of an object of study. This assessment is based on a predefined ideological position. An evaluation creates a language use–human factor connection, but the analysis is largely zoomed out from an object of study (i.e., demonstrating how an ideological position is relevant to the data presented).

1. Reacquaint yourself with the interview data in Object of Study 3.5. What is your feeling about the teacher's experience? Can you construct an assessment of the employer's photo request? For example, is it acceptable or ethical to ask teachers to create fictitious identities?
2. Carefully read Example Analysis 3.4, which uses the teacher's experience to evaluate the English language teaching profession. The explicit assessment is that neoliberalism is bad for the English language teaching profession (i.e., dehumanizes and exploits). This assessment is based on the ideological position that neoliberalism is a broken economic system. Is it possible to create a positive assessment of the teacher's experience? For example, are there positive aspects of neoliberalism that can be used to evaluate this data?
3. Neoliberalism is an exogenous theory. That is, the theory is relevant to the data excerpt, but was not created to understand this specific object of study. What other situations are influenced by neoliberalism? Conversely, what other ideological positions can be used to understand this object of study?
4. Where is the language use–human factor connection? That is, what language use feature is being analyzed through the lens of neoliberalism? Is there is specific word or phrase that is referenced in the analysis?

Object of Study 3.5 Teacher Interviews

The following excerpt comes from an Asian American teacher reporting on her experiences working at a school:

"… the hiring manager made comments about how I had a 'great English native speaker voice' … When I next met the hiring manager to review the job requirements and lesson plans, they instructed me to tell students that I was a White female from California and showed me (what looked to be a stock photo of) a picture of a blonde female with blue eyes that they would be sending to all of my students. Their justification was that it fit with the company's mission statement of employing only 'English native speakers.'"

Example Analysis 3.4 Evaluation

Neoliberal market forces are bad for the English language teaching profession (Block, 2017), as they perpetuate racist ideologies in and through the selling and buying of instruction. In the interview excerpt, for example, the largely unlegislated neoliberal education system that has employed this teacher has a financial incentive to sell English language teaching as a "Western" experience (Appleby, 2013), which dehumanizes the Asian American teacher: the request to use a White female as a profile image treats the teacher as a form of capital (Chomsky, 1999). Neoliberalism allows employers to maximize their profits by exploiting problematic stereotypes (English is best spoken by White people), which perverts societal belief systems.

Evaluations include in-text citations that help readers identify your ideological position and assess the validity of your explicit assessment. Example Analysis 3.4 includes three references that evaluate the object of study from two ideological positions: neoliberalism is bad (Chomsky, 1999; Block, 2017) and the English language teaching profession dehumanizes (Block, 2017; Appleby, 2013). Evaluations often begin with the human factor (e.g., neoliberal market forces are bad), but somewhere during the analysis you are expected to refer to specific language use features (e.g., the request to use a different photo).

Evaluations are again based on predefined ideological positions which come from exogenous theories (e.g., feminist theory), theoretical frameworks (e.g., critical discourse analysis), or paradigmatic movements (e.g., postmodernism). Although the range of ideological positions makes it difficult to identify an object of study or select an analytic focus, it is useful to begin the research process by simply thinking of a human factor for which you hold an interest or possess a strong opinion (e.g., climate change, political tribalism, war). Discourse analysts that use evaluations are often passionate about a particular human factor, which allows them to identify objects of study that fit their ideological positions. To this end, Table 3.7 lists four common "tools" that possess ideological positions from which evaluations can be made.

The ideological positions identified in Table 3.7 are oversimplifications that only represent a part of what could be said using a particular evaluation tool. Furthermore, there are different versions and interpretations of evaluation tools: further reading is required to establish a more comprehensive understanding of the nuances that exist within and across evaluation tools.

It must also be noted that while evaluations tend to be critical, what this actually means in an analysis will vary from one study to another. More importantly, possessing a critical focus does not mean that positive evaluations should be avoided. Critical theories can be used to assess objects of study positively, which is central to transformative analyses.

Table 3.7 Evaluation tools

Evaluation tool	Ideology	Reference
Postcolonial theory	Life in postcolonial regions is influenced by a history of cultural Othering by colonizers. Although no longer colonized, the experiences of subjugation continue to shape present-day ideologies and behaviors.	Gandhi (2019)
Critical discourse analysis	A theoretical framework that possesses several schools of thought; however, the main idea is societies are based on systems of power and domination.	Wodak & Chilton (2005)
Critical pedagogy	Societies are made up of marginalized communities and institutions in positions of power. Power imbalances exist in all aspects of life.	Morrow & Torres (2002)
Critical race theory	Societies, including their legal systems, are founded on racialized power imbalances. The world is based on racial hierarchies that oppress minority and marginalized groups.	Spencer (2006)

Summary 3.7

1. Evaluations make explicit assessments of objects of study.
2. Evaluations are based on predefined ideological positions.
3. Evaluations are largely concerned with the human factor.

3.8 Level: Transformation

A transformation *identifies positive solutions* to a situation relevant to an object of study. Like evaluations, transformations are based on ideological positions that view the world in a particular way. However, whereas evaluations tend to focus on "what is wrong," transformations are concerned with "what can be done." Transformations are concerned primarily with the human factor: they are conducted to improve a social, cultural, or political issue.

Identifying a positive solution begins with an ideological position, such as the belief that patriarchy oppresses women in society (the human factor); in this example, the transformation would use an object of study that demonstrates the existence of patriarchy, such as unequal turn-taking rights during family conversations, to explore what can be done to *transform* family relationships. Again, the goal of a transformation is not to show that something is wrong, bad, or broken, but rather to see an object of study as an opportunity to create positive solutions.

Learning Activity 3.9 Providing a Transformative Analysis

A transformation identifies positive solutions to a situation. A positive solution is based on an evaluation of an object of study, but is constructed to improve a social, cultural, or political issue. Transformations create language use–human factor connections, though the analysis is largely zoomed out from an object of study.

1. Reacquaint yourself with the interview data in Object of Study 3.6. The evaluation analysis in the previous section determined that the teacher's experience is an example of racial discrimination. Can you identify solutions or make suggestions that would improve the teacher's professional situation that she finds herself working in?
2. Carefully read Example Analysis 3.5, which identifies several solutions that may help eradicate racial discrimination. These solutions focus on improving teacher training programs, which possess long-term outcomes. Do you agree with these recommendations? Can you think of any short-term solutions?
3. The positive solutions in Example Analysis 3.5 are based on critical race theory and critical pedagogy. Are there other evaluation tools that can be used (refer to the previous section for help)?
4. Where is the language use–human factor connection? That is, what language use feature is referenced in the transformation analysis? Is there a specific word or phrase that is referenced or does the transformation focus on the data excerpt as a whole?

Object of Study 3.6 Teacher Interviews

The following excerpt comes from an Asian American teacher reporting on her experiences working at a school:

"… the hiring manager made comments about how I had a 'great English native speaker voice' … When I next met the hiring manager to review the job requirements and lesson plans, they instructed me to tell students that I was a White female from California and showed me (what looked to be a stock photo of) a picture of a blonde female with blue eyes that they would be sending to all of my students. Their justification was that it fit with the company's mission statement of employing only 'English native speakers.'"

Example Analysis 3.5 Transformation

The problematic experience of this teacher demonstrates the need to revamp teacher training programs. Specifically, the request to use a fictitious photo of a White female teacher is evidence that teacher training programs are not doing enough to confront the racial capitalism that exists in the teaching profession (Kubota, 2020). A possible solution to creating a more inclusive teaching profession is to decolonize the images and ideologies that occupy English language spaces (Bhattacharya, Jiang, & Canagarajah, 2020). For example, teacher training programs can increase racial diversity amongst their faculty and deliver courses on world Englishes and multiculturalism, which would circulate competing discourses and celebrate alternative voices and faces. An effort to decolonize White spaces will help future educators understand the complex relations between race and language, as well as promote laws and practices that protect teachers from discrimination (Jenks & Lee, 2020).

Transformations use in-text citations to point readers to publications that support your suggestions. Example Analysis 3.5 includes three references. The first citation supports the claim that racial capitalism exists in the teaching profession. The second citation points readers to a study that makes a similar suggestion regarding the benefits of diverse spaces. The third citation identifies a study that also explores the benefit of decolonizing White spaces. All three citations are based on the teacher being asked to lie about her racial identity.

Transformations use evaluation tools to create positive solutions. Identifying a positive solution requires possessing extensive knowledge of the situation from which your object of study exists. Like evaluations, it is useful to begin the research process by simply thinking of a human factor for which you hold an interest or possess a strong opinion (e.g., genocide, human rights, censorship). In addition to thinking of what is problematic about a particular human factor, transformations require you to think of what can be done to address the problem. Table 3.8 uses the same evaluation tools identified in Section 3.7 to identify how an ideology can be transformed into a positive outlook.

Table 3.8 Transformation examples		
Evaluation tool	**Ideology**	**Transformation**
Postcolonial theory	Life in postcolonial regions is influenced by a history of cultural Othering by colonizers. Although no longer colonized, the experiences of subjugation continue to shape present-day ideologies and behaviors.	Positive solutions often focus on ways communities can decouple themselves from their colonial past.
Critical discourse analysis	A theoretical framework that possesses several schools of thought; however, the main idea is societies are based on systems of power and domination.	Positive solutions often focus on how systemic power can be equally distributed across all segments of the population.

Table 3.8 (cont.)		
Critical pedagogy	Societies are made up of marginalized communities and institutions in positions of power. Power imbalances exist in all aspects of life.	Positive solutions often focus on activism, and how knowledge can be transferred to students, giving them the power to bring out change in their communities.
Critical race theory	Societies, including their legal systems, are founded on racialized power imbalances. The world is based on racial hierarchies that oppress minority and marginalized groups.	Positive solutions often focus on how the humanity of racial minorities can be validated and protected.

Positive solutions take many forms, as they vary according to both situational variables and transformation goals: the examples provided in Table 3.8 represent a fraction of what can be done with transformations using evaluation tools. That said, all transformations that are analytically insightful and socially impactful are based on extensive knowledge of theory (e.g., critical pedagogy) and praxis (e.g., understanding how a classroom can benefit from an evaluation tool such as critical pedagogy).

Summary 3.8	1. Transformations identify positive solutions. 2. Transformation are based on evaluations. 3. Transformations aim to improve a social, cultural, or political issue. 4. Transformations are often based on a societal issue.

Learning Accomplishments

The chapter has provided an overview of the analysis in discourse analysis. This section identifies how each learning outcome has been addressed in this chapter.

1. You will understand that discourse can be analyzed from different, sometimes overlapping, perspectives: language use, the human factor, and the connections between these two vantage points.

Analytic perspectives were discussed in relation to the following question: What do you see in your object of study? The telescope analogy was used to address this question: you must determine whether you wish to "zoom in" or "zoom out" after selecting your object of study.

2. You will understand that there are different levels of discourse analysis: summation, description, interpretation, evaluation, and transformation.

The level of analysis that you conduct can be understood by asking the following question: What do you want to say about your object of study?

This question was addressed by showing that the analytic process is bound to many theoretical and methodological principles. Levels of analysis place varying degrees of importance on language use and the human factor.

3. You will understand that the analytic process is multifaceted; it can combine different perspectives and levels of analysis.

It was discussed throughout the chapter that perspectives and levels of analysis do not exist independently of each other.

Key Themes

Language Use Themes

1. Language use is not small in terms of empirical significance.
2. Seeing discourse as language use requires zooming in with your telescope.
3. Language use features are immediately visible or hearable.
4. Making connections is often accomplished inductively.
5. Seeing discourse as language use does not mean ignoring the human factor.

The Human Factor Themes

1. The human factor is not large in terms of empirical significance.
2. Seeing discourse as the human factor requires zooming out with your telescope.
3. The human factor exists independently and outside your object of study.
4. Making connections is often, but not always, accomplished deductively.
5. Seeing discourse as the human factor does not mean ignoring language use.

Summation Themes

1. Summations require paying special attention to an object of study.
2. Summations are not good analytic observations.
3. Summations do not provide new analytic insights for the reader.

Description Themes

1. Descriptions provide technical observations.
2. Descriptions uncover the forms and functions of objects of study.
3. Descriptions are typically concerned with language use features.

Interpretation Themes

1. Interpretations establish connections between language use and the human factor.
2. Interpretations use exogenous theories to assign meaning to objects of study.
3. Interpretations help readers understand the significance of objects of study.

Evaluation Themes

1. Evaluations make explicit assessments of objects of study.
2. Evaluations are based on predefined ideological positions.
3. Evaluations are often based on a human factor.

Transformation Themes

1. Transformations identify positive solutions.
2. Transformations are based on evaluations.
3. Transformations aim to improve a social, cultural, or political issue.
4. Transformations are often based on a human factor.

Reading List

Gee (2011) This popular book offers one perspective on the analytic process; however, the book provides many discourse examples (objects of study) with some practical exercises. The last three chapters focus on the analytic process.

Hart (2020) This student guide to researching discourse is organized around different analytic approaches. The book can be used as a reference guide for specific methodological guidelines that are based on the different perspectives and levels of analysis discussed in this chapter.

Paltridge (2021) The author presents a number of foundational concepts and ideas in an engaging writing style and with reflection exercises. The book is one of the more accessible introductions that are helpful for novice discourse analysts. In this updated edition, Paltridge reviews several objects of study and approaches to discourse analysis.

4 What Is the Role of Context in an Analysis?

CHAPTER OUTLINE

Learning Outcomes

This chapter reviews the different interpretations of, and approaches to, *context*. The aim of the chapter is to establish how context factors into the analysis of your object of study.

The contents of the chapter are organized according to the following learning outcomes. After reading this chapter:

1. You will understand what context is and why it is important to the analysis of your object of study;
2. You will be able to study context using different models and constructs;
3. You will understand how discourse and context work together to create meaning.

4.1 Definitions of Context

Context is broadly defined as all the conditions that influence how discourse is structured and used. In this sense, when an analyst speaks of context, what is often being referred to are conditions (see Figure 4.1).

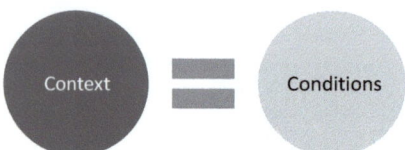

FIGURE 4.1
Context equals conditions

Context is an exceptionally important construct in discourse analysis, as all researchers regardless of their disciplinary background are expected to consider how conditions factor into the analysis of their objects of study. That is to say, all discourse analysis involves showing (1) how discourse is influenced by context, and (2) how context influences discourse. In this sense, not only does context shape discourse, but discourse can also redefine context (for an early and seminal understanding of context, see Malinowski, 1923).

For example, a classroom lesson on prepositions is a context that influences how a teacher uses discourse, such as testing for understanding by asking questions or correcting student contributions while they provide answers to a grammar exercise. However, the discourse between the teacher and students may also redefine the context from a lesson on prepositions to a casual conversation should the participants decide to talk about, for example, what they did over the weekend or their favorite movies. In this situation, the participants are still in the **setting** of a classroom, but their context transforms as they communicate. Accordingly, context and setting are different constructs, and should not be used synonymously. Setting merely refers to the (physical or digital) space in which an object of study occurs.

The role of context in your analysis can be expressed in the following question: What are the conditions that influence, and are being influenced by, discourse? Six ways of understanding context are discussed in this chapter: systemic functional linguistics, the SPEAKING model, frames, indexicality, contextualization cues, next-turn proof procedure.

However, before introducing these six examples, it is necessary to establish a few more general statements about context.

4.1.1 Context Continuum

What are the different conditions that may factor into understanding your object of study? A practical way of answering this question is to think of context as existing along a continuum with one side representing global conditions and the other end symbolizing local conditions. Figure 4.2 provides a visual illustration of this continuum.

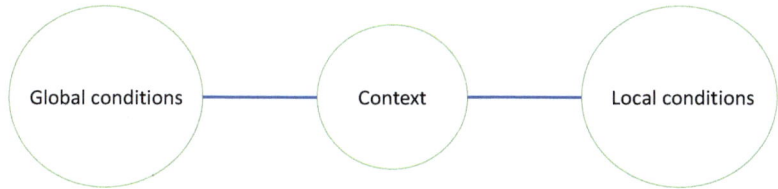

FIGURE 4.2
Context continuum

Local conditions are contextual dimensions that exist within the immediate **time** and **space** in which an object of study occurred or was produced. Objects of study possess different local conditions, so it is important to provide a specific example here. Take, for example, two strangers from different economic backgrounds discussing rain in front of a bus stop. Local conditions – that is, what is happening during the time and space of this discussion – are the weather, the words used to describe the rain, the turn-taking practices of the two interlocutors, the prosodic features of their utterances, and the physical configuration of the bus stop, to name a few. Local conditions are linguistic (e.g., verbal language), interactional (e.g., turn-taking), spatial (e.g., distance between the strangers), and semiotic (e.g., the meaning that is derived from a bus stop symbol). In short, local conditions are anything within the time and space that communicates meaning for the people involved in the discourse (e.g., the background noises of the buses and how it influences voice amplitude).

Global conditions are contextual dimensions that exist outside the immediate time and space in which an object of study occurred or was produced, but are nonetheless important to the context (for a popular interpretation of global conditions, see Fairclough, 1989). For the bus stop example, global conditions are the language policy of the country, class dynamics and tensions, the pragmatic norms that shape whether it is acceptable to engage in small talk, and the culture of complaining about the weather, to name a few. While these global conditions may exist within the local context, they exist outside the immediate time and space of the object of study because they were established before the bus stop encounter took place. Global conditions are historical (e.g., the history of talking about the weather), political (e.g., the extent to which it is normal to talk across class lines), cultural (e.g., the culture of complaining), and societal (e.g., the normalcy of taking public buses).

In between the two ends of the continuum are conditions that do not exist precisely within or outside the time and space in which an object of study occurred or was produced. Take, for example, cognitive and psychological conditions, which transcend time and space in that they are based on past events but are present in so far as they exist within the discourse and discourse producers. Cognitive and psychological conditions that are relevant to the bus stop example include anxiety, fear of speaking, emotional states, and fatigue, to name a few.

Conditions do not exist independently of one another, but are rather connected in complex ways. For example, the cultural history of complaining about the weather (global condition) may shape how the language used in front of a bus stop is structured and whether communication takes place at all (local conditions). Conversely, the topic of discussion between the two interlocutors (local condition) may reinforce the pragmatic expectation to engage in small talk in public spaces (global condition). Of course, cognitive and psychological conditions influence how discourse is structured and unfolds; so, for example, the two interlocutors may be feeling exceptionally talkative because they are both well rested, thoroughly caffeinated, and ready to start the workday.

Figure 4.3 provides a visual illustration of the different conditions that may shape discourse: the first row under "conditions" represents global conditions; the bottom row represents local conditions; the middle row represents the conditions that fall between the global and the local. While this figure represents neither a complete list nor the only way of thinking about context, the illustration provides a practical overview of the conditions that may shape discourse.

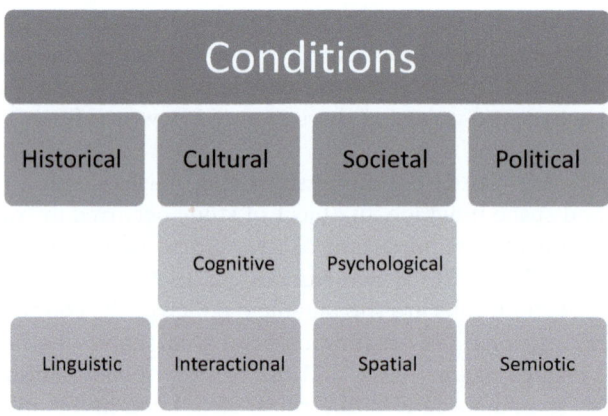

FIGURE 4.3
Types of conditions

Learning Activity 4.1 Identifying Conditions

In this exercise, the learning objective is to reflect on the different conditions that may shape discourse. The object of study for this exercise is a government report on global warming. The report is written in English with supporting images and figures. It is a public document that was written by an American politician. The politician is also on the board of a Dutch petrol company.

An example is provided for each condition in the middle column. Please provide a second example for the right column. Remember that you are identifying conditions that may possibly – and not definitively – shape this discourse example.

Category	Condition example 1	Condition example 2
Historical	national dependency on oil	
Cultural	American car culture	
Societal	capitalism	
Political	campaign finance laws	
Cognitive	neoliberal belief systems	
Psychological	apathetic views of the environment	
Linguistic	the language of skepticism	
Interactional	pre-report dialogues with politicians	
Spatial	US Letter paper size	
Semiotic	the symbolism of refuting science	

This exercise demonstrates that there are numerous conditions that could shape discourse. Although most researchers agree that there are many conditions that are potentially relevant to discourse, there is great diversity in how they demonstrate that a particular condition is indeed influencing an object of study. This point is summarized in Cicourel's (1987) discussion of the importance of using global conditions to understand the communication of medical encounters:

While many researchers will agree that talk and some notion of "context" shape each other as part of an emergent process that changes through time and space, not all students of language use will concede that ethnographic material, participant attributes, and patterns of social organization that are constitutive of talk need to be included in studies of the structure of conversation or discourse.

(Cicourel 1987, p. 217)

Put differently, although all discourse analysts accept that context is an important analytic variable, the precise conditions that end up being studied vary from one theory and methodology to another. This variation in how context is studied exists because researchers draw from a range of theoretical frameworks and methodological principles that dictate what conditions should or can be incorporated into an analysis.

Although it is beyond the scope of this book to review how and why researchers use different theories and methodologies (for examples, see Flowerdew, 2014), it is possible to discuss several models and constructs that can be used to understand how context is relevant to discourse. Before introducing these models and constructs, it is important to summarize why context is important to your object of study.

> **Summary 4.1**
> 1. Context is all of the conditions that influence discourse.
> 2. Context and setting are not the same construct.
> 3. Many conditions exist within a context.
> 4. Researchers have different ways of understanding and approaching context.
> 5. Context is central to all approaches to discourse analysis.

4.2 Systemic Functional Linguistics

The systemic functional linguistics (SFL) model, which is discussed in Halliday and Hassan (1989) and informed by the work of J. R. Firth (see Firth, 1957), offers one way of understanding and studying context. The SFL model suggests that context can be mapped onto a system of three interrelated discourses or what the researchers call "context of situation": field of discourse ("what is going on"), tenor of discourse ("who is talking part"), and mode of discourse ("role assigned to language").

The SFL model requires studying the relationship between context and discourse by applying these three interrelated discourses to an object of study. The underlying assumption is that all objects of study, from a billboard sign in a busy urban space to a highly confidential conversation between government officials, are made up of meanings that fall within field of discourse, tenor of discourse, and mode of discourse. In this sense, the SFL model views context as a network of meanings. More specifically, experiential meaning, interpersonal meaning, and textual meaning are connected to field of discourse, tenor of discourse, and mode of discourse, respectively, as Figure 4.4 illustrates.

In their original discussion of context, Halliday and Hasan use a Christian broadcast as an object of study to explain how meanings can be mapped onto their three interrelated discourses. However, a classroom lecture will be used for this section as an example, as it is a more universally relatable situation.

Field of discourse	Tenor of discourse	Mode of discourse
Experiential meaning	Interpersonal meaning	Textual meaning

FIGURE 4.4
The SFL model

1. **Field of discourse**: relates to the conditions that shape discourse in and through (as "realized by") experiential meanings, including the language being used, what it is used for, and the purposes it fulfills. For a university lecture, field of discourse may include the words and phrases used to convey an academic topic, the purpose of the lesson, and the goals of the participants. For example, the technical words used by a professor (see local conditions) to explain geography terminology signals to her students that their encounter is an academic lecture (and not, for example, a random non-academic discussion that happens to take place in a classroom).

2. **Tenor of discourse**: refers to the conditions that shape discourse in and through (as "realized by") interpersonal meanings, such as the roles assigned to classroom participants and the communicative expectations that are historically attached to teachers and students (see global conditions). These roles and expectations are established *in situ* (within the immediate time and space of the classroom lecture), using a range of language and communicative resources (see local conditions), such as the professor testing learning by asking students to answer questions, the students asking the professor to address points of mis- or non-understanding, or the terms of address (e.g., Professor or Doctor as opposed to John or Jane) used by students to treat their professor as an authority figure.

3. **Mode of discourse**: relates to the conditions that shape discourse in and through (as "realized by") textual meanings, such as the medium and style of communication adopted during lectures. In this sense, textual is not limited to written communication, but refers to all modes of language that convey meaning. For example, the PowerPoint slides used by the professor, and her monologue discussion of geography topics, signal that a classroom lecture is taking place, allowing students to participate accordingly. The PowerPoint slides and monologue establish a set of expectations and behaviors (i.e., meanings), such as taking notes while the professor is talking, raising a hand to signal a need to ask a question, and setting a mobile phone to vibration mode to avoid disruption. Therefore, mode of discourse can help participants recognize that they are communicating in a classroom lecture, and this recognition is based on both local and global conditions.

The challenge in studying context lies in identifying how meanings are relevant to a particular object of study. One way of approaching this challenge is to think about how the meanings that are relevant to one object of study may not be important in other objects of study. The SFL model adopts the term **register** to understand the variation that exists in how meanings change from one object of study to another. Register is used to capture the meanings that are unique to an object of study.

The idea of a register is helpful in uncovering important details regarding how people make sense of each other and their environment. For example, a job interview is an object of study with a **closed register** in that what is communicatively possible is somewhat narrow and fixed: the meanings that are expressed through discourse are largely related to questions and answers based on predictable topics. A job interview could also be characterized as possessing a **formal register**: institutional or professional language with established and technical language. Conversely, a text exchange between two friends is an object of study with an **open register** in that what is communicatively possible is wide and indeterminate: the friends could talk about anything from serious to trivial topics using a range of linguistic resources from text abbreviations to multimedia memes. A conversation between two friends could also be characterized as having an **informal register**: casual language with fewer established communicative expectations or set rules.

The use of register to understand the job interview and friendly conversation demonstrates that there are different contextual expectations and constraints that determine how discourse is structured and understood. This variation exists because all objects of study possess a set of unique meanings that allows individuals to make sense of their context. As a discourse analyst, however, you must do more than simply categorize an object of study as being closed, open, formal, or informal. It is your responsibility as an analyst to identify conditions that are specific to an object of study, and explore how they may influence discourse (and vice versa). The SFL model again proposes that you complete this task by considering field, tenor, and mode of discourse in relation to experiential, interpersonal, and textual meanings.

Learning Activity 4.2 The SFL Model

In this exercise, the learning objective is to use the SFL model to understand the relationship between context and discourse. The object of study for this exercise is a job interview. Please answer the questions below for each SFL category.

Field of Discourse

1. What happens between an interviewer and an interviewee that tells them that they are actively taking part in an interview?
2. What local conditions, such as question types and word choice, define an encounter as an interview?

Tenor of Discourse

1. What type of language does an interviewer use?
2. What type of language does an interviewee use?
3. What is the objective of the interviewer and how is it expressed in language?
4. What is the objective of the interviewee and how is it expressed in language?

Mode of Discourse

1. What communication practices are needed to conduct an interview?
2. How does an interviewee use language to secure a job offer?
3. When is informal language used during an interview and what purpose does it serve?

Your answers to these questions offer examples of how contexts are shaped by shared norms and expectations with regard to language and communication. Can you think of other communicative situations that possess similar or dissimilar contexts and discourse examples, such as a police interrogation or a friendly argument?

An interesting thought experiment for the current discussion is to reflect on what would happen during a job interview (or any context) if the participants decide to deviate from established communicative norms and expectations. This sort of exercise is based on what is commonly referred to as a **breaching experiment**, which is simply a conscious effort to violate the social norms that are tied to a particular context. The goal of breaching experiments, which were popularized by the works of Harold Garfinkel (for an overview of breaching experiments, see Rafalovich, 2006), is to study how people reveal their shared understandings of context in and through their responses to such violations.

For example, what would happen if the interviewee relied on informal language or refused to answer questions from the interviewer? How would the interviewee be treated and what would happen during the interview? Your answers to this question reveal an important aspect of context: that is, our ability to communicate in meaningful and appropriate ways is based on the shared meanings that we bring to, and negotiate during, communicative situations. Our objects of study, therefore, are also bound to shared meanings that form the basis of what is referred to as context.

One way of identifying the shared meanings that are tied to objects of study is to use the SPEAKING model.

Summary 4.2

1. An SFL understanding of context is based on three interrelated discourse categories.
2. The SFL model views context as a network of meanings.
3. The SFL model adopts the term *register* to understand contextual variation.

4.3 The SPEAKING Model

The SPEAKING model is the work of Dell Hymes, which is devoted to the ways in which communicative competence is developed within speech communities. Hymes's work is particularly helpful in understanding context, as he argues that the conditions that make up a communicative situation, such as those variables identified in the continuum above, form the basis of communicative competence. In other words, for Hymes, context provides a window into communicative competence. By identifying what is needed to exhibit communicative competence, a researcher is also uncovering the context of an object of study.

The SPEAKING model offers one way of identifying what is needed to exhibit communicative competence. SPEAKING is a mnemonic construction which represents eight categories of context that collectively make up what it means to possess communicative competence: Setting, Participants, Ends, Act sequence, Keys, Instrumentalities, Norms, and Genres. Each category within the SPEAKING model can be thought of as a set of conditions that potentially influences how discourse is structured and used.

Below, the SPEAKING model is introduced by making connections with the ideas and terminology used in this book (e.g., object of study, global conditions, local conditions). Although Hymes does not use such language, the ideas and terminology used in this book provide more concrete examples of how the SPEAKING model is related to context.

A political debate will be used to discuss how the SPEAKING model can be applied to an object of study.

1. Setting	This category of conditions refers to the time and place of an object of study, including local conditions. Hymes also includes "scene" within this category, which relates to the cognitive and psychological conditions identified at the beginning of this chapter (see Hymes, 1972, p. 60). In a political debate, setting includes the physical stage, the microphones used to project opinions, and the desire of politicians to win over hearts and minds, to name a few.

2. Participants

This category of conditions includes the people that occupy or make up an object of study, such as speakers, recipients, interlocutors, or audience members, to name a few. Like tenor of discourse within the SFL model, this category refers not only to who the participants are, but also what they are expected to communicate given their role (see Hymes, 1972, pp. 60–61).

In a political debate, the main participants are the debaters, which includes their unique positions that are based largely on political affiliation, as well as the mediator.

3. Ends

This category of conditions refers to the purpose of an object of study, which comprises two contextual variables: outcomes and goals. An outcome of an object of study, such as the winner of a political debate, is different from its goals, which is within this example the intention of winning that presumably all the debaters possess (see Hymes, 1972, pp. 61–62).

4. Act sequence

This category of conditions refers to the types of speech acts that occur within an object of study, such as when debaters assert, claim, promise, and pledge during a political debate (see Hymes, 1972, p. 62). Act sequence also includes the order of speech events, such as how debaters respond to opposing assertions and claims.

5. Keys

This category of conditions is closely related to act sequence, and refers to the "tone, manner, or spirit" of speech acts (see Hymes, 1972, p. 62), such as the extent to which a political debate is friendly or confrontational.

6. Instrumentalities

This category of conditions includes the "channels" and "forms of speech" of an object of study (see Hymes, 1972, p. 63).

Channels refer to both the medium of communication, such as speaking versus reading, and modes of use, such as whispering or yelling versus reading a script or paraphrasing written notes.

Forms of speech refer to the ways in which an object of study can be communicated, such as using formal or informal language during a political debate.

7. Norms

This category of conditions refers to two types of norms: norms of interaction and norms of interpretation (see Hymes, 1972, pp. 63–64). Norms of interaction are the normative communicative features that are tied to an object of study, such as the mediator allocating turns or asking questions during a political debate. Norms of interpretation are meanings that are ascribed to norms of interaction, such as the differences in how debaters from different political parties diverge in their interpretations regarding whether it is acceptable to talk over someone else during a debate.

8. Genres

This category of conditions includes all the contextual features that make an object of study unique or particular, such as the formalized discourse features that define a political debate (e.g., a mediator allocates turns, topics are prearranged, and contention is built into the speech event). Like other familiar speech events, such as a "poem, ... proverb, ... commercial, [and] form letter" (see Hymes, 1972, p. 65), genres are based on communicative traditions that are co-constructed over time, creating an expectation within societies regarding how a particular object of study ought to be organized or used. For example, viewers of political debates possess an expectation that what they are about to watch will possess familiar discourse features, such as a mediator allocating turns or politicians engaging in argumentative turns.

Using the SPEAKING model to understand the context of an object of study, such as a political debate, requires considering how all eight categories may interact with each other. In other words, the SPEAKING model is best utilized when all eight categories are taken into consideration and the researcher accepts the possibility that one category may be interacting with another category. For example, the manner of communication (**Key**) during a political debate, such as confrontational talk, will likely influence how debaters address and respond to each other (Act sequence). With that said, not all eight categories of the SPEAKING model may be relevant to some objects of study: for example, it may be difficult to apply "Act sequence" to a billboard that only contains an image of a face. Furthermore, it is often the case that a researcher will not know the precise purpose (see Ends) of an object of study, such as hand gesture or storefront sign.

Learning Activity 4.3 The SPEAKING Model

In this exercise, the learning objective is to use the SPEAKING model to understand the relationship between context and discourse. The object of study for this exercise is a face-to-face interaction between a car salesman and a potential customer looking for a new automobile.

  Below, two conditions are provided for each category. Please try to identify two or more additional conditions for each category.

Category	*Condition*
Setting	car lot
	salesman's office
Participants	customer
	salesman
Ends	to buy
	to sell
Act sequence	seeking information
	answering questions
Keys	casual talk
	serious negotiation
Instrumentalities	spoken communication
	written contract
Norms	establishing intent to buy
	establishing trust
Genres	business transaction

  Can you think of other contexts that share the same or similar conditions as this sales encounter? Cars can be sold and purchased online and even without an encounter with a human. What conditions exist in these other contexts of car sales?

The SPEAKING model offers a practical tool for identifying and describing context. In particular, the eight categories call to mind the multifaceted nature of context. Like all models or frameworks, the true value in using the SPEAKING model lies in its ability to establish a holistic contextual account of an object of study.

In addition to offering a holistic overview, discourse analysts have at their disposal a number of tools and metaphors to examine context. Four such tools and metaphors are discussed in this chapter: frames, contextualization cues, indexicality, and next-turn proof procedure.

Summary 4.3

1. The SPEAKING model consists of eight categories of context.
2. The SPEAKING model views competence as a lens through which to understand context.
3. The SPEAKING model is best used to provide a holistic account of a context.

4.4 Frames

A frame is a contextual resource that helps establish how to interpret meaning within a given situation. Frames are important to co-constructing meaning, as any segment, feature, or stretch of discourse can be potentially interpreted in a number of ways. For example, Bateson (1972), who introduced the term based in part on his observations of animal behavior in zoos, observes that frames allow monkeys to assess whether a physical action, such as a push or shove, should be interpreted as an act of play or aggression. In other words, there is something within the global–local context continuum (e.g., social, psychological, and interactional conditions) that establishes a frame, allowing monkeys to determine that play is commencing. In this context, once play has commenced, the discourse of the monkeys can be referred to as a "play frame." In this sense, a frame can, but need not, have a beginning, middle, and end. Bateson uses the term **meta-message** to refer to the process of using conditions to make interpretations – to understand, for example, when a frame is beginning or ending. Like conditions, meta-messages allow individuals to make sense of the discourse that they are encountering.

Language is often the key resource for establishing, maintaining, and ending a frame, but frames are also based on other factors, such as historical, cognitive, and spatial conditions. For example, a stop sign uses language (the word *STOP*) to frame an ensuing action: to stop. However, a stop sign relies on other conditions to frame the same action. Consider, for instance, Figure 4.5, which offers a visual depiction of a stop sign without the word *STOP*.

It is reasonable to assume that many people would interpret this sign as a stop frame. The red octagon is a semiotic condition that people recognize as a request (or meta-message) to stop. The spatial location of the stop sign is yet another condition that offers the appropriate frame of interpretation. Of course, historical and cognitive conditions, such as a

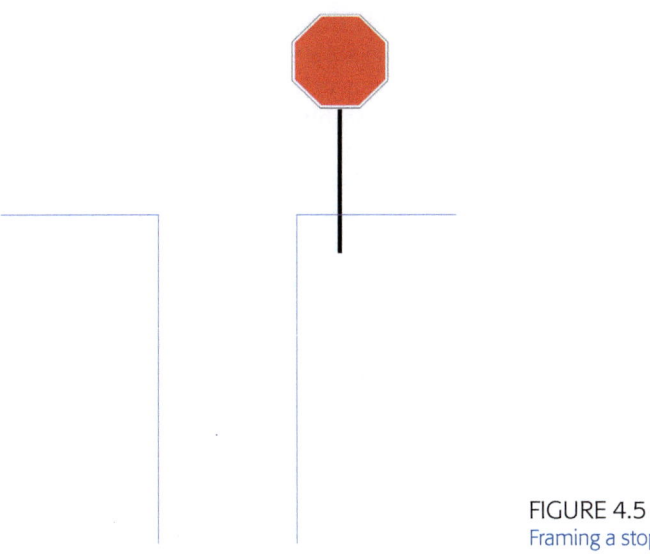

FIGURE 4.5
Framing a stop

lifetime of experiences with stop signs, factor into this interpretation process. That is, there are numerous conditions that are relevant to how frames are interpreted.

Furthermore, multiple frames can exist within a given communicative situation. This situation exists, in part, because people possess diverse ways of making sense of their surroundings. Goffman (1986) – who is responsible for popularizing the use of frames – uses the term **lamination** to capture how frames can be built on, or exist in competition with, one another within a single communicative situation. Imagine, for example, a crossing guard standing near a stop sign at an intersection. Figure 4.6 offers a visual depiction of this situation.

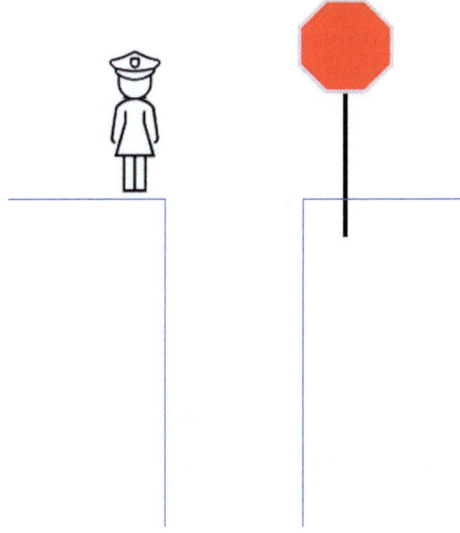

FIGURE 4.6
Stop frame with a crossing guard

At least two frames exist within this situation, creating a lamination of different interpretations. First, the stop sign potentially establishes a stop frame through the interpretive work discussed in the first illustration. Second, the crossing guard establishes a different frame that potentially overrides the stop sign. For example, the crossing guard could wave pedestrians through the intersection without stopping if she gestures to do so – though how people interpret this gesture and whether they follow the sign or the human will vary from one individual to another. Alternatively, the crossing guard could establish a stop frame by raising the palm of her hand. In both situations, the existence of the crossing guard at the intersection could be interpreted as a directive to ignore the stop sign and follow the directions of the human. Whatever interpretation is made, two frames are established through a process of lamination.

The stop sign example demonstrates that frames come in many forms and are based on potentially numerous conditions. A frame can be anything from a road sign that explicitly establishes how to behave to a subtle change in facial expressions that implicitly signals a shift in emotional states. **Framing** is the action of signaling or telling people how to come to an understanding of an object of study or communicative situation. Frames can help interpret whether an email is hostile, the purpose of a commercial, the underlying motives of a political speech, and changes in levels of formality during an interview, to name a few.

Learning Activity 4.4 Frames

In this exercise, the learning objective is to apply frames to the study of context. The context here is a university campus with walking paths.

In the image of the paths, please identify what your frame of interpretation is for each established walking path: the sidewalk and the small trail that has been created as a result of students taking a shortcut. Imagine yourself or someone else walking from the bottom of the image with the intention of turning left down the westward path.

Please think of what conditions help you come to your interpretation. In other words, what meaning – that is, discourse – is communicated when you consider both walking paths?

Would your interpretation change if you witnessed students taking a particular path? For example, if no one is taking the concrete path, then would you too take the shortcut if this was not your original decision? Your interpretation of what other students are doing is an example of discourse communicating meaning, which also influences your decision to walk a particular path.

The frames that are relevant to the campus pathways are contextual resources that help us understand how to navigate the need to turn left. Frames, which are potentially based on a range of conditions, help individuals co-construct meaning. For example, the path established by many students taking a shortcut may communicate to you that it is acceptable to walk through the grass. For other students, however, it is more important to avoid damaging the grass and therefore a different frame may be communicated. Our diverse ways of interpreting meaning, as well as our divergent intentions and goals, mean that objects of study may possess multiple frames, creating a lamination process that requires further interpretation. Indexicality is one such contextualization process that helps people make sense of their environment or communicative situation.

Summary 4.4

1. A frame helps people understand their context and how to behave within it.
2. A frame can have a beginning, middle, and end.
3. A frame contains a meta-message that helps people make interpretations of their context.
4. A frame can be any condition located in the context continuum.
5. Framing is the action of signaling how a context should be understood.

4.5 Indexicality

Indexicality is discourse pointing to something within a communicative situation. Using a finger to point out a person in a crowded room is an example of indexicality. This act of pointing is referred to as **indexing**, which creates meaning by connecting discourse and context. For instance, using a finger to point out a person in a crowded room can create meaning by connecting a name with a face. Of course, there are numerous other aspects of discourse that can create the same meaning, such as uttering the words *him* or *over there*. Whether it is verbal, embodied, interactional, or related to any other condition, discourse that points to something within a communicative situation is called an **index**. A pointing finger is an index. The words *him* and *over there* are **indexes**.

It is important to note that discourse requires context in order for it to be considered indexical. For example, the words *him* and *over there* spoken without context are not indexical, as their meanings exist in relation to some referential point. Put differently, it is difficult to understand the words *him* or *over there* without information to which *him* or *over there* is pointing. This observation can easily be tested by beginning the next conversation you have with a friend or family member with the word *him* or *over there* – confusion is likely to ensue (cf. breaching experiments). Indeed, there are numerous words and expressions that require context in order for them to be meaningfully interpreted, such as *then, now, soon, enough, you, that,* and *I*. These context-dependent words and expressions are examples of **deixis**. Deictic words and expressions are related to time (e.g., *now* and *then*), place (e.g., *here* and *this*), quantity (e.g., *more* and *enough*), and person (e.g., *we* and *they*). Such words and expressions are indexical, as they are pointing devices that connect discourse and context.

All discourse analysts are concerned with indexicality: the juncture between context and discourse is again central to discourse analysis. Although the term is not often explicitly named in research, all approaches to discourse analysis possess a unique way of thinking about and studying indexicality. Readers that are interested in a more theoretical overview of indexicality that attends to the history and application of the term, as well as its role in discourse analysis, should refer to the work of R. Moore (2020).

Learning Activity 4.5 Indexicality

In this exercise, the learning objective is to understand how context transforms the meaning of indexical words. The object of study is a political debate between two interactants. The focus of analysis within this context are the indexical words *he*, *him*, and *it*.

The conversation is presented below as a transcript, which begins with a contextual overview of the conversation.

((KM and CQ are debating on live television why the father of an accused terrorist supports the presidential candidate that they endorse))

1	KM:	what attracted the father of the Orlando terrorist to your candidate
2	CQ:	he's a mentally ill individual
3	KM:	oh that's what attracted him
4	CQ:	who ran for president
5	KM:	I get it.

First, identify what is being pointed at with the words *he, him,* and *it*. Do the words *he* and *him* point to the same thing? Second, is it clear what *it* is referring to in line 5? How would you respond to this statement if you do not know what is being referred to with *it*? Third, what do these indexical words tell you about how people use language? For example, why do KM and CQ use *he* and *him* instead of names?

The exercise demonstrates that indexicality offers a window into the relationship between discourse and context. By looking at indexical words and expressions, it is possible to see how discourse points to specific things within a particular situation or encounter, creating meaning for the people involved in, or part of, a context. Indexical words and expressions, such as *he* and *him*, contain meaning in relation to something within a particular situation or encounter (i.e., context), but the exercise also demonstrates that people have different referential points and ways of interpreting discourse. Thus, context also reflects the meaning that people construct in and through discourse, such as with contextualization cues.

Summary 4.5
1. Indexicality is discourse pointing to something within a communicative situation.
2. This process of pointing is referred to as indexing.
3. A discourse that points to something is called an index.
4. Context-dependent words and expressions are deixes.

4.6 Contextualization Cues

Contextualization cues are linguistic resources that point to some aspect of context. Thus, contextualization cues are indexical resources; they reveal the ways in which meaning is created within context. For Gumperz (1982, p. 131), the scholar that coined and operationalized the term, contextualization cues are "any feature of linguistic form" that allow people to understand their context.

Gumperz (1992, p. 231) divides contextualization cues into four linguistic resources (what he calls "levels of speech production"): prosody, paralinguistic signs, code choice, and formulaic expressions.

1. **Prosody**: is the level of speech production that includes "(a) intonation, i.e. pitch levels on individual syllables and their combination into contours; (b) changes in loudness; (c) stress, a perceptual feature generally comprising variations in pitch, loudness, and duration; (d) other variations in vowel length; (e) phrasing, including utterance chunking by pausing, accelerations

and decelerations within and across utterance chunks; and (f) overall shifts in speech register" (Gumperz, 1982, p. 100). These prosodic examples demonstrate that meaning can be derived from the most minute details of talk. For example, prosody in the form of turn-ending intonation helps children explain game instructions by signaling information about what the next turn will likely entail (Kern, 2007).

2. **Paralinguistic signs**: are the level of speech production that includes "tempo, pausing and hesitation, conversational synchrony, including latching or overlapping of speaking turns, and other ... expressive cues" (Gumperz, 1992, p. 231). These paralinguistic cues provide meaning to context by signaling information about how a conversational exchange should be managed, such as knowing when a turn at talk should be taken or relinquished. Like all contextualization cues, paralinguistic signs interact with other levels of speech, such as prosody.

3. **Code choice**: is the level of speech production that entails selecting one way of speaking from a linguistic repertoire, such as switching between different languages, adjusting registers, modifying grammatical constructions, and raising voice amplitude. These examples demonstrate that the meaning tied to contextualization cues is not limited to language, but may also be embedded within the choices that people make as they communicate. For example, the decision to use English – rather than a language commonly spoken within a particular context or region – could be interpreted as an attempt to establish power over other people or to engage in some identity work.

4. **Formulaic expressions**: are the level of speech production that covers the ways in which people organize interactional sequences, such as exchanging greetings at the beginning of an encounter or saying goodbyes at the end of a conversational exchange. Formulaic expressions also include lexical constructions and phrases, such as metaphors, colloquial sayings, and analogies. These examples demonstrate that meaning can be derived from how a communicative situation or encounter is organized, such as the expectation that an interview will require an interviewee to answer many questions.

Like frames, contextualization cues help people make sense of what is being said, who the speaker or discourse producer is, how a situation must be interpreted, and why a communicative act is taking place. Gumperz (1992, p. 230) refers to these functions as "contextualization," which is the "use of verbal and nonverbal signs to relate what is said at any one time and in any one place to knowledge acquired through past experience." According to this quote, meaning not only comes from contextualization cues, but is also inextricably tied to historical and cognitive conditions.

Gumperz (1992, p. 230) identifies three aspects of contextualization that are important to understanding the juncture between discourse and context: situatedness, inferencing, reinterpretation.

1. **Situatedness**: is the observation that meaning can only be constructed in relation to the situation (or context) in which the discourse occurs, which includes not only language and interaction, but also the people involved in the communicative encounter. In other words, meaning is context-dependent.
2. **Inferencing**: is the observation that meaning is based on the presuppositions (or established assumptions) that people use to make inferences about discourse and context. Inferences can turn out to be incorrect (e.g., misinterpreting the meaning of an utterance), which can be rectified during a process of reinterpretation.
3. **Reinterpretation**: is the observation that although people frame communicative situations according to their presuppositions (i.e., inferencing), these assumptions must be tailored to contexts. Reinterpretation is thus the process of negotiating meaning according to context.

Applying these three aspects of contextualization to a communicative situation is straightforward. Take, for example, an immigration counter at an airport. The type of discourse that occurs within this context is *situated* (contextualization aspect 1): the immigration counter is an institutional encounter that requires an officer to determine formally whether a traveler is allowed to enter a country, which involves checking documents and asking questions. Both experienced and inexperienced travelers will possess their own *inferences* about how to interact at the immigration counter (contextualization aspect 2), which could shape how they understand and respond to the officer. Such inferences may turn out to be incorrect: a traveler could, for example, approach the situation as an informal encounter, engaging in small talk with the officer. The traveler will have to *reinterpret* the situation if the officer asks for silence or ignores the attempt to engage in small talk (contextualization aspect 3).

In the immigration counter example, the contextualization cues that the officer uses to signal to the travel that her interpretation is incorrect may include, but are not limited to, the four levels of speech production discussed previously: prosody, paralinguistic signs, code choice, and formulaic expressions. For instance, the officer could give a look of annoyance or disapproval by lowering his eyebrows, clenching his jaw, or tensing his lips.

Learning Activity 4.6 Contextualization Cues

In this exercise, the learning objective is to discuss how contextualization cues establish meaning within a communicative situation. The object of study is roughly based on a conversational exchange that the author had with an immigration officer at an airport.

Please identify any aspect of speech that functions as a contextualization cue. Use the four levels of speech production to identify your cues (i.e., prosody, paralinguistic signs, code choice, and formulaic expressions). Remember that contextualization cues – that is, what the traveler and officer are saying and doing – tell us something about context – that is, the immigration encounter.

1	Officer:	((motions with hand for the traveler to come to the counter))
2	Traveler:	((walks to the counter))
3		hello. nice weather outside today.
4	Officer:	passport, please!
5	Traveler:	sorry. here you go.
6	Officer:	what is the purpose of your visit?
7	Traveler:	I am here to attend a conference.

What contextualization cues are used in line 1 to initiate the encounter? Do these cues establish any particular meaning, such as that the encounter is institutional and formal? How did you come to this interpretation? In what other contexts or situations would you find these cues being used?

What contextualization cues does the traveler use in line 3? Do these cues align with or match the meaning established by the officer? For example, what cues does the officer use in line 4 to establish a particular frame?

What does this overall exchange tell us about how contextualization cues are used to establish meaning? Can misinterpretations be prevented using different contextualization cues?

This exercise demonstrates that contextualization cues are resources that people use to make sense of their communicative situation. Like all indexical resources, contextualization cues establish meaning by pointing to something within a context in and through discourse, such as the immigration officer maintaining his institutional role by refusing to engage in small talk or the traveler treating the situation as an informal encounter. In this sense, contextualization cues also build context by revealing how a particular situation ought to be managed or understood. One particularly useful, albeit narrow, way of analyzing how people understand context is called next-turn proof procedure, which is discussed in Section 4.7.

Summary 4.6	1. Contextualization cues are linguistic resources that point to some aspect of context.
	2. Contextualization cues can be divided into four linguistic resources.
	3. The process of contextualization can be divided into three aspects of context.

4.7 Next-Turn Proof Procedure

The frameworks and constructs presented thus far view context holistically, accounting for some or many of the conditions in the global–local continuum that were identified at the beginning of this chapter. While these holistic perspectives are suitable for most researchers, there is a branch of discourse analysis that seeks answers from an incredibly "local" level. This branch of discourse analysis is called **conversation analysis** (see the descriptive approaches in Chapter 3) and can be studied in greater detail in Schegloff (2007).

Conversation analysis uses next-turn proof procedure to analyze how people create meaning within their local context. For conversation analysts, local context refers to the turn-taking system that people rely on to communicate. What this "rule" means is relatively simple in principle: next-turn proof procedure requires a researcher to look at how one turn reveals an understanding of its prior turn. This narrow way of analyzing an object of study is based on the theoretical principle that a researcher can only make an observation about context that has been made relevant (or is spoken about) by the people communicating.

The theory behind next-turn proof procedure is based on an **emic** understanding of context, which simply refers to a participant-based approach to analyzing discourse. For instance, when a speaker uses one turn to respond to a previous turn, the response creates meaning, revealing how the participants make sense of their context. In this sense, next-turn proof procedure sees turn-taking as a lens through which to understand context. Take, for example, the conversation between Rose and Felipe that takes place at the former friend's house late in the evening.

1   Rose: Feels late, right?

At the beginning of this exchange Rose asks Felipe a question. The turn spoken by Rose reveals her understanding of the communicative situation (i.e., context): Rose could be revealing her feelings about the time and is simply seeking confirmation from Felipe (this observation is referred to as Option A). Alternatively, Rose could be revealing her feelings about the time and is suggesting that Felipe should leave (this observation is referred to as Option B).

A researcher could make an educated observation about what is the most valid option using any of the frameworks or constructs introduced in this chapter. However, a researcher using next-turn proof procedure cannot say for certain how Rose is interpreting the context, as an emic understanding requires looking at how the participants themselves co-construct meaning. Again, next-turn proof procedure requires looking at how one turn reveals an understanding of its previous turn:

2   Felipe: No, not really.

Felipe reveals his understanding of the previous turn in responding to Rose. That is, Felipe treats Rose's question as seeking confirmation about the time (Option A), but not necessarily as a request to leave (Option B). However, Felipe's turn does not reveal what Rose was thinking – only how Felipe interprets Rose's question. That is, according to next-turn proof procedure, Rose's understanding of the situation is still unknown. In order to attempt to reveal how Rose is interpreting the context, it is necessary to keep looking:

3   Rose: Well, Lilly needs to sleep now.

Rose in line 3 states that her daughter needs to sleep. In so doing, Rose reveals her understanding of the context, aligning with Option B by providing a more explicit contextualization cue to her friend that it is time for Felipe to leave:

4   Felipe: Oh, okay. I will leave now.

The exchange between Rose and Felipe demonstrates how context can be understood from a local, turn-taking perspective. Next-turn proof procedure requires a researcher to withhold any assumptions about context, and instead focus on how speakers reveal their understanding of a communicative situation from one turn to another – conversation analysts refer to this principle as **procedural consequentiality** (Schegloff, 2007). For example, it took three turns of talk in order to provide an emic perspective of Rose's understanding of context. This length of time is also precisely the number of turns that it took Felipe (in line 4) to finally realize that Rose's first utterance was a cue to leave. Even though a researcher may have a strong indication of what Rose's first utterance was attempting to do, next-turn proof procedure requires a researcher to make observations about context that are based on, or situated within, the turn-by-turn moments of discourse.

Learning Activity 4.7 Next-Turn Proof Procedure

In this exercise, the learning objective is to follow next-turn proof procedure in an object of study. The object of study is the same conversational exchange presented in the previous section.

   This exercise requires two analytic steps for each line. First, please identify the different interpretations that you could make for what is being said or done. Second, please identify how the following turn orients to the previous one. For example, identify at least one way of interpreting line 1 and then see if line 2 matches any of your interpretations. Remember that next-turn proof procedure requires using the interpretation made in the next line/turn (and not necessarily what the researcher believes is happening).

1	Officer:	((motions with hand for the traveler to come to the counter))
2	Traveler:	((walks to the counter))
3		hello. nice weather outside today.

4	Officer:	passport, please!
5	Traveler:	sorry. here you go.
6	Officer:	what is the purpose of your visit?
7	Traveler:	I am here to attend a conference.

In order to provide some pedagogical guidance, a few example observations will be provided for the beginning of this exchange.

In line 1, the hand motion can be interpreted as a request for the traveler to approach the counter. However, we cannot say for certain until seeing what happens in the next turn. To this end, in line 2, the traveler walks to the counter and therefore interprets the hand motion according to our original observation. In this two-part exchange, we can say that both the officer and traveler interpret the context as the start of their encounter.

In line 3, the traveler provides a greeting and offers an assessment of the weather. We can assume that these utterances are attempts to engage in small talk, be nice, or mitigate the potentially stressful situation that is associated with such encounters, to name a few possible interpretations. Although these interpretations seem logical given the context, next-turn proof procedure again requires us to see what happens next. To this end, in line 4, the officer responds to the traveler by requesting his passport. We cannot say for certain what the traveler is attempting to do in line 3, but it is possible to conclude that the officer does not see this context as a space for casual or informal talk. In other words, the traveler and officer in lines 3 and 4 do not have the same understanding of their context.

Please continue with your analysis of the context using next-turn proof procedure for lines 4–7.

Next-turn proof procedure is based on the belief that there are potentially multiple ways to interpreting any given utterance or segment of discourse, and therefore the most "locally" sensitive way of understanding context is to see how the participants themselves make sense of their communicative situation. In practice, this principle means that a researcher cannot say anything for certain until seeing the next turn(s) or how a stretch of communication unfolds. In so doing, a researcher is providing a local (or emic) understanding of context.

Summary 4.7

1. Next-turn proof procedure is based on a local understanding of context.
2. Next-turn proof procedure looks at how one turn reveals an understanding of its prior turn.
3. Next-turn proof procedure offers an emic or participant-based understanding of context.
4. Next-turn proof procedure is based on a turn-taking understanding of context.

4.8 Concluding Remarks on Context

Context is fundamental to doing discourse analysis. It can be generically defined as all of the conditions that shape how discourse is structured and used. However, great variation exists in how context is defined and accounted for in analytic approaches, making it difficult for novice (and indeed seasoned) discourse analysts to make sense of this construct. It is thus necessary to provide further guidance on context as a way of concluding this chapter.

Although the definitions, ideas, models, and constructs reviewed in this chapter offer sufficient coverage for introductory purposes, there are several aspects of context and related analytic issues that can be included in the present discussion to provide a more comprehensive account of the topic. These aspects of context and related analytic issues are discussed below in no particular order of importance: situational knowledge, situatedness, and situational resources.

1. **Situational knowledge**: relates to how much information a researcher possesses of the context being investigated (for more information on the role of the researcher in discourse analysis, see Chapter 5). A researcher with little situational knowledge of a context will typically have a harder time understanding an object of study than someone with expertise of the same communicative situation. For example, a researcher investigating the discourse of surgeons with no medical knowledge will struggle to understand the context. Therefore, not only is context an important aspect of discourse analysis, it also requires a level of situational knowledge that is sufficient for analyzing an object of study. The practical implication is that it is more often than not better to investigate contexts and objects of study of which you possess situational knowledge. It is, however, entirely possible and not even uncommon to develop situational knowledge before investigating a context (e.g., a discourse analyst training to be a driving instructor to investigate instruction-giving in cars).

2. **Situatedness**: refers to how the same context can vary in meaning across time and space. A context evolves over time and space because the conditions that are important to a situation are not stable. For example, how people answer phones has changed over time as a result of technological advancements (e.g., caller ID or video calling). What is contextually relevant and meaningful in one context for one person may not apply to other people communicating in the same situation. In this sense, context is dynamic and somewhat unpredictable, which leads the discussion to the next point.

3. **Situational resources**: refer to how people use context as a resource or means to engage in discourse. That is to say, context is something that people use for their own intentions and purposes,

which results in different discourse features. For example, two students in the same classroom may approach a learning task with different motivations, ambitions, and goals. For instance, the highly motivated student may take more turns at talk, communicate longer, and frequently take the initiative to ask the teacher questions. This example demonstrates that context is co-constructed and adaptable.

While these three aspects of context are important to how all analysts conduct research, there is great variation in how each methodological approach deals with the conditions that shape discourse. What is deemed an important or relevant aspect of context in one methodology will likely be different for other methodologies. For example, while descriptive approaches, such as conversation analysis, typically privilege local conditions, evaluative approaches, such as critical discourse analysis, often look at global conditions. Readers who are interested in understanding context in greater detail and in relation to a specific methodology should refer back to the Chapter 3 references.

Summary 4.8	1. Situational knowledge is needed to understand a context fully. 2. Situatedness refers to how context is dynamic and somewhat unpredictable. 3. Situated resources refer to how context is used as a means of engaging in discourse. 4. Context is understood in many different ways and according to theory and methodology.

Learning Accomplishments

The chapter has reviewed the different interpretations of, and approaches to, context. The discussion established how context factors into the analysis of your object of study. This section identifies how each learning outcome has been addressed in this chapter.

1. You will understand what context is and why it is important to analyzing your object of study.

Context was defined as all of the conditions that influence how discourse is structured and used. Many conditions were identified and discussed in relation to a global–local continuum. It was stated that context is an exceptionally important construct in discourse analysis, as all researchers regardless of their disciplinary background are expected to consider how conditions factor into their objects of study. It was also argued that context is important to an object of study because discourse shapes context, and context shapes discourse.

2. You will be able to study context using different models and constructs.

In addition to discussing context as a set of conditions existing along a global–local continuum, several models and constructs were introduced. Two models were discussed in this chapter: the systemic functional linguistics model and the SPEAKING model. Furthermore, four constructs were introduced: frames, indexicality, contextualization cues, and next-turn proof procedure.

3. You will understand how discourse and context work together to create meaning.

All the models and frameworks discussed in this chapter demonstrated how meaning is embedded within context. This meaning may come from a communicative act, contextualization cue, or turn at talk, to name a few. Meaning may also exist within institutions, cultural knowledge, and historical events that shape how people approach, and communicate within, a particular situation. The chapter established that although different models and constructs exist, they all have their own ways of identifying the meaning that is embedded within context.

Key Themes

Context and Its Importance

1. Context is all of the conditions that influence discourse.
2. Context and setting are not the same construct.
3. Many conditions exist within a context.
4. Researchers have different ways of understanding and approaching context.
5. Context is central to all approaches to discourse analysis.

The Systemic Functional Linguistics Model

1. An SFL understanding of context is based on three interrelated discourse categories.
2. The SFL model views context as a network of meanings.
3. The SFL model adopts the term register to understand contextual variation.

The SPEAKING Model

1. The SPEAKING model consists of eight categories of context.
2. The SPEAKING model views competence as a lens through which context is understood.
3. The SPEAKING model is best used to provide a holistic account of a context.

Frames

1. A frame helps people understand their context and how to behave within it.
2. A frame can have a beginning, middle, and end.
3. A frame contains a meta-message that helps people make interpretations of their context.
4. A frame can be any condition located in the context continuum.
5. Framing is the action of signaling how a context should be understood.

Indexicality

1. Indexicality is discourse pointing to something within a communicative situation.
2. This process of pointing is referred to as indexing.
3. A discourse that points to something is called an index.
4. Context-dependent words and expressions are deixes.

Contextualization Cues

1. Contextualization cues are linguistic resources that point to some aspect of context.
2. Contextualization cues can be divided into four linguistic resources.
3. The process of contextualization can be divided into three aspects of context.

Next-Turn Proof Procedure

1. Next-turn proof procedure is based on a local understanding of context.
2. Next-turn proof procedure looks at how one turn reveals an understanding of its prior turn.
3. Next-turn proof procedure offers an emic or participant-based understanding of context.
4. Next-turn proof procedure is based on a turn-taking understanding of context.

General Contextual Issues

1. Situational knowledge is needed to understand a context fully.
2. Situatedness refers to how context is dynamic and somewhat unpredictable.
3. Situated resources refer to how context is used as a means of engaging in discourse.
4. Context is understood in many different ways and according to theory and methodology.

Reading List

Duranti & Goodwin (1992) In this seminal edited collection, the contributors provide a range of perspectives to context using different methodological approaches. Although the book does not provide an introductory overview of context, the chapters offer concrete examples of how to account for context in discourse analysis.

Flowerdew (2014) The edited collection offers engaging and easily to follow examples of how context is approached from multiple, applied linguistic perspectives. Each chapter uses a different social phenomenon or communicative situation to demonstrate how meaning emerges from the juncture between discourse and context.

van Dijk (2009) The author provides an understanding of context that is related mostly to the societal, political, and cognitive conditions that were identified in the global–local continuum. The book explores how and why discourse is based on situations or contexts.

Learning Outcomes

This chapter reviews how being a researcher shapes the analytic process and why it is important to think about this influence. The aim of the chapter is to establish that every researcher imprints their own personal and professional *subjectivities* onto the analytic process, which includes collecting and analyzing an object of study.

The contents of the chapter are organized according to the following learning outcomes. After reading this chapter:

1. You will understand that discourse analysis research is inherently subjective;
2. You will understand that a researcher's cultural familiarity with an object of study is crucial to doing discourse analysis;
3. You will be able to identify and adopt multiple analytic perspectives;
4. You will be able to apply reflexive practices to the analytic process;
5. You will understand, and know how to deal with, the power dynamics that exist in discourse analysis research.

5.1 Objectivity and Subjectivity

In experimental studies that rely on statistical computations of controlled dependent variables, it is traditional to view the role of the researcher as an independent participant *detached* from the analytic process. The goal in such research is to be as "objective" as possible, removing any biases of the researcher that may influence how data is collected and analyzed. Notwithstanding the question of whether objectivity is fully achievable even in experimental studies, the concept of removing subjectivities and biases is not viewed the same way in discourse analysis.

In discourse analysis, the researcher is often *attached* to the analytic process, making adjustments to a study as it progresses. For example, a discourse analyst investigating teacher questions as an object of study may need to change the placement and angles of cameras while collecting data in order to reflect both predetermined and evolving research objectives. Such changes may be necessary because a camera is not capturing the right type of discourse, the researcher selects a different object of study after viewing an earlier recording, or it is concluded that more data is needed after an ethnographic visit to a site of investigation, to name a few. The point here is that a researcher using discourse analysis plays an active role in shaping the analytic process as the research progresses.

While playing an active role in the analytic process is not a catastrophic problem in objectivity (for a list of things to avoid when analyzing discourse, see Antaki *et al.*, 2003), a discourse analyst should follow guidelines set forth by theories that establish what you should and should not do while analyzing an object of study (for an overview of different frameworks, see De Fina & Georgakopoulou, 2020). This expectation exists because there are concrete differences in how the role of the researcher is viewed within discourse analysis. For instance, a critical discourse analyst and a conversation analyst will have different interpretations of what it means to participate actively in the analytic process (see, for example, Wooffitt, 2005), including collecting data and analyzing an object of study from a particular analytic perspective (see Section 5.3 on emic and etic perspectives).

Readers interested in the specific theoretical and methodological differences that exist in how researchers view their role in discourse analysis should refer to Hammersley (2003), Henwood (2007), and Nikander (2008) for more advanced – though not comprehensive – discussions of the topic. For now, it is important to establish an introductory foundation for the role of the researcher in discourse analysis.

In order to provide an introductory account, it is important to establish the ways in which a researcher has a role in the analytic process first. The role of a researcher in discourse analysis refers to the extent to which your personal experiences, life subjectivities, and empirical objectives influence how an object of study is identified and understood. Another way of conceptualizing the role of a researcher is to think of how the analytic process is shaped according to the relationship that you have with the things or people that you are investigating. This influence or relationship can be expressed as personal (e.g., biases, life experiences) and professional (e.g., theoretical position and disciplinary expectations) knowledge. Personal and professional knowledge shape how you select and analyze an object of study. Such knowledge is discussed in the following order: cultural familiarity, emic and etic perspectives, reflexivity, power relations, and autoethnography.

Summary 5.1

1. A discourse analyst actively shapes the analytic process.
2. Theory and methodology determine the role of the researcher in discourse analysis.
3. Experiences, subjectivities, and research objectives influence the analytic process.
4. An analysis can include personal, subjective, theoretical, or contextual information.

5.2 Cultural Familiarity

Cultural familiarity is the level of knowledge that a researcher possesses of an object of study. This knowledge can be based on anything from a semiotic object, such as the cultural familiarity of a symbol used by a luxury company, to the oral history of a speech community, such as the cultural familiarity with a marginalized ethnic group. In short, cultural familiarity is based on any aspect of discourse (i.e., language use and the human factor). Cultural familiarity is fundamental to doing discourse analysis, as it is impossible to analyze an object of study if a researcher has no knowledge of what is being examined. For example, a monolingual English-speaking American political scientist will not be able to analyze how the Russian media reports on state politics. Minimally, the political scientist will need to have the media reports translated into English, though it could be argued that cultural familiarity with Russian politics is also needed.

The minimal level of cultural familiarity that is needed to investigate an object of study is referred to in this book as **entry-point knowledge**. Objects of study possess different entry-point knowledge requirements. For example, investigating a luxury symbol may not demand much cultural familiarity; on the other hand, understanding how a marginalized ethnic group lives in a city requires extensive linguistic, cultural, and social knowledge. Therefore, it is important to know what is needed of (and from) you in terms of cultural familiarity when considering a particular object of study.

Learning Activity 5.1 Reflecting on Entry-Point Knowledge

In this exercise, the learning objective is to reflect on how objects of study are connected to different expectations regarding cultural familiarity.

For each object of study identified below, please name at least three different aspects of cultural familiarity that are needed to conduct a discourse analysis investigation. Examples for the first object of study are provided below for your reference.

Object of study	Cultural familiarity
1. explaining math problems	mathematical formulas pedagogical theories teaching practices
2. political adverts in the Netherlands	
3. speeches at the European Parliament	
4. English lyrics in Korean popular music	
5. introductions during business meetings	

Now that several aspects of cultural familiarity have been identified, it is helpful to reflect on whether you possess the knowledge to analyze these five objects of study. To this end, if you do not possess the knowledge to examine any particular object of study, then what would you need to do to develop the necessary cultural familiarity? Would developing these aspects of cultural familiarity make the discourse analysis project feasible?

Beyond entry-point knowledge, a researcher must determine how much cultural familiarity will be used to report on an object of study. Using cultural familiarity in this way entails using your knowledge to describe an object of study, which is often based on people or communities, such as a community of graffiti artists, but could also be semiotic (e.g., a brand of spray paint), discursive (e.g., the language painted on walls), or multimodal (e.g., the images and icons that are used alongside words). This type of reporting is needed, as it allows readers to understand your object of study better. Using cultural familiarity to describe an object of study is referred to as **reporting knowledge**. The following two-paragraph description offers an example of what reporting knowledge may look like when describing an object of study (this description would typically be found in a section called "The Study" or "The Methods").

Reporting Knowledge Description

The data are based on the interactions of 50 university students communicating on Zoom: 25 research participants from a Dutch university and 25 research participants from a Hong Kong university. The students were at the time of recording between 19 and 21 years of age. All the research participants speak English as an additional language, and were tested by their universities to be at the B1 level of proficiency.

The students were enrolled in a first-year academic writing course at their respective university. Nearly all of the research participants at both universities were first-generation students, meaning that they had no prior family history of university-level academic writing. The writing course required the students to discuss their writing assignments two times per week for 16 weeks. These interactions took place on Zoom. Although the students understood that they could use the text-based chat function, they often relied on video communication.

In your analysis of an object of study, which is often broken into smaller fragments of data (see Chapter 2), reporting knowledge is also used to answer research questions; but more specifically, reporting knowledge allows you to demonstrate how an object of study can be understood from a unique or noteworthy cultural perspective. For example, reporting knowledge can be used to demonstrate how the cultural values of graffiti artists are communicated in public spaces – information that presumably many readers will not possess. Including cultural knowledge in discourse analysis helps readers better understand both your object of study and analytic observations. It is common to share this type of cultural familiarity immediately before presenting each excerpt within what would typically be called the "Findings" or "Results" section. The following analysis of a roadside billboard offers an example of what reporting knowledge may look like when analyzing an object of study. Special attention should be placed on the last sentence of the analysis (following the image) where the author's cultural familiarity with the local area is used to analyze the roadside billboard.

Reporting Knowledge Analysis

Roadside billboards are ideological signposts, and their messages help drivers create and reaffirm belief systems while providing a sense of national belonging. Such messages can also be symbolic, performative, and ornamental. In this roadside billboard, for example, an "American" identity is constructed through a combination of characteristics, such as wearing fur and owning guns, that are not necessarily suggestions for how to live, but are rather ideal symbols of what it means to belong to this identity category.

This billboard, which is located on a major highway in rural southeast South Dakota approximately thirty minutes north of the state's flagship university, ideologically aligns with many of the residents in the area who are indeed meat-eaters and hunters.

The ideas underpinning cultural knowledge are similar to other constructs used in qualitative research. For example, in ethnomethodology (e.g., Maynard & Clayman, 1991), as well as ethnomethodological conversation analysis (e.g., Lynch, 2000), **membership knowledge** is a construct that represents both a topic of investigation and a methodology to examine an object of study. Membership knowledge refers to the competences that members of societies possess to manage their daily lives, including taking part in a meeting, running a family, learning a language, participating in a conversation, and playing a game, to name a few. In ethnomethodology and ethnomethodological conversation analysis, these competences that members of societies possess are the same capabilities that researchers are expected to have for researching objects of study. This knowledge that is shared between society and researchers forms an interpretive framework, allowing scholars to understand why and how discourse is used in particular ways (for an overview of membership knowledge, see ten Have, 2005). In this sense, membership knowledge is more specialized or esoteric than cultural knowledge. Both constructs are, however, helpful in thinking about the role of the researcher in the analytic process.

Similarly, in ethnography, it is expected that researchers attain a deep understanding of their participants, developing over time a level of cultural familiarity that will provide the foundation for a **thick description**. According to Geertz (1973, p. 312), who is responsible for popularizing the construct, a thick description is "the object of ethnography," which is in its most basic form a comprehensive analysis. A thick description entails looking at, and accounting for, the complex, multifarious, and interconnected ways in which an object of study can be understood. Thick descriptions require more than entry-point knowledge. Within the tradition of ethnography, a thick description requires having the same (or very similar) level of cultural familiarity of the research participants. This may entail a discourse analyst that is studying a tribe in a distant region of the world living as a member of the community, practicing the cultural traditions, and acquiring the local language (for a seminal book-length publication on ethnomethodology and conversation analysis, see Moerman, 1988). In this sense, a thick description is a type of reporting knowledge.

Learning Activity 5.2 Reflecting on Reporting Knowledge

In this exercise, the learning objective is to reflect on how cultural familiarity can be used to report on an object of study.

The object of study for this exercise is based on something that you possess a high level of cultural familiarity with: your communicative practices with a family member during a specific encounter or situation. Using the guiding questions for the research participants below, please identify the different characteristics of you and your family member that may help the reader understand your communicative practices. Now using the guiding questions for the context, please identify the different contextual variables that will help the reader understand your communicative practices.

Guiding questions for the research participants

How old are the research participants?
What is the relationship between the two research participants?
What languages do the research participants speak?
How close are the research participants?
Do they speak to each other often?

Guiding questions for the context

Why are the research participants communicating?
Where are the research participants communicating?
How are the research participants communicating?
Are there any communication technologies being used?
What is the topic of conversation?

Now that you have identified the different aspects of cultural familiarity that could be used to report on an object of study, it may be helpful to practice writing out what these descriptions may look like. Please refer to the reporting knowledge examples provided in this section for reference.

Cultural familiarity is related to a number of empirical issues that determine how your role as a researcher shapes the analytic process. These empirical issues are summarized below in four research processes: knowing, locating, utilizing, and trusting.

1. **Knowing**: is the part of cultural familiarity that is related to the level of knowledge that a discourse analyst possesses of an object of study. This knowing can be based on any aspect of discourse. Knowing can be divided into two categories: entry-point knowledge and reporting knowledge.

2. **Locating**: is related to how cultural familiarity is used to locate objects of study or research topics. It is common for researchers to gravitate towards objects of study or research topics of which they possess cultural knowledge. For instance, it is natural for a researcher that was, or is, a teacher to be interested in classroom discourse or pedagogical topics as objects of study.

3. **Utilizing**: is related to the ways in which cultural familiarity is utilized to make specific analytic observations of an object of study. While researchers can use theoretical or methodological principles to make analytic observations, they can also utilize specialized, technical, or even personal knowledge to reveal something important about an object of study.

4. **Trusting**: is related to how cultural familiarity allows researchers to establish trust with the people that are being investigated. Researchers need to have a certain level of cultural familiarity to investigate an object of study, but this knowledge is also helpful in establishing trust. Trusting helps research participants "open up" and behave or communicate in an authentic way.

Cultural familiarity is central to how researchers approach and shape the analytic process. The construct of cultural familiarity not only represents the knowledge needed to research discourse, but is also a tool for researchers to provide unique insights into objects of study. In practical terms, what this means is that your role as a researcher is first to determine if you have the necessary cultural familiarity to carry out a research project, and then to decide how this knowledge will be used to report on an object of study.

To this end, a researcher can shape the analytic process by determining what perspective to take when examining an object of study. In Section 5.3, two analytic perspectives, which underpin all approaches that exist in discourse analysis, will be introduced.

Summary 5.2

1. Cultural familiarity is the knowledge that a researcher possesses of an object of study.
2. Entry-point knowledge is the minimal level of cultural familiarity that is needed.
3. Objects of study possess different entry-point knowledge requirements.
4. Reporting knowledge is using cultural familiarity to describe or analyze an object of study.
5. Researchers have different ways of understanding and using cultural familiarity.

5.3 Emic and Etic Perspectives

Using cultural familiarity to report on an object of study requires a researcher to select an analytic perspective. Analytic perspectives are commonly associated with specific discourse analysis approaches (e.g., critical discourse analysis versus conversation analysis). Although readers could begin the analytic process by studying a specific discourse analysis approach, this path requires extensive reading and close mentorship from an experienced researcher. A more practical way of learning how a researcher shapes the analytic process is to consider **emic** and **etic** perspectives, which underpin all discourse analysis approaches.

That is, before committing to a specific discourse analysis approach, a researcher can begin the analytic process by determining whether an object of study will be examined from either an emic or etic perspective – in practice, however, a researcher will typically use a bit of both perspectives. This decision is partly based on how much of your cultural familiarity will be used while analyzing an object of study. In very simple terms, emic perspectives do not generally support researchers using their cultural familiarity to report on an object of study (unless they are researching themselves; see autoethnography in this chapter), while etic perspectives are comparatively open to different analytic possibilities. Although this is a crude distinction, the characterization demonstrates that cultural familiarity is connected to all the empirical issues presented in this chapter.

The notion of emic and etic perspectives comes from the work of Pike (1967) in his attempt to understand human behavior in relation to language. Pike created the constructs emic and etic from the words phon*emic* and phon*etic*, respectively. Phonemic being, of course, the *internal* system from which speakers of a language construct meaning, while phonetic is an *external* classification system that researchers use to understand the sounds of all languages.

First, a researcher can select an emic perspective, which is a participant or inside(r) view of an object of study. According to Pike (1990, p. 28), an emic perspective accounts for an object of study as it is "treated by insiders as relevant to their system of behavior." This notion of "treated" can be followed through in two ways. On the one hand, a researcher can ask participants – through interviewers, for example – why or how they communicate or behave in a particular way (e.g., How do they "treat" or feel about a particular object of study?). On the other hand, a researcher can observe what participants do in and through their communication or behavior (e.g., How do they "treat" or orient to a particular object of study in and through their communication?). In both emic perspectives, the researcher relies on the "internal" or **endogenous** resources of the participants, revealing the ways in which they make sense of an object of study. For example, a researcher studying how university students address their professors in emails will select an object of study from the data or what appears to be demonstrably important for the research participants in their written communication to each other.

Emic perspectives focus on phenomena *during* data collection and analysis. For example, a researcher investigating how children communicate during recess or playtime will withhold any preestablished commitment to communication theories, and only analyze a particular discourse feature when it is revealed in the data that the participants themselves treat the object of study as important to their encounter. In this sense, emic perspectives are not only endogenous, but they are selected **in situ**.

Emic perspectives are commonly employed when a researcher wants to discover an object of study that is important for the research participants (rather than, again, selecting an object of study before data collection and analysis; see etic perspectives below). In some cases, a discourse analysis approach, such as conversation analysis, will require a researcher to rely on the endogenous resources that participants use to make sense of themselves and the world around them. In so doing, objects of study are identified in and through the communication of the research participants. That is, objects of study are discovered during data collection and analysis.

Learning Activity 5.3 Emic Perspectives

In this exercise, the learning objective is to understand how an emic perspective can be applied to an object of study, which is a brief exchange between a police officer and driver.

The encounter is presented below as a transcript, which begins with a contextual overview of the conversation.

> ((A driver has just been pulled over in the United States by a police officer for unknown reasons. The transcript begins when the police officer exits his car and approaches the other car))

| 1 | Police officer: | good afternoon, sir. |

2	Driver:	what are you pulling me over?
3	Police officer:	license and registration, please.
4	Driver:	((hands over driving license and car registration))

Please make an observation of the encounter using an emic perspective. Remember that emic perspectives focus on the "internal" or "endogenous" resources that the research participants use to communicate.

For example, what can you say about the encounter that is visible in the transcript? It is possible, for instance, to say that the driver does not know why he is being pulled over, as demonstrated in his question in line 2. What else can you observe from an emic perspective?

Conversely, it is not possible from an emic perspective to make an observation about the emotional state of the driver, as he does not reveal this in the transcript. The driver would have to, as one possibility, display anger through words or recognizable sounds that express this emotion.

Second, a researcher can select an etic perspective, which is a researcher or outside(r) view of an object of study. An etic perspective engages in the analytic process using theories taken from *outside* an object of study. For example, a researcher studying how kids ridicule each other while playing online games may use theories taken from different settings or contexts, such as research on how football players engage in verbal sparring. Such theories are "external" or **exogenous**, as they have been taken from one situation (football) and applied to another (online games).

Etic perspectives are also based on theories developed *before* data collection and analysis. For example, even if the researcher was an online gamer with a high level of relevant cultural familiarity, any personal insights into the object of study are considered etic because they are based on ideas or concepts developed prior to the research participants communicating. In this sense, etic perspectives are not only exogenous, but they are also selected **a priori**.

Etic perspectives are commonly employed when a researcher investigates a new context, setting, or phenomenon. For example, a researcher wishing to investigate a new social media platform will have no prior cultural familiarity with the online space, thus requiring the use of exogenous or *a priori* theories. Etic perspectives are also commonly used when researchers need to bring in their own ways of understanding an object of study, such as the previous example of a new social media platform. By relying on exogenous or *a priori* theories, etic perspectives tell the researcher what the object of study is. That is, objects of study are part of, or connected to, exogenous or *a priori* theories. For instance, an exogenous theory may contend that people are inherently kind when they communicate in face-to-face settings; this theory could then be used to understand to what extent kindness is a factor in how communication unfolds on a social media platform.

Learning Activity 5.4 Etic Perspectives

In this exercise, the learning objective is to understand how an etic perspective can be applied to an object of study, which is the same exchange between a police officer and driver presented above.

The encounter is presented below as a transcript, which begins with a contextual overview of the conversation.

		((A driver has just been pulled over in the United States by a police officer for unknown reasons. The transcript begins when the police officer exits his car and approaches the car))
1	Police officer:	good afternoon, sir.
2	Driver:	what are you pulling me over?
3	Police officer:	license and registration, please.
4	Driver:	((hands over driving license and car registration))

Please make an observation of the encounter using an etic perspective. Remember that etic perspectives use "external" or "exogenous" theories or ideas to understand objects of study.

For example, what can you say about the encounter that is *not* visible in the transcript, but is logical or valid from a particular theoretical perspective? It is possible, for instance, to use theories of "police states" (van Dijk, 1993) to say that the encounter is based on an asymmetrical distribution of power where citizens – in this case, the driver – does not have the same communicative rights as the officer.

What else can you observe from an etic perspective? What theories or ideas did you use to make such an observation?

External or exogenous theories can also be based on historical issues and events, as well as your cultural familiarity with the setting or situation. Is there anything that you know about powerful societal institutions, being stopped by the police, or driving in the United States that would offer logical or valid observations of this encounter? For instance, is there an emotional state that you associate with such encounters that may help you understand what the driver may have felt during the stop?

This discussion of emic and etic perspectives establishes a crucial point in the role of the researcher in discourse analysis. As a qualitative researcher, it is important to be cognizant of the ways in which your decisions during the research process influence how you collect and analyze objects of study. To this end, the Section 5.4 introduces the concept of reflexivity.

> **Summary 5.3**
>
> 1. An emic perspective is a participant or inside(r) view of an object of study.
> 2. Emic perspectives rely on the internal or endogenous resources of the participants.
> 3. An etic perspective is a researcher or outside(r) view of an object of study.
> 4. Etic perspectives use external or exogenous theories to study an object of study.

5.4 Reflexivity

Reflexivity is self-awareness of how you – the researcher – shape the research process from beginning to end. This self-awareness is different from **reflection**, which is when a researcher thinks about the research process *after* it ends. Reflexivity can be thought of more specifically as the understanding that a researcher actively shapes the analytic process, which includes selecting, collecting, analyzing, and disseminating data. Reflexivity is thus the acknowledgement that a researcher creates a subjective understanding of an object of study. In its most basic form, reflexivity entails sharing, often through writing, how research decisions, such as selecting a methodology, are founded on personal experiences and professional assumptions. As discussed below, reflexive practices also include collaborating or partnering with research participants to collect data and analyze objects of study.

A central reason for engaging in reflexive practices is to maintain research integrity. In discourse analysis, the principal way of maintaining research integrity is to select and apply an approach or methodology that is appropriate for an object of study. Reflexivity, more generally, allows qualitative researchers to maintain moral integrity (i.e., "doing the right thing"): this entails thinking about and sharing how you have influenced the analytic process. In so doing, reflexivity offers much needed transparency in qualitative research, allowing readers to understand and ultimately evaluate the empirical decisions made by you during the analytic process.

Reflexivity requires a discourse analyst to interrogate – again through some form of sharing or communication – the ways in which personal experiences, subjectivities, and research objectives influence the analytic process. This begins during the conceptualization stage, interrogating for example how personal belief systems or experiences may differ from the people or discourses that are considered for investigation. Researchers may also consider to what extent their identities shape how research participants interact with them and during the analytic process. For instance, researchers planning to investigate people or places with which they are familiar should consider how professional or occupational relationships and identities alter what type of data is collected and how it is analyzed. Take, for instance, a teacher researcher wishing to investigate question–answer sequences in classrooms at her own school. The following writing sample illustrates one way this teacher researcher could report on her reflexive practices that occurred during the conceptualization stage.

Reporting Reflexive Practices: Conceptualization Stage

Locating a classroom to investigate involved considering to what extent my status as a teacher would influence how I analyze the object of study. A decision was made before data collection not to investigate my own students, as I did not want the power dynamics of being a teacher to potentially shape how the research participants communicate while being recorded. Accordingly, I asked several colleagues to consider my empirical objectives and the extent to which the research would disrupt the teaching that occurred in their classrooms.

In this writing sample, reflexivity entails thinking about the extent to which professional identity and occupational role impose power dynamics into the analytic process. For an informative discussion of **in-group** and **out-group** dynamics in qualitative research, see Hellawell (2006). For example, is it possible, problematic, desirable, or beneficial to research a group of people if a discourse analyst is intimately involved in the object of study? Although there are many "correct" ways of answering this question, it can be said more generally that reporting statements like the one provided in the example above improve research integrity, as reflexivity allows researchers to understand how their subjectivities and experiences shape the analytic process.

Furthermore, subjectivities, such as overly sympathetic feelings for an object of study (e.g., marginalized communities), may cloud or color the analytic process; reflexivity must therefore account for such emotional states, as the feelings a researcher has for an object of study will likely influence the analytic process. It is possible, for example, to investigate an object of study through a political lens rather than from an analytic perspective, which may create a depiction that is based on a researcher's sensibilities rather than an issue that is grounded in an established methodology. Although political accounts of objects of study are the norm in some discourse analysis traditions (e.g., critical discourse analysis), it is advisable to engage in reflexive practices because writing about how researcher biases influence the analytic process is helpful for readers to understand the observations and conclusions made of an object of study better. Whatever reflexive practices are followed, it is important to remember that reporting on such biases and subjectivities is better than completely omitting such information, as establishing research integrity is again dependent on transparency.

In the same vein, the relationship that research participants have with researchers, especially with intimate partners or close colleagues (e.g., researching the communication practices of your family or co-workers), may shape what is said and done during the analytic process, creating a reality that does not reflect how people normally communicate in their daily lives. Reflexivity is thus being cognizant of not only how a researcher shapes the analytic process through personal biases and professional assumptions, but also the ways in which research participants influence data collection and analysis as a result of their relationship with the people researching them.

During the analytic process, when the researcher is collecting and analyzing an object of study, reflexivity can take many forms in discourse analysis research. These forms can be expressed within a continuum, as illustrated in Figure 5.1.

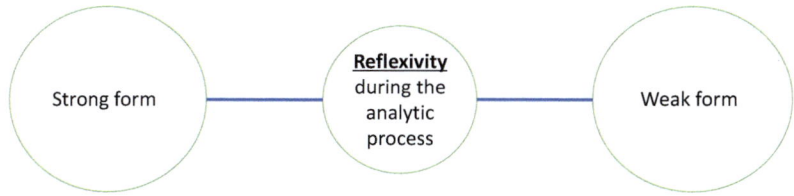

FIGURE 5.1
Reflexivity continuum

The strongest form of reflexivity begins with acknowledging that a researcher creates a subjective understanding of an object of study through professional biases and personal experiences; but more importantly, the strongest form of reflexivity views this subjective positioning of the researcher as an opportunity to collaborate or partner with the people responsible for the discourse under investigation. This may entail asking research participants to help collect data. The following list includes four reasons for asking research participants to collect data according to the empirical goals of the researcher; these reasons may also apply to analyzing objects of study.

1. **Situational knowledge**: includes experiences and competences that the researcher may not possess, such as working in a hospital or participating in a community on a social media platform. Researchers may ask research participants to collect data in situations like these: this request may be based on the researcher not having the situational knowledge to understand what type of data to collect and when. Situational knowledge includes cultural familiarity (cf. membership knowledge), which was discussed earlier in this chapter and is related to the next situation.

2. **Unfamiliarity**: refers to discourses or people that are unfamiliar, and thus inaccessible, because of a gap in language or culture between the researcher and object of study. Research participants may be asked to collect data in such situations because they are part of, or have access to, the community or object of study that is of interest to

the researcher. Example situations include researching a community that speaks a language that is different from the one spoken by the researcher or collecting data from people who do not wish to reveal their identities or personal information, which is related to the next situation.

3. **Sensitive information**: includes data that should not be revealed to either the general public or the academic community, such as psychiatric diagnoses, financial consultations, and family-related matters. A researcher may ask research participants to collect such data because they have a more robust understanding of, or better access to, personal or sensitive information.

4. **Naturalness**: refers to the environmental or contextual factors that ordinarily shape how an object of study is organized or unfolds. For instance, the trust that two friends share will shape how they communicate about a range of topics. A researcher wishing to investigate these two friends should avoid disrupting the natural state of their communication. One way of accomplishing this is to ask one of the friends to collect data, though the presence of a recording device will, to some extent, disrupt the environmental factors that naturally shape their communication.

These four situations offer examples of how the researcher is active in data collection. In addition to data collection, the strongest form of reflexivity may entail asking research participants to co-construct an understanding of an object of study through some form of collaborative analysis (for an extended discussion of reflexive theory and practice, see Finlay, 2002). The following list identifies four reasons for asking research participants to help analyze data according to the empirical goals of the researcher; these reasons may also apply to collecting data.

1. **Existing relationship**: refers to situations when the researcher has an established connection to the research participant in some capacity and typically outside academia, such as at work or in a family. In such situations, it may be helpful to collaborate on an analysis because the researcher and the research participant are jointly involved with, and responsible for, the object of study. For example, the researcher and the research participant may be co-workers at a school, and having the input from all perspectives is needed to offer a more robust and comprehensive account of an object of study.

2. **Lack of proficiency**: covers situations when the researcher does not have the proficiency to understand an object of study fully. For example, the object of study may be in a language that the researcher does not comprehend, such as researching historical translations or multilingual encounters. Alternatively, the object of study may deal with technical knowledge or specialized information that the researcher does not possess, such as researching how air traffic controllers use professional jargon to communicate with pilots. In situations like these, the researcher will need to recruit someone

to help analyze (or translate) the object of study, which may entail asking research participants to collaborate in the analytic process.

3. **Impact**: refers to the benefits that are gained by a research participant from co-analyzing an object of study. For example, a researcher wishing to investigate inclusive workplace and hiring practices at an international marketing company may ask a research participant working at this organization to help with data analysis. By co-analyzing the object of study, the research participant will gain a deeper understanding of, and as a result provide benefits to, the international marketing company by uncovering the ways in which the organization promotes diversity and equity through hiring practices.

4. **Empowerment**: is the process of giving research participants more control over how the academic community understands their life circumstances or discourses. Having more control or power over the analytic process is especially important when researching marginalized communities, as they are often already overlooked in mainstream society. Reflexive collaboration and analytic partnerships empower research participants by giving them a voice during the analytic process, creating findings or observations that better reflect the circumstances and viewpoints of the people that are being studied.

As demonstrated with these four examples, the strongest form of reflexivity views collaboration as an empirical opportunity: working with research participants during the analytic process is thought to produce observations of an object of study that are more nuanced or detailed than what researchers offer working independently. Furthermore, the strongest form of reflexivity is based on the idea that the researcher's involvement in the analytic process should be balanced with a participant or emic perspective.

Conversely, the weakest form of reflexivity begins with accepting that a researcher creates a subjective understanding of an object of study through professional biases and personal experiences, but it does not see this subjective positioning as an opportunity to get research participants actively involved in the analytic process. Rather, the weakest form of reflexivity only asks that a researcher consider how professional biases and personal experiences may influence data collection and analysis, and to make relevant decisions that maintain research integrity throughout this process. The previous writing sample of how to report on reflexive practices during the conceptualization stage represents a weak form of reflexivity, which is reproduced below.

An Example of a Weak Form of Reflexivity

Locating a classroom to investigate involved considering to what extent my status as a teacher would influence how I analyze the object of study. A decision was made before data collection not to investigate my own students, as I did not want the power dynamics of being a teacher to potentially shape how the research participants communicate while being recorded. Accordingly, I asked several colleagues to consider my empirical objectives and the extent to which the research would disrupt the teaching that occurred in their classrooms.

It is important to note that a weak form of reflexivity does not amount to doing bad research. Any form of reflexivity strengthens a discourse analysis project whether it entails collaboration with research participants or being cognizant of your role as the researcher in the analytic process. Indeed, the example of a weak form of reflexivity provided above represents good research practice.

Learning Activity 5.5　Reflexivity through Researcher Biographical Statements

In this exercise, the learning objective is to practice one form of reflexive practice and to think about how your role as the researcher may influence the analytic process.

The reflexive practice used in this exercise is called a researcher biographical statement, which is simply an account of your experiences and ideologies as they pertain to an object of study. That is, a researcher biographical statement should only include information about yourself that helps readers understand how your role as the researcher may have influenced the analytic process. Example topics and themes to include in a researcher biographical statement are previous jobs, research motivations, professional relationships, educational background, and social identities, to name a few. Researcher biographical statements can be put in any part of a research paper that helps readers understand your writing better.

For the first part of this exercise, please write a short paragraph detailing your research biography as it pertains to an object of study. An example is provided below for your reference.

The researcher has over a decade of experience working with children from marginalized communities. This professional interest is a reflection of the researcher's experiences growing up in a community that was discriminated against and marginalized because it spoke a minority language. The researcher's memories of being ridiculed as a child are now used as motivation to investigate children living in similar conditions.

In the second part of this exercise, please use your researcher biographical statement to think about how the stated topics and themes may influence the analytic process. Four questions related to the example statement above are provided for your reference.

How may the researcher's extensive work experience shape the analytic process? How may the researcher's own experience with discrimination shape the analytic process? How may the researcher's proximity to the research participants shape the analytic process?

How may the researcher's personal motivations shape the analytic process?

Minimally, all discourse analysts should consider how their personal circumstances, empirical goals, and professional expectations shape the analytic process. Although the strongest and weakest forms of reflexivity offer vastly divergent solutions to the subjectivity "problem" in qualitative discourse analysis, potentially leading to distinct analytic observations, most discourse analysis studies in practice are situated in the middle of the continuum. In between the strongest and weakest forms of reflexivity are many complementary ideas and approaches. Indeed, a number of reflexive principles and practices have been proposed in recent years, offering numerous opportunities for researchers to explore where their research falls within the continuum and whether their objects of study would benefit from a strong, weak, or moderate form of reflexivity. For example, the edited volume by Consoli & Ganassin (2023) includes diverse and numerous examples of how researchers approach reflexivity in applied linguistic research, which is a field of study that has a long history of working with discourse analysis.

An underlying idea that exists across all reflexive principles and practices is the observation that researchers bring their professional background to a research site, imprinting most notably unique research experiences and specialized training onto objects of study. This influence over the analytic process is commonly referred to as the researcher's gaze (see also professional vision; Goodwin 1994). The role of the researcher is to understand how this gaze transforms data collection and analysis. The researcher's gaze is neither a strong nor weak form of reflexivity; rather, it reflects the simple reality that researchers, like all humans, are subjective beings that see the world in divergent ways. On the one hand, the researcher's gaze may be beneficial to the analytic process in that it allows researchers to use their unique experiences to pick up or identify aspects of an object of study that would be overlooked by an untrained eye. On the other hand, the researcher's gaze may be problematic to the analytic process in that it can encourage researchers to overlook important aspects of an object of study because specialized training is inherently myopic and narrow in perspective.

Summary 5.4

1. Reflexivity is self-awareness of how the researcher shapes the analytic process.
2. A central reason for engaging in reflexive practices is to maintain research integrity.
3. Reflexive principles and practices are diverse and varied, existing along a continuum.
4. Reflexivity is the acknowledgement that researchers possess subjective biases and perspectives.

5.5 Power Relations

Power refers to the ability to influence the behavior, thoughts, or language of an individual or group of people. This influence often comes from other individuals or groups of people. However, power can also come from the meanings that are created by societies, such as language and ideas that influence how people think and behave. Consider, for example, how a police officer has the power to stop drivers, issue tickets, and therefore alter the ways in which people talk, feel, and behave. In this example, power is not limited to the dynamics between the police officer and the driver. Power extends to, and is embedded within, many aspects of society, such as education and law. For instance, education can socialize children into fearing police officers or law can establish an understanding that the police can exert control over ordinary members of society. In both examples, power comes from the fear and obedience that society discursively constructs in relation to the police.

Such power dynamics exist in research. Like most qualitative, participant-based scholarship, the power that exists in discourse analysis research is based on the relationship between the researcher, research participants, and object of study. This relationship, however, is not limited to the personal or professional ties that a researcher may have with research participants and objects of study. Power in discourse analysis research also comes from the meanings that are assigned by society in relation to who the researcher and research participants are, the state of their relationship, what is being studied, and how the investigation is conducted. These different, yet related, dimensions of power operate within two, interrelated levels: local power and remote power.

1. **Local power**: refers to the influence that a researcher has over the behavior, thoughts, or language of research participants. This influence may come from who the researcher is, be based on an object of study, or both. For example, a teacher researching her students has a responsibility to impart knowledge, administer tests, grade assignments, and discipline recalcitrant behavior, to name a few. These teaching practices exert local power over students by encouraging them to, for instance, communicate in a way that aligns with their expectation of what the teacher wants from them. An object of study may also exert local power over students; for instance, asking students to talk about their cultural identities or attempts at learning a subject in school may trigger emotional states and thoughts that they would rather avoid.

2. **Remote power**: is the influence that societies have on the behavior, thoughts, or language of the researcher and research participants. This influence exists because societies establish belief systems that influence how people, including researchers and research participants, communicate and participate in the world. A researcher does not control remote power, but is rather influenced

by it. Specifically, cultural traditions, historical events, education systems, ethnic relations, and government policies, to name a few, may influence how a researcher and research participants think and talk about an object of study. For example, a teacher from one ethnic background researching her students from different ethnic backgrounds will approach the analytic process with preconceived beliefs and ideas about racial categories that she developed over a lifetime of socialization. In this example, it is the responsibility of the researcher to think about how remote power may shape her understanding of the object of study and research participants.

Learning Activity 5.6 Reflecting on Power Relations

In this exercise, the learning objective is to practice identifying local and remote power in the analytic process. The power that is embedded within the analytic process is complex and variable. It is therefore necessary to reflect on local and remote power by considering one research topic.

In the first part of this exercise, please read the following research topic. Put yourself in the position of the researcher. Please reflect on the social, cultural, and political dynamics of researching the topic identified. Refer back to the discussion on reflexivity to explore how you can critically examine your role in this particular research topic.

Research Topic

You are researching how homeless people talk about their living situation. In order to gain access to, and the trust of, the research participants, you buy them lunch over a period of one week. You interview the research participants while eating lunch, asking them questions based on a previous study that you conducted on homeless people from a different city. Although you are generally interested in how homeless people talk about their living situation, you use the interviews to identify more specific objects of study, including their identities.

In the second part of this exercise, please think of how local and remote power may shape the analytic process, such as the ways in which the power dynamics between you and the research participants complete the interviews. Questions are provided below for your guidance.

Guiding Questions

1. How does the money involved in buying lunch shape the analytic process?
2. How do societal meanings of homelessness influence the analytic process?
3. How does your identity as a researcher shape the analytic process?

4. How does your social class, or economic status, influence the analytic process?
5. What forms of local or remote power have you identified in the questions above?

The power that is embedded within a research topic is difficult, if not impossible, to change or eradicate; yet it is possible to conduct a reflexive and robust empirical study that is sensitive to the social, cultural, and political aspects of a research project. In identifying the social, cultural, and political aspects of a research project, a researcher can uncover the power dynamics that may shape how the analytic process unfolds. However, this heightened state of awareness requires action in order to change the analytic process according to local and remote power.

Although power exists in all discourse analysis research, it is possible to remove the local power from the analytic process. The most effective way of doing this is to analyze an object of study that existed or has been created prior to a research project. For example, a teacher researcher could analyze essays written many years before by a co-worker's students or a business communication scholar may wish to study the mission statements of established companies. Using existing data removes the local power that a researcher may exert over and during the analytic process, though it is still important to reflect on remote power.

In other words, the practice of using existing data for the analytic process does not allow a researcher to ignore the consequences of remote power. For example, the content of a student essay – even when written many years before – should be examined in relation to the societal meanings that exist at the time of analysis (e.g., an old essay that contains reflections of race will be understood from the racial meanings that are created by the society to which the researcher belongs).

In many research contexts, however, the analytic process is shaped by both local and remote power. Considering how power influences the analytic process entails reflecting on the researcher, research participants, and object of study, as well as the relationship between them. How such considerations are put into practice varies considerably from one research project to another. For example, a researcher that adopts an emic perspective (see Section 5.3 above) may not be motivated to reflect on local power while a scholar interested in transformative discourse analysis (see Chapter 3) will think deeply about all aspects of power. Despite such methodological variation, there are three steps that a researcher can follow to plan and conduct a study that is more sensitive to local and remote power: acknowledge, identify, and adjust.

1. **Acknowledge**: is the first step that a researcher can take when considering how local and remote power factor into the analytic process. This step entails accepting that a researcher has local power when collecting data from research participants. Although this first step is ostensibly simple, many researchers ignore or forget the

power dynamics that can potentially shape how an investigation is planned and unfolds. It is difficult to return to an earlier stage of the analytic process, so it is important to consider this first step early in the planning stages. Acknowledgment can take many forms, including simply making a mental note that local and remote must be addressed during the analytic process or explicitly planning an investigation according to power dynamics (for a discussion of planning research according to power dynamics, see Flyvbjerg, 2002).

2. **Identify**: is the second step that a researcher can take when considering how local and remote power factor into the analytic process. This step entails identifying specific aspects of the analytic process that are shaped by local and remote power. Identification can take many forms, including asking a collaborator or colleague to create a list of questions or issues that they see as being problematic or influential to the analytic process, searching the literature for examples of how other researchers have confronted power in their research, or maintaining a journal while collecting data so that it is possible to reflect on the effects of local or remote power.

3. **Adjust**: is the third step that a researcher can take when considering how local and remote power factor into the analytic process. This third and final step entails making adjustments to the analytic process as a result of the identification step. Adjustments are not always needed, however, as simply knowing, or reporting on, how power is influencing the analytic process is all that can be done or is necessary. With that said, adjustments should be made to the analytic process when local or remote power negatively influences the behavior, thoughts, or language of the research participants. For instance, knowing that your role as a researcher is a source of fear for the research participants may require you to reconsider your research topic or locate a different person for data collection. Research situations that may require such actions include examining as an outsider (i.e., no membership knowledge) the business practices of office workers, graffiti artists' communicative resources, or how family members discuss personal affairs, to name a few.

It is possible, and in some cases advisable, to include in your research paper (e.g., in the "Methods" section) what you have identified, and reflected on, in Step 2. If adjustments were also made to the analytic process during Step 3, then such changes should also be mentioned in your final report.

Summary 5.5	1. Power is the ability to influence an individual or group of people.
	2. Power exists within two interrelated levels of influence: local power and remote power.
	3. Local power can be removed from the analytic process by using existing data.
	4. Three steps can be taken to address power: acknowledge, identify, and adjust.

5.6 Autoethnography

The chapter has thus far established that the role of the researcher in the analytic process can be discussed in relation to several aspects of research, such as cultural familiarity, reflexivity, and power relations. Each aspect of research is integral to the analytic process, though putting them all together into a coherent set of research practices is difficult to accomplish with no established methodology. Although there are no methodologies within discourse analysis devoted to exploring the role of the researcher in the analytic process, there are qualitative approaches that practice many of the principles and ideas identified in this chapter. One such approach is called **autoethnography** (see also interpretive phenomenology; Engward & Goldspink, 2020).

Autoethnography is a qualitative approach that explores the experiences of the researcher, which may include a language practice, a critical life moment, or an unusual communicative encounter, to name a few. Accordingly, autoethnography requires critically evaluating the role of the researcher in the analytic process because collecting and analyzing data is intimately connected to personal experiences. In other words, in autoethnography, the object of study is the researcher.

An autoethnography is not an autobiography. The latter simply reports on personal experiences without utilizing the concepts introduced in this chapter. For example, an autobiography uncritically reports on a life event without considering alternative or competing analytic perspectives. Conversely, autoethnography adopts multiple analytic perspectives, using theoretical positions to critically evaluate the researcher. These positions can be discussed in relation to the five principles of autoethnography as discussed in L. Anderson (2006, p. 378): "complete member researcher status," "analytic reflexivity," "narrative visibility of the researcher's self," "dialogue with informants," and "commitment to theoretical analysis."

1. **Complete member researcher status**: is the idea that a researcher is completely immersed and thus a member of the phenomenon under investigation (see cultural familiarity). A teacher researcher could, for example, investigate her teaching practices in her own classroom.
2. **Analytic reflexivity**: is again acknowledging that a researcher creates a subjective understanding of an object of study. The teacher researcher could, for instance, evaluate how her personal subjectivities and institutional responsibilities shape, but are also shaped by, the teaching practices utilized in the classroom.
3. **Narrative visibility of the researcher's self**: is the idea that a researcher must be visible in the analytic observations made in a research report. In reporting on her teaching practices, for example, the teacher researcher must establish herself as a central subject in her findings, which often comes in the form of narratives.

4. **Dialogue with informants**: refers to the need to understand how the experiences of the researcher are shaped by personal and professional relationships and encounters. Although the researcher is the object of study, a study that strives to be more reflexive must be situated beyond the Self. For instance, the teacher researcher could evaluate how her students think about her teaching practices and tie this data into her narrative accounts.

5. **Commitment to theoretical analysis**: is the principle that analytic observations can be related to personal subjectivities, but such accounts must be grounded in theory and reflexive practice. For example, the teacher researcher could reflect on her personal feelings regarding a particular teaching approach, but this reflection must be additionally evaluated according to a theory that offers a triangulated account of the object of study. In other words, commitment to theoretical analysis requires engaging in multiple levels of analysis (see Chapter 3).

Learning Activity 5.7 Reflecting on Autoethnography and the Role of the Researcher

In this exercise, the learning objective is to think about how an autoethnography offers a window into the role of the researcher in the analytic process.

In the first part of this exercise, please think about a disagreement that you have had recently. This disagreement could be a friendly debate that you had in class or a heated argument with a family member.

In the second part of this exercise, please address the following questions related to the disagreement.

1. What emotions were you feeling during the disagreement?
2. Why did you have these emotions?
3. How would you describe the disagreement?

In the third part of this exercise, please reflect on how the other person would interpret the disagreement.

1a. What would the other person say about the emotions that you were feeling?
1b. What would the other person say about their emotions?
2a. What would the other person say about why you had these emotions?
2b. What would the other person say about why they experienced their emotions?
3. How would the other person describe the disagreement?

Thinking about how two people interpret the same disagreement provides opportunities to understand the interpretive work that is involved in both participating in, and analyzing, a communicative encounter. For example, as the researcher, you may interpret a situation in ways that differ from how the research participants understand the same encounter. This difference is not necessarily problematic; yet, as discussed in this chapter, it is important to understand how and why differences exist. Autoethnography provides the tools to evaluate the interpretive work that is involved in discourse analysis. That is, reflecting on how people approach situations with different interpretive frameworks helps discourse analysts understand their own ways of understanding objects of study.

Investigating the role of the researcher in the analytic process, or more specifically analyzing the researcher as the object of study, is an underdeveloped yet fascinating area of discourse analysis research. Autoethnography is based on several principles that can be followed to conduct an analysis of the researcher as the object of study. Although these principles can be interpreted and followed in various ways (for a collection of different interpretations, see Jones, Adams, & Ellis, 2013), leading to diverse forms of discourse analysis research, most autoethnographies share a set of analytic practices. Chang (2016) offers an extensive discussion of these practices, which are summarized below.

1. **First person**: is the practice of writing analytic observations from the perspective of the researcher. In other words, discourse analysis findings should be reported in the first person in an autoethnography. This practice establishes a system of writing that makes it easy for readers, and the writer, to evaluate the subjectivities of the researcher.
2. **Story-based**: is the practice of writing analytic observations as stories. Story-based writing is integral to adhering to each analytic practice (e.g., depth and evocative), as well as weaving together all the practices into a coherent and compelling set of discourse analytic observations. This practice helps the researcher adopt multiple analytic perspectives (e.g., emic and etic).
3. **Depth**: is the practice of privileging nuance and detail over breadth and coverage when writing analytic observations. As an object of study, the researcher must be treated as a complex individual with a rich history of experiences and encounters. Reporting on such experiences and encounters, while reflexively attending to multiple analytic perspectives, requires great attention to detail. This practice helps the researcher showcase the value in possessing cultural familiarity when using discourse analysis.
4. **Personal**: is the practice of writing analytic observations so that the personal subjectivities of the researcher are the object of study. This practice does not entail generating singular analytic observations

that are anchored to biased feelings. Rather, this practice involves using emic and etic perspectives to understand how the researcher is involved in a larger social network of influential relationships. The practice of analyzing personal subjectivities helps readers, as well as the writer, critically evaluate the role of the researcher in the analytic process.

5. **Evocative**: is the practice of writing a compelling account of the researcher as an object of study intimately shaped by a complex set of emotional and psychological states. As an object of study, the ideas, thoughts, and feelings of the researcher are important to the analytic process, as they demonstrate the interpretive work that goes into researching language and communication. In other words, the analytic practice of writing evocative narratives allows the researcher to reveal the interpretive and subjective work that is involved in the analytic process.

Discourse analysts can use narrative analysis to respect and investigate the subjectivities of the researcher. This approach requires adopting narrative analysis (analytic practice 1; see De Fina & Georgakopoulou, 2019), explaining in great detail how life experiences are understood and organized (analytic practice 2), sharing personal and sometimes intimate social relationship information (analytic practice 3), uncovering feelings and thoughts about the story being told (analytic practice 4), and rejecting the possibility that complete objectivity is possible when doing research on human language and communication (analytic practice 5).

> **Summary 5.6**
> 1. Autoethnography investigates the experiences of the researcher.
> 2. Autoethnography adopts multiple and diverse theoretical and analytic perspectives.
> 3. Autoethnography offers tools to evaluate the role of the researcher in the analytic process.
> 4. Autoethnography is a type of critical narrative analysis.

Learning Accomplishments

The chapter has reviewed how being a researcher shapes the analytic process. The chapter established that every researcher imprints their own personal and professional subjectivities onto the analytic process, which includes collecting and analyzing an object of study. This section identifies how each learning outcome has been addressed in this chapter.

1. You will understand that discourse analysis research is inherently subjective;

The chapter established that although objectivity is an important aspect of many experimental and quantitative studies, discourse analysis research is inherently subjective in that the researcher is often attached to the analytic process, making adjustments to a study as it progresses. Specifically, it was established that a researcher's personal and professional experiences and subjectivities, as well as empirical objectives, influence how an object of study is identified and understood.

2. You will understand that a researcher's cultural familiarity with an object of study is crucial to doing discourse analysis;

Cultural familiarity was defined as the level of knowledge that a researcher possesses of an object of study. The chapter argued that cultural familiarity is fundamental to doing discourse analysis, as it is impossible to analyze an object of study if a researcher has no knowledge of what is being examined.

3. You will be able to identify and adopt multiple analytic perspectives;

Two analytic perspectives were introduced in this chapter: emic perspective and etic perspective. The chapter argued that a researcher will often privilege one perspective over the other, but in practice a combination of both perspectives is used. In selecting an analytic perspective, it was established that a researcher imprints their own subjectivities onto the analytic process. Autoethnography was introduced as one approach that is equipped to understand, as well as investigate, the subjectivities that go into the analytic process.

4. You will be able to adopt reflexive practices in the analytic process;

The chapter defined reflexivity as possessing a self-awareness that a researcher shapes the analytic process in both positive and negative ways. Several examples of practicing reflexivity were provided, including the practice of writing about how personal experiences and professional assumptions shape the analytic process. It was argued that a central reason for engaging in reflexive practices is to maintain research integrity.

5. You will understand, and know how to deal with, the power dynamics that exist in discourse analysis research.

The discussion argued that power dynamics exist in all discourse analysis research in the form of local power and remote power. Although researchers deal with power in diverse and diverging ways, the chapter established that there are three steps that can be taken to plan and conduct a study that is more sensitive to such power dynamics: acknowledge, identify, and adjust.

Key Themes

Objectivity and Subjectivity

1. A discourse analyst actively shapes the analytic process.
2. Theory and methodology determine the role of the researcher in discourse analysis.
3. Experiences, subjectivities, and research objectives influence the analytic process.
4. An analysis can include personal, subjective, theoretical, or contextual information.

Cultural Familiarity

1. Cultural familiarity is the knowledge that a researcher possesses of an object of study.
2. Entry-point knowledge is the minimal level of cultural familiarity that is needed.
3. Objects of study possess different entry-point knowledge requirements.
4. Reporting knowledge is using cultural familiarity to describe or analyze an object of study.
5. Researchers have different ways of understanding and using cultural familiarity.

Emic and Etic Perspectives

1. An emic perspective is a participant or inside(r) view of an object of study.
2. Emic perspectives rely on the internal or endogenous resources of the participants.
3. An etic perspective is a researcher or outside(r) view of an object of study.
4. Etic perspectives use external or exogenous theories to study an object of study.

Reflexivity

1. Reflexivity is self-awareness of how the researcher shapes the analytic process.
2. A central reason for engaging in reflexive practices is to maintain research integrity.
3. Reflexive principles and practices are diverse and varied, existing along a continuum.
4. Reflexivity is the acknowledgement that researchers possess subjective biases and perspectives.

Power Relations

1. Power is the ability to influence an individual or group of people.
2. Power exists within two interrelated levels of influence: local power and remote power.

3. Local power can be removed from the analytic process by using existing data.
4. Three steps can be taken to address power: acknowledge, identify, and adjust.

Autoethnography

1. Autoethnography investigates the experiences of the researcher.
2. Autoethnography adopts multiple and diverse theoretical and analytic perspectives.
3. Autoethnography offers tools to evaluate the role of the researcher in the analytic process.
4. Autoethnography is a type of critical narrative analysis.

Reading List

Consoli & Ganassin (2023) This edited collection offers interdisciplinary examples of how scholars think about and practice reflexivity in the study of intercultural communication, language teaching and learning, as well as bilingual interaction. The book represents a diverse range of methodological approaches, so readers get many suggestions regarding how reflexivity can be practiced in their research.

Moerman (1988) The author offers an early and seminal book-length account of using cultural familiarity to investigate discourse from different analytic perspectives. Moerman uses ethnographic tools and conversation analysis to investigate how inequality is discussed within the Thai context, demonstrating to readers how a researcher is embedded within the analytic process.

Pike (1967) The book is a necessary read for any researcher concerned with analytic perspectives in general or using the emic and etic constructs in particular. Pike offers one of the earliest accounts of how objects of study can be categorized into linguistic systems of analysis, though the term has since evolved into different, and sometimes competing, interpretations of what it means to adopt an emic or etic perspective.

What Is the Role of Theory in an Analysis?

Learning Outcomes

This chapter introduces what *theory* is, and discusses why it is important to the analytic process. The aim of the chapter is to help you understand how theory is a part of doing discourse analysis. This will be done by defining theory, identifying the different theories that exist in discourse analysis, and explaining how theoretical principles relate to the topics and issues discussed in previous chapters.

The contents of the chapter are organized according to the following learning outcomes. After reading this chapter:

1. You will know how to define theory;
2. You will understand how theory relates to the analytic process;
3. You will understand the difference between a theory of knowledge and an applied theory;
4. You will be able to identify the different types of applied theory that exist.

6.1 Theory

A theory is an idea that explains *what* discourse is, *how* discourse should be understood, or both. Put differently, theories in discourse analysis help you understand *what* is in front of you and *how* to understand what is happening in front of you. Figure 6.1 illustrates these two functions of theory.

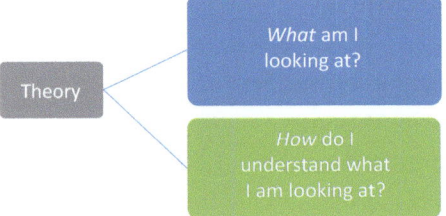

FIGURE 6.1
Two main functions of theory

These two questions are crude examples of what you will do with theories for your research. That is, a theory provides a system for *identifying* and *making* observations of an object of study. Figure 6.2 offers a visual overview of these two functions in relation to the discourse analysis flow chart presented in Chapter 3.

This visual overview of the what and how questions demonstrates that theory is central to discourse analysis. Theory defines discourse analysis; it also establishes the parameters from which discourse analysis research is evaluated. As shown in Figure 6.2, all perspectives and levels of discourse analysis rely on a theory or theories. This theory may help describe a communicative practice, form the foundation from which you understand the social impact of a particular discourse feature, or

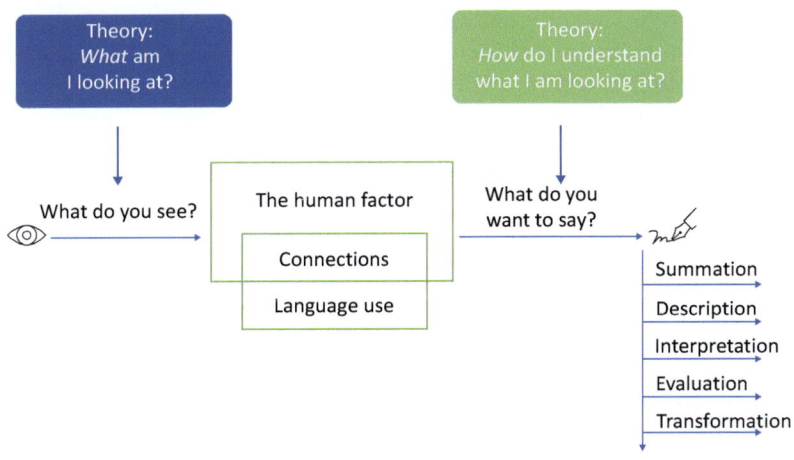

FIGURE 6.2
The functions of theory

offer a lens through which to uncover the hidden meanings within a text, to name a few of many possibilities.

A theory is not an opinion, thought, or belief, which are simply intuitions without an explanatory framework. For example, you can have an opinion about how politicians use social media to convey policy issues, such as "social media is bad for politics," but a theory is needed to explain why this intuition is so.

Theories may be specific to a context, such as Giles's (2016) theory of communication accommodation, which contends that people try to minimize the differences between them by adjusting their speech according to their fellow interlocutors. One example object of study related to communication accommodation theory is accent changes in conversations (e.g., Dong & Blommaert, 2009). In this example, there are a number of methods and methodologies that can be used to apply or test communication accommodation theory, such as recording an exchange between strangers (method) and using conversation analysis (methodology) to see how adjustments in accents are made in situ.

Other theories are more general, and relate to questions of how discourse is structured or why it is important to human sociality. For example, heteroglossia is a theory developed by Bakhtin (1981) that argues there are multiple voices, or ways of thinking about and expressing the world, within a given language. One example object of study related to heteroglossia is language ideologies. In this example, there are a number of methods and methodologies that can be used to apply or test heteroglossia, such as asking people within the same speech community to write down their thoughts about the language(s) that they use (method) and applying narrative analysis (methodology) to see how ideologies converge and diverge around different social issues (e.g., Jenks & Lee, 2016).

Both communication accommodation and heteroglossia are examples of applied theories. An applied theory is simply an idea about an object of study. Applied theories may form larger methodologies, frameworks, or approaches. The different applied theories that can be used for your analysis are the focus of this chapter. Before discussing applied theories in more detail, however, it is important to review momentarily what a theory of knowledge is.

6.1.1 Theory of Knowledge

A theory of knowledge is an idea related to the principles of inquiry. Simply put, a theory of knowledge concerns how we know what we know. A theory of knowledge helps establish what discourse analysis is and why it approaches the study of language and communication in a particular way.

Theories of knowledge are not the same as applied theories. As discussed previously, applied theories can help researchers understand a specific object of study or a general aspect of language. That is to say, applied theories possess an application value: they are applied to objects of study during the analytic process.

Conversely, theories of knowledge help explain what discourse analysis is, and how this way of investigating language and communication is different from other fields of study, such as psycholinguistics. Discourse analysis is informed by several theories of knowledge (for a more comprehensive discussion of theories of knowledge, see Ladyman, 2002), such as poststructuralism (e.g., Williams, 2014), leading to a theoretically diverse and inherently interdisciplinary field of study. With that said, it is important to provide a concrete example of a theory of knowledge related to discourse analysis. To this end, there is one theory of knowledge that helps explain what many researchers do while using discourse analysis. This theory of knowledge is called social constructivism.

Social constructivism contends that human knowledge, which includes how people view themselves and the world around them, is constructed in and through language and communication (Lynch, 2016). The theory is relevant to discourse analysis, as social constructivism views language as a social phenomenon that is bound to the contexts in which communication occurs. In other words, social constructivism informs discourse analysis, as the theory states that language cannot be separated from the context in which it is used (see Chapter 4). For a discourse analyst, this means that while language is made up of grammatical rules and pragmatic expectations, such meanings come from the encounters, histories, desires, and feelings that humans experience and possess.

This social constructivist view of language is different from, for example, the theory of knowledge that is adopted by scholars informed by cognitive and psycholinguistic theories, such as Chomsky and his study of generative grammar (Chomsky, 2021). These and related notions of language are often based on positivism (Park, Konge, & Artino, 2020), which is a theory of knowledge that seeks out universal laws that explain and predict. Relatedly, the study of generative grammar is partly based on the universal law that language is a set of logical and innate rules, thus allowing people to communicate and co-construct meaning. The study of generative grammar is positivistic, as scholars gather empirical data to validate the "law" that language is an innate human ability.

Despite the theoretical diversity that exists in discourse analysis and allied fields of study, all theories form and inform. A theory of knowledge forms, as it establishes the boundaries in which discourse analysis operates (e.g., social constructivism). An applied theory informs, as it tells researchers what object of study to investigate and how to conduct such an analysis (e.g., speech accommodation theory). Figure 6.3 offers an illustration of where theories of knowledge and applied theories are situated within discourse analysis.

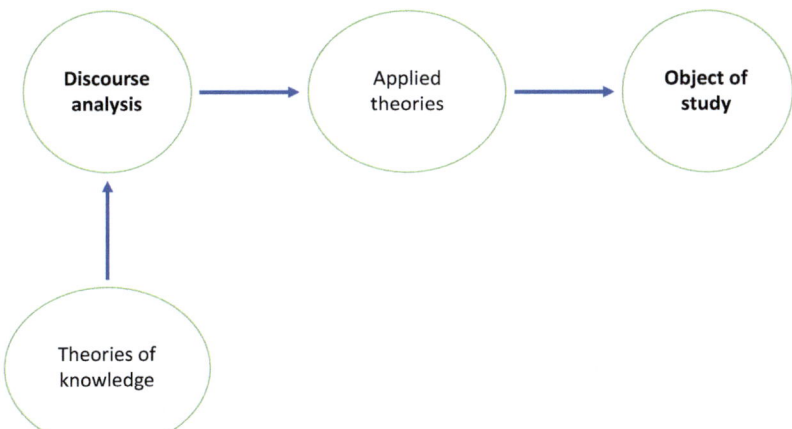

FIGURE 6.3
Theories of discourse analysis

Although theories of knowledge offer important philosophical direction, they provide little practical guidance for the novice discourse analyst. Therefore, this chapter is devoted to discussing the practical implications of applied theories.

Summary 6.1
1. A theory is an idea that explains how a discourse phenomenon should be understood.
2. All perspectives and levels of discourse analysis are based on a theory.
3. An applied theory is an idea about discourse that can be used to study an object of study.
4. Applied theories may form larger methodologies, frameworks, or approaches.
5. A theory of knowledge is an idea about the principles of inquiry.

6.2 Applied Theories

An applied theory is an idea specific to an object of study. Applied theories are needed for all perspectives and levels of analysis (see Chapter 3). Many applied theories are used in discourse analysis, so it is important to understand why and how they are employed for your analysis.

Applied theories are needed, as they provide a way of demonstrating that your analysis is based on an established and "tested" idea. Such ideas often map out how to analyze an object of study; they may also pinpoint something important or interesting about a particular aspect of discourse. Furthermore, applied theories provide rigor and nuance to your analysis, as they are made up of principles that can be followed in a systematic way.

At a more fundamental level, applied theories are needed, as they help formulate and answer research questions. Without an applied theory, it is difficult to answer research questions with just the perspectives and levels of analysis discussed earlier in this book. For example, a researcher that adopts a language use perspective to analyze counselors giving advice at the level of description will still need an applied theory to pinpoint what to describe and how to make sense of it. In this scenario, the researcher knows the perspective (language use) and level (description) of analysis that will be adopted, as well as the object of study (advice giving), but is missing an applied theory. In this research example, an applied theory, say next-turn proof procedure (see Chapter 4), would help the researcher understand how clients in counselor settings respond to, and make sense of, advice giving within a turn-taking system (for an example study, see Waring, 2007).

Applied theories can be used to generate research questions in two basic ways. The first way entails using an applied theory to generate a research question *after* identifying an object of study. Here the researcher first identifies an object of study based on an existing interest, say advice giving, then generates a research question given what a theory can offer analytically, such as next-turn proof procedure's focus on how people co-construct meaning within a turn-taking system. In this example, next-turn proof procedure, like other applied theories, tells the researcher how to understand, and thus generate research questions based on, the object of study.

The second way entails using an applied theory to generate a research question *before* identifying an object of study. Here the researcher first identifies an applied theory that is of interest, say next-turn proof procedure, then selects a suitable object of study. In this example, next-turn proof procedure is concerned with how the meaning of one turn is understood by a person that responds to it, so any object of study with an interactional exchange between two or more people would be a suitable object of study. A research question can then be formulated, as the applied theory will again possess ideas about what object of study to investigate and how to conduct such an analysis. Figure 6.4 illustrates where applied theories are situated within discourse analysis.

The figure shows how applied theories and research questions shape the selection and analysis of an object of study. While a research question need not come from an applied theory, it is often the case that the two complement each other. It is for this reason that applied theory and research question(s) are presented in the same bubble in Figure 6.4.

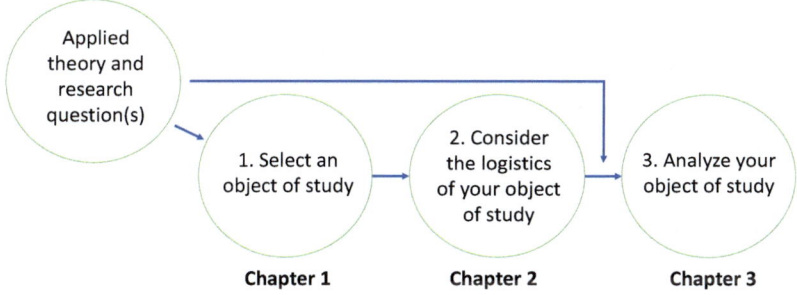

FIGURE 6.4
Applied theories
flowchart

Although the beginning of this book presented discourse analysis in three "simple" steps, in practice, a researcher must understand what applied theories are, and why and how they are used. As the figure illustrates, applied theories and their associated research questions can be identified before selecting an object of study. Alternatively, applied theories and their associated research questions may be considered after selecting an object of study.

Numerous reasons influence when a researcher selects an applied theory. A researcher will often select an object of study before an applied theory because of an existing interest in an aspect of discourse or a communication situation. This interest may stem from a personal or professional familiarity with the object of study, such as a counselor wishing to investigate her colleague's advice-giving practices. In this situation, the applied theory aids the counselor in seeing the advice-giving practices beyond her normal professional understanding and training (see professional vision; Chapter 4).

Alternatively, a researcher will select an object of study after an applied theory because the motivation to do discourse analysis is based on a theoretical idea rather than an existing interest in a context or setting. That is, for many researchers, doing discourse analysis means applying the same theories to different objects of study. For example, a researcher who is devoted to critical discourse analysis, which is made up of a set of applied theories, may be motivated to uncover the power dynamics in a range of contexts from government policy documents to family conversations.

Learning Activity 6.1 Reflecting on Applied Theories

In this exercise, the learning objective is to reflect on how applied theories are used to identify research settings and their related objects of study. An easy way to accomplish this task is to use one applied theory as an example.

To this end, please return to Giles's (2016) communication accommodation theory, which again contends that people try to minimize the differences between them by adjusting their speech according to their fellow interlocutors. Please identify three different research settings and their related objects of study that communication accommodation theory can be used to analyze. Two examples are identified for your reference.

Communication accommodation theory:

Possible research settings	Possible objects of study
1. immigration control at an airport	1. traveler's change in register/ style of speech
2. service encounter at a computer store	2. employee's choice of technical words
3.	3.
4.	4
5.	5.

In both examples provided above, the communication accommodation is done by one speaker (e.g., traveler and employee). Is this the same for your three examples?

The reasons for someone to adjust their speech are diverse and context-specific. In the first example, the immigration officer has the power to grant entry into the country, encouraging the traveler to speak in deference and possibly even in fear. In the second example, the employee at the computer store has technical knowledge that may not be understood by the customer, creating a need to simplify the language used to sell a product. In both examples, speech accommodation theory helps the researcher ground the observation to an established idea of discourse, which is needed to provide some level of quality to an analysis.

This exercise could also be completed in reverse, starting with research settings and objects of study. In this order, the exercise would require you to identify an applied theory that could explain what is happening within a particular context or setting. Of course, completing the exercise in reverse would require you to know more about what an applied theory is and what applied theories exist for your analysis. These issues are topics of discussion below.

The discussion of applied theory has thus far addressed why and how they are used for your analysis. It is also important to know what applied theories are. That is, what types of applied theories exist?

Numerous applied theories exist in, and are used for, discourse analysis. In the interest of simplicity, these applied theories are represented as four interrelated and overlapping categories: applied discourse theories, applied social theories, applied context theories, and applied frameworks.

6.2.1 Applied Discourse Theories

An applied discourse theory is concerned with language and communication, and more specifically the aspect of discourse referred to as "language use" in Chapter 1. Applied discourse theories establish ideas about *how* to understand objects of study, and can thus help you identify *what* to investigate in your discourse analysis project. For example, a speech act is an object of study, but it is also an applied theory in that it is based on ideas about how to study language and communication. In this sense, an applied discourse theory can be both an object of study and a way of understanding language use.

Example applied discourse theories include, but are not limited to, register, turn-taking, speech acts, and texture. It is helpful to note that some applied discourse theories are not referred to as a theory in the literature partly because they may also be objects of study (e.g., turn-taking). In addition, some researchers possess a narrow understanding of what constitutes a theory, and therefore do not see objects of study as being theoretical. When looking for a theory to guide you in your analysis, it is important to remember that an applied discourse theory is at its most basic level an idea about language use, so many of the topics and themes discussed in this book are in fact theoretical whether or not the literature refers to them as such.

6.2.2 Applied Social Theories

An applied social theory is related to the social aspects of language and communication, and more specifically the aspect of discourse referred to as "the human factor" in Chapter 1. Like applied discourse theories, applied social theories establish ideas about *how* to understand objects of study, and can thus help you identify *what* to investigate in your discourse analysis project. For instance, neoliberalism is an applied social theory: it possesses ideas about how economic issues shape the ways in which people behave and use language. Neoliberalism is also an object of study in that it can represent the main focal point in your analysis. In this sense, an applied social theory can be both an object of study and a way of understanding the human factor in discourse. Example applied social theories include, but are not limited to, power, race, class, ethnicity, neoliberalism, and colonialism. Applied social theories are discussed exhaustively in allied disciplines, including Critical Literary Studies, Sociology, Law, Education, and Anthropology. Readers can refer to such disciplines for lengthy and more nuanced discussions of applied social theories.

6.2.3 Applied Context Theories

An applied context theory is related to the conditions that shape discourse, such as the contextual issues discussed in Chapter 4. Applied context theories establish ideas about *how* to understand the contextual dimensions of objects of study, and can thus help you identify *what* to investigate in your discourse analysis project. Like other applied theories, an applied context theory can be both an object of study and a way of understanding discourse. For instance, contextualization cues are linguistic resources that point to some aspect of context. These cues, such as prosody and code choice, help researchers understand how and why people communicate in a particular way (i.e., the *how* question). Contextualization cues are also objects of study (i.e., the *what* question), representing the focal point in your analysis.

Chronotope is an applied context theory that is not discussed in Chapter 4, but is included below in the present chapter for its usefulness in studying discourse.

6.2.4 Applied Frameworks

An applied framework is a collection of applied theories that form a coherent analytic system. For example, it is common for applied frameworks to consist of applied discourse theories and applied context theories.

Applied frameworks specify what theoretical positions to take in relation to discourse, such as the general idea that all language is bound to power (e.g., critical discourse analysis), or the belief that meaning is jointly established as people communicate (e.g., conversation analysis). Applied frameworks may also establish ideas about how to investigate objects of study, such as the idea that identities can be analyzed by looking at the words that people use (e.g., membership categorization analysis and narrative analysis). Several applied frameworks are referenced in Chapter 1 at the end of each section that introduces an object of study.

Applied frameworks are often referred to as an approach or methodology. More specifically, an analytic framework can be an approach or a methodology. However, approach and methodology are not precisely the same construct. For example, critical discourse analysis is a set of applied theories, but it does not tell researchers how to analyze an object of study. Rather, critical discourse analysis tells researchers what position to take in relation to discourse. In this sense, critical discourse analysis is more of an approach than a methodology.

Conversely, conversation analysis is a set of applied theories that establishes how to analyze discourse (e.g., next-turn proof procedure). Because conversation analysis is fundamentally about how to look at discourse, it is more of a methodology than an approach. However, the distinction between approach and methodology never perfectly captures what applied frameworks do. For example, conversation analysis also possesses ideas about what position to take in relation to discourse, such as the belief that meaning is co-constructed as communication unfolds.

Summary 6.2	1. An applied theory is an idea specific to an object of study.
	2. All perspectives and levels of analysis rely on applied theories.
	3. Applied theories can be used to generate research questions.
	4. Applied theories allow you to show that your analysis is based on an established idea.

6.3 Some Example Theories and Theorists

The chapter has thus far established what a theory is and how it shapes the analytic process.

Previous sections also focused on why and how applied theories are used, and identified the types of applied theories that exist. The current section builds on these discussions by using specific applied theories and theorists to make sense of the topics introduced in previous chapters. For example, applied theories are introduced and discussed in relation to perspectives and levels of analysis, showing how a theory fits within the research process. Furthermore, the example applied theories and theorists in this section demonstrate what a theory can do.

A total of ten applied theories and theorists are identified in this section: five example applied theories and five example theorists. Although this number represents a fraction of the theories and theorists that can potentially be used for an analysis, the examples presented in this section offer sufficient coverage for readers getting acquainted with discourse analysis. Further, it is important to note again that many of the themes and topics identified in previous chapters can be categorized as an applied theory; throughout the book, theorists have also been referenced and discussed. Readers are encouraged to revisit each chapter when considering how theory can benefit their discourse analysis project.

6.3.1 Example Applied Theories

The example applied theories discussed in this section are capital, chronotope, community of practice, conversational maxims, and enregisterment. These applied theories have been randomly selected and do not collectively represent an overarching theme.

Each applied theory is accompanied with a brief definition. Definitions are followed by a discussion of how the theory relates to the perspectives and levels of analysis introduced in previous chapters. Practical suggestions are offered for each theory. Each applied theory ends with a reflection exercise and a reference for further reading.

Capital

Applied Theory

Capital is an applied social theory that argues societies are organized and divided according to the advantages that individuals possess over others. Pierre Bourdieu, for instance, observes that individuals possess social capital, economic capital, and cultural capital; each type of capital will influence how people think, communicate, and behave in society. For example, an individual with high social capital may have access to privileged communities, such as being a member of a country club or a student at an elite private school, which creates life opportunities and ways of thinking that other members of society with less social capital may not experience and possess.

Perspective of Analysis

Capital begins from the human factor perspective, but connections are often made to language use when it is used with an applied discourse theory.

Level of Analysis

Capital can be used to describe, interpret, evaluate, and transform an object of study.

Practical Application

Capital is a useful applied social theory for readers interested in showing how language and communication are shaped by what people know and possess. The applied social theory is also useful for readers intrigued by how power maps onto society and influences how people think, communicate, and behave.

Reflection Exercise

Can you think of a unique thing that you know or possess that influences how you think, communicate, or behave? Your example of capital may be an experience, such as a vacation, a material object, such as a car, or knowledge, such as proficiency in a language. Does your example of capital afford you opportunities that other members of society may not experience? What does your example of capital tell you about how societies are organized? What does your example of capital tell you about language and communication?

Reference Example

Thurlow & Jaworski (2006) The alchemy of the upwardly mobile: Symbolic capital and the stylization of elites in frequent-flyer programmes.

Chronotope

Applied Theory

Chronotope is an applied context theory developed by Mikhail Bakhtin that sees literature as being a representation of time (chrono) and space (tope). In the context of discourse analysis, chronotope views time and space as a single unit of understanding for language and communication. In other words, the language that people use and the ways in which they communicate are historical artifacts that traverse different settings and contexts.

Perspective of Analysis

Chronotope is concerned with context, as well as language use. In combination with other applied social theories, chronotope can be used to understand the human factor.

Level of Analysis

Chronotope can be used to describe, interpret, evaluate, and transform an object of study.

Practical Application

Chronotope is a helpful applied context theory for readers wanting to show how language and communication can be understood by referencing past (and even potential future) events and phenomena. The theory is also used to demonstrate how an object of study that is being investigated is shaped by different settings and contexts.

Reflection Exercise

Is there an aspect of your language use that is shaped by something that is removed from your immediate life and social network, such as a past event, people living in a different country, or a context that is unfamiliar to you? For example, words have histories dating back many decades or even centuries and often start as a different language. Can you think of a word that you use that is influenced by such examples?

Reference Example

Blommaert (2017) Commentary: Mobility, contexts, and the chronotope.

Community of Practice

Applied Theory

Community of practice is an applied social theory developed by Jean Lave and Etienne Wenger that describes how people with common interests or goals communicate with each other and learn from one another. It is a theory that developed from situations where a new member joins an existing "community" or group, such as in a workplace setting. The applied social theory observes that the apprentice or neophyte in a community of practice will develop over time the ways in which the group thinks, behaves, and communicates.

Perspective of Analysis

Community of practice is an applied social theory that is often used with other applied discourse theories to describe how social factors influence language use. In this sense, community of practice can also be used to understand the human factor.

Level of Analysis

Community of practice can be used to describe, interpret, evaluate, and transform an object of study.

Practical Application

Community of practice is a useful applied social theory for readers wanting to identify and describe how language use is shaped by the shared interests or common goals of a group. This description of language use can then be used to understand how the human factor, such as the institutional norms of a company or school, may factor into how community members think, behave, and communicate.

Reflection Exercise

Do you belong to a community of practice? What are your shared interests or common goals? How do these shared interests or common goals influence how you think, behave, and communicate?

Reference Example

Moore E. (2006) "You tell all the stories": Using narrative to explore hierarchy within a community of practice.

Conversational Maxims

Applied Theory

Conversational maxims are an applied discourse theory. The theory is concerned with principles of cooperative communication, which was developed by Paul Grice. The applied discourse theory describes how individuals ought to interact with each other. Four conversational maxims exist: the maxim of quantity (communication ought to be based on appropriate amount of information), the maxim of quality (communication ought to be truthful), the maxim of relevance (communication ought to be relevant to the context), and the maxim of manner (communication ought to reflect contextual expectations, such as avoiding unnecessary jargon).

Perspective of Analysis

Conversational maxims are fundamentally concerned with language use.

Level of Analysis

Conversational maxims are typically used to describe, but can be used to interpret, evaluate, and transform.

Practical Application

Conversational maxims are useful for readers interested in how people follow, or deviate from, established communicative expectations. Conversational maxims are not rules or guidelines, but rather reflect the expectations of a particular context. Some contexts may provide opportunities to deviate from one or some of the four maxims (e.g., friends communicating via text messages), which is a phenomenon that represents an interesting discourse analysis project.

Reflection Exercise

Is there a context that you are familiar with that requires strictly following one or some of the conversational maxims? What makes this context so strict in terms of communicative expectations? Is there a context that you can think of that does not require strictly following one or some of the conversational maxims? What makes this context flexible in terms of communicative expectations?

Reference Example

Pellegrini, Brody, & Stoneman (1987). *Children's conversational competence with their parents.*

Enregisterment

Applied Theory

Enregisterment is an applied discourse and social theory conceptualized by Asif Agha, which observes how the forms and functions of a language (i.e., what people say and how they communicate) become recognized by, and associated with, a group of people, including their ideologies and identities. An accent or slang term, for instance, could become enregistered when it is adopted by, and recognized as belonging to, a speech community. Enregisterment transforms mundane language features into central identity characteristics and ways of thinking about social relations.

Perspective of Analysis

Enregisterment is concerned with language use (e.g., accents and dialects), and is therefore an applied discourse theory. However, like many applied theories, enregisterment is also concerned with the human factor (e.g., ideologies and identities), and is therefore an applied social theory.

Level of Analysis

Enregisterment is used to describe, but descriptions are often employed as a springboard to interpret, evaluate, and transform.

Practical Application

Enregisterment is a useful theory for readers wishing to investigate how the belief systems and identities of an individual or speech community are tied to language features. The theory is also useful to uncover the indexicality nature of language, or more specifically how linguistic features point to different social phenomena, such as the values of a speech community.

Reflection Exercise

Are your ideologies and identities connected to the way you write or talk? Try to think of a specific word or a unique way of pronouncing it that may be connected to an ideology or identity. Do your examples of enregisterment vary according to the language being used? For example, how does your identity change when using a language other than English? What do these differences tell you about how people view the status and value of English and your other language example?

Reference Example

Silva & Lee (2021) *"Marielle, presente": Metaleptic temporality and the enregisterment of hope in Rio de Janeiro.*

6.3.2 Example Theorists

The key theorists discussed in this section are Erving Goffman, Paul Grice, Michael Halliday, Harvey Sacks, and Ron Scollon. These theorists have been randomly selected and do not collectively represent an over-arching research agenda or theoretical framework.

A concise overview is provided for each theorist. Practical suggestions for research opportunities are also offered. Perspectives and levels of analysis are discussed in relation to each theorist. One example reference is identified for each theorist.

Readers interested in learning more about these theorists should begin with online sources. Numerous websites that are devoted to these theorists can be found online and at no cost, which offer detailed overviews and extensive reference lists.

Erving Goffman

Erving Goffman is a theorist best known for his work on face-to-face communication. His book publications cover a range of topics that are central to discourse analysis, including the idea that human communication is a performance. Erving Goffman developed frame analysis, which begins from the perspective of language use, but can be used to understand the human factor. Frame analysis is often employed to generate descriptions, but is also helpful to engage in interpretations, evaluations, and transformations.

Readers may wish to draw from the work of Erving Goffman if they are interested in showing how social variables, such as a widespread belief system or an institutional rule, shape the ways in which people communicate, including the words that they use.

Reference Example

Goffman (1986). *Frame Analysis: An Essay on the Organization of Experience*.

Paul Grice

Paul Grice is a theorist best known for his work in the philosophy of language, and more specifically the study of meaning (recall that discourse is at its most basic form meaning). His study of conversational implicatures is perhaps the most useful for novice discourse analysts. Conversational implicatures are indirect speech acts; it is a useful applied discourse theory to study language use, as a conversational implicature is about the meaning that is derived from how an utterance is communicated rather than what is said.

Readers may wish to draw from the work of Paul Grice if they want to investigate how the syntactic structure of a sentence may not reveal what is being done with said utterance. For instance, the statement "it is loud here" offers an observation, but can or should be interpreted as a request to close the office door. An interesting discourse analysis project could look broadly into what is said versus what is understood within a specific context.

Reference Example

Grice (1991). *Studies in the Way of Words*.

Michael Halliday

Michael Halliday is a theorist who is best known for introducing systemic functional linguistics, which is an applied framework for viewing language as a system of functions and meaning-making actions. Systemic functional linguistics is adopted in many disciplines as a way of describing language and understanding the context in which it is used, though many critical discourse analysts use this applied framework to make interpretations, evaluations, and transformations.

Readers interested in describing what language does or accomplishes should refer to systemic functional linguistics and the works of Michael Halliday. For instance, readers may wish to look at how utterances or sentences can be divided into, and described according to, who the participants are, what the mode of communication is, and how the communication should take place. Collectively, by describing language according to functional categories, readers can demonstrate how language functions to create meanings relevant to a particular context (see Chapter 4, Section 4.2).

Reference Example

Halliday & Matthiessen (2014). *Halliday's Introduction to Functional Grammar.*

Harvey Sacks

Harvey Sacks is best known for developing conversation analysis, which is an applied methodology. However, his earlier lectures on the study of talk offers the most insightful observations regarding how conversations are structured. His work on the structure of conversations includes several topics, including turn-taking order, topic organization, and storytelling practices.

Readers interested in describing the minute details of conversations should refer to Harvey Sacks's work on turn-taking and preference organization. His earlier lectures on the study of talk have been transcribed and published as a two-volume book which offers numerous theoretical insights for readers interested in describing conversations in general, and using conversation analysis in particular.

Reference Example

Sacks (1992). *Lectures on Conversation.* Volumes 1 and 2.

Ron Scollon

Ron Scollon is best known for developing mediated discourse analysis, which is an applied methodology that examines the mediation of discourse, agency, and practice. Unlike other common applied frameworks and methodologies that attempt to singularly describe or interpret discourse through one theoretical lens, Ron Scollon argues that discourse should be understood as mediated action (i.e., action as being mediated by setting and context). His work on the discourse of spaces and places has also been extremely influential.

Readers interested in exploring the intersection between descriptions and interpretations should refer to the many studies published by Ron Scollon, as well as his partner, former students, and collaborators. His work on uncovering the mediation between language use and the human factor has been applied to numerous topics, including intercultural communication, public signs, news discourse, and technology.

Reference Example

Scollon (2001). *Mediated Discourse: The Nexus of Practice*.

This section has offered a short, but detailed, overview of some of the applied theories and theorists can be referred to when conceptualizing a discourse analysis project. In Chapter 7, a practical model for doing discourse analysis is introduced. In this model, research questions are defined and discussed in relation to the research process. It may be helpful to refer back to these ten examples when considering how to apply this practical model for doing discourse analysis, as applied theories and theorists are central to selecting and analyzing an object of study.

Summary 6.3	1. Applied theories come from different disciplines and are inherently multifaceted.
	2. Applied theories can be used to understand discourse, society, or context.
	3. Numerous applied theories exist in, and can be used for, discourse analysis.
	4. Applied theorists can help readers think about a topic for investigation.
	5. Applied theories are often needed to develop a research question.

Learning Accomplishments

The chapter has introduced what theory is, and has discussed why it is important to the analytic process. The aim of the chapter was to help you understand how theory is a part of doing discourse analysis. This was done by defining theory, identifying the different theories that exist in discourse analysis, and explaining how theoretical principles relate to the topics and issues discussed in previous chapters. This section identifies how each learning outcome has been addressed in this chapter.

1. You will know how to define theory;

The chapter established that a theory is an idea that explains what discourse is and how discourse should be understood. However, a theory is not an opinion, thought, or belief, which are simply intuitions without an explanatory framework.

2. You will understand how theory relates to the analytic process;

Discussions throughout the chapter argued that all perspectives and levels of discourse analysis rely on a theory or theories. Theory can assist in the analytic process in numerous ways, including but of course not limited to describing a communicative practice, forming the foundation from which you understand the social impact of a particular discourse feature, or offering a lens through which to uncover the hidden meanings within a text. It was argued that theories in discourse analysis help you understand what is in front of you and how to understand what is happening in front of you. These functions of theory were expressed as two questions. What am I looking at? How do I understand what I am looking at? The chapter also discussed theory as a system for identifying and making observations of an object of study.

3. You will understand the difference between a theory of knowledge and an applied theory;

The chapter established that a theory of knowledge is an idea related to the principles of inquiry: it concerns how we know what we know. A theory of knowledge helps establish what discourse analysis is and why it approaches the study of language and communication in a particular way. It was argued that theories of knowledge are not the same as applied theories. Applied theories help researchers understand a specific object of study or a general aspect of language. That is to say, applied theories possess an application value: they are applied to objects of study during the analytic process. Conversely, theories of knowledge help explain what discourse analysis is, and how this way of investigating language and communication is different from other fields of study.

4. You will be able to identify the different types of applied theory that exist.

The end of this chapter offered a total of ten applied theories and theorists for readers to consider. Although this number represents a fraction of the theories and theorist that can potentially be used for an analysis, it was argued that the examples offer sufficient coverage for readers getting acquainted with discourse analysis. It was also noted that many of the themes and topics identified throughout the book can be categorized as an applied theory. Readers were encouraged to revisit each chapter when considering how theory can benefit their discourse analysis project.

Key Themes

What a Theory Is

1. A theory is an idea that explains how a discourse phenomenon should be understood.
2. All perspectives and levels of discourse analysis are based on a theory.
3. An applied theory is an idea about discourse that can be used to study an object of study.
4. Applied theories may form larger methodologies, frameworks, or approaches.
5. A theory of knowledge is an idea about the principles of inquiry.

Theory of Knowledge

1. A theory of knowledge is an idea related to the principles of inquiry.
2. A theory of knowledge concerns how we know what we know.
3. A theory of knowledge helps establish what discourse analysis is.
4. A theory of knowledge helps explain why discourse analysis is unique.

Applied Theory

1. An applied theory is an idea specific to an object of study.
2. All perspectives and levels of analysis rely on applied theories.
3. Applied theories can be used to generate research questions.
4. Applied theories allow you to show that your analysis is based on an established idea.

Theory Examples

1. Applied theories come from different disciplines and are inherently multifaceted.
2. Applied theories can be used to understand discourse, society, or context.
3. Numerous applied theories exist in, and can be used for, discourse analysis.
4. Applied theorists can help readers think about a topic for investigation.
5. Applied theories are often needed to develop a research question.

Reading List

Jaworski & Coupland (2014) The popular volume include some influential publications on using, discourse analysis. The book presents chapters by key theorists in discourse analysis such as Norman Fairclough, Barbara Johnstone, and Teun van Dijk. Chapters are organized according to themes and topics, such as power, identity, and social relationships. The book can be used to complement the discussions in this chapter.

Johnstone, B. (2018) The book offers numerous examples of applied theories in each chapter, which are organized according to themes and topics, such as discourse and the world, discourse structure, and discourse and medium. Applied theories discussed in this book range from indexicality and contextualization cues to language ideology and identities.

Dunn & Neumann (2016) The authors provide an excellent overview of discourse analysis by breaking the research process into two themes: theories in discourse analysis and analytic points to consider when doing discourse analysis. The first theme offers examples of theories of knowledge. The second theme is related to applied theories. The authors discuss these themes in relation to specific research topics, such as formulating a research question and organizing an analysis.

Learning Outcomes

This chapter summarizes the main points established in this book and reviews how research questions factor into doing discourse analysis. The aim of the chapter is to help you synthesize the different aspects of conducting discourse analysis research into a coherent set of *principles*. This will be done by introducing a practical model for doing discourse analysis.

The contents of the chapter are organized according to the following learning outcomes. After reading this chapter:

1. You will be able to recall the mains points of doing discourse analysis;
2. You will be able to use a model for doing discourse analysis to conduct research;
3. You will know a number of practical tips for doing discourse analysis;
4. You will be able to construct research questions that are relevant to discourse analysis research.

7.1 Summarizing the Book

This book presented a practical overview of discourse analysis that can be used by researchers working in a number of varied disciplines. A practical interpretation of discourse analysis begins with an object of study. How you select and analyze an object of study is based on multiple research considerations from thinking about the practical implications of examining a particular type of discourse (e.g., text versus spoken language) to developing an understanding of the theories involved in adopting a specific analytic perspective. Such themes and topics were addressed throughout the book. Although each chapter deals with a specific theme or topic, discourse analysis is in practice an interrelated research process. Nevertheless, it is helpful to briefly summarize the foci for each chapter.

Chapter 1 offered a definition of discourse analysis, provided examples of discourse, and discussed the importance of objects of study. Chapter 2 reviewed how to organize an analysis around an object of study, offered examples of what data excerpts look like, and gave several examples of how to organize an analysis.

Chapter 3 showed that objects of study can be analyzed from different, sometimes overlapping, perspectives and levels of analysis. Chapter 4 provided a definition of context, demonstrated why it is important to discourse analysis, and identified numerous models and constructs that can be used to uncover the contextual dimensions of objects of study. Chapter 5 argued that discourse analysis is inherently subjective, and discussed the many ways that a researcher shapes the research process from using cultural familiarity for data collection and analysis to being reflexive and attending to the power dynamics involved in examining human communication.

Chapter 6 offered a definition of theory, and demonstrated how theories factor into discourse analysis.

The present chapter synthesizes these chapters by providing a model for doing discourse analysis. This chapter also builds on previous chapters by offering numerous suggestions regarding how to interpret this model, which includes a discussion of how to write research questions.

> **Summary 7.1**
> 1. Chapters 1 and 2 are devoted to selecting an object of study.
> 2. Chapters 3 through 6 are devoted to analyzing an object of study.
> 3. Chapter 7 presents a practical model for doing discourse analysis.
> 4. Chapter 7 offers ten practical tips for doing discourse analysis.
> 5. Chapter 7 reviews the importance of research questions in discourse analysis research.

7.2 A Practical Model for Doing Discourse Analysis

A practical model for discourse analysis views the research process as a series of interrelated steps. The model begins with selecting an object of study and ends with incorporating theory. While theory is central throughout the research process, a practical model for doing discourse analysis places it at the end for consideration. This way of sequencing the research process allows readers to focus on the fundamental practices related to discourse analysis without being weighed down by complicated theoretical discussions. Students of discourse analysis can deviate from this model after they have become knowledgeable about a particular theory or methodology.

Two questions are central to how a practical model for doing discourse analysis sees the transition from selecting to analyzing an object of study. First, what do you see once you have selected an object of study? Second, what do you want to say about this object of study?

Figure 7.1 illustrates this practical model in relation to the chapters presented in this book.

Selecting an object of study requires understanding what discourse is. Discourse, as discussed throughout this book but especially in Chapter 1, consists of three major aspects: language use, the human factor, and their interconnectedness. Most discourse analysis research considers all three aspects, but will in practice favor one aspect over the other two. For readers getting started with discourse analysis, it is helpful to focus on one aspect of discourse rather than thinking about how to incorporate all three.

Determining what aspect of discourse to "see" can be done by drawing from personal interests, life experiences, academic expectations, professional objectives, methodological principles, or theories. While it

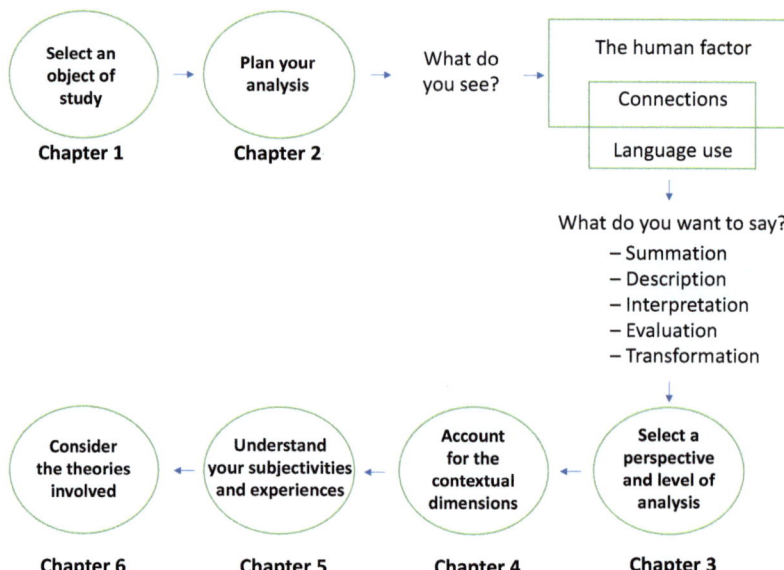

FIGURE 7.1
A practical model for
doing discourse analysis

is possible to select an object of study by first picking a methodology or theory, this approach is not recommended for readers who are new to discourse analysis. Selecting a theory before an object of study requires knowing what theories are available and understanding why one is the most suitable for your research, which entails extensive reading and a significant amount of time. Furthermore, selecting a methodology or theory before identifying an object of study will lock you into a specific way of thinking, limit your empirical possibilities as a result, and may not align with your personal or professional interests.

A more practical way of selecting an object of study is to draw from personal or professional situations, reflecting on what is interesting, important, and feasible to you and your life situation.

7.2.1 Selecting Your Object of Study

Discourse is your object of study. Thus, selecting an object of study requires a broad understanding of discourse and its research implications. As depicted in Figure 7.2, discourse can be interpreted in numerous ways.

Selecting an object of study requires understanding how the different interpretations of discourse exist in society. However, before selecting an object of study, it is important to consider the logistical implications of a particular type of analysis, as discussed extensively in Chapter 2. This planning stage determines whether it is feasible to investigate an object of study. It may be necessary to return to Chapter 1 if it is determined that you do not have the time, resources, or competences to analyze a particular object of study. Selecting an object of study is thus an iterative process that entails repeating this planning step until an appropriate and feasible object of study is selected (see Figure 7.3).

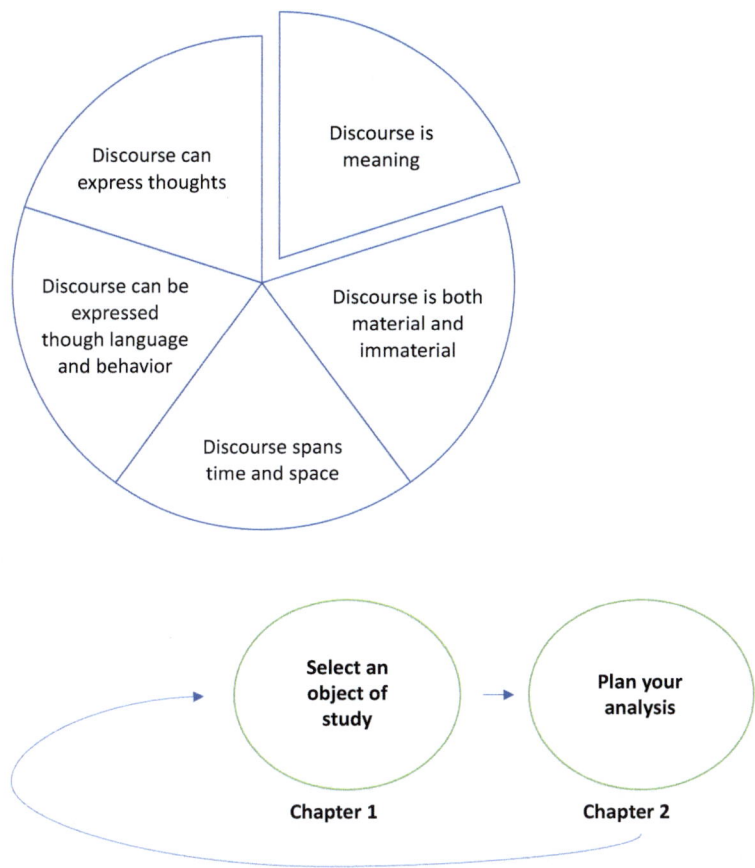

FIGURE 7.2
Interpretations of discourse

FIGURE 7.3
Selecting an object of study

Planning your analysis requires knowing what a data excerpt is, how it is organized in relation to your research questions, and the time and resources that it takes to collect and present your object of study, to name a few. The planning considerations that go into selecting an object of study are based on a range of research issues that were discussed at the beginning of this book. In addition to the topics addressed in Chapter 2, it is important to pay special attention to how much time you have and how much is needed to conduct a particular analysis, as this research variable will ultimately determine whether it is feasible to investigate an object of study. The six example questions that are presented in Figure 7.4 demonstrate that the issue of time is relevant to many research situations.

The time commitment involved in selecting an object of study is based on numerous empirical situations, ranging from the ostensibly simple, such as determining how many data excerpts will be used in a report, to the highly technical, such as learning a programming language to tailor an application according to your research questions. While it is beyond the scope of this book to address all the different planning considerations that come with selecting an object of study, it is possible to discuss

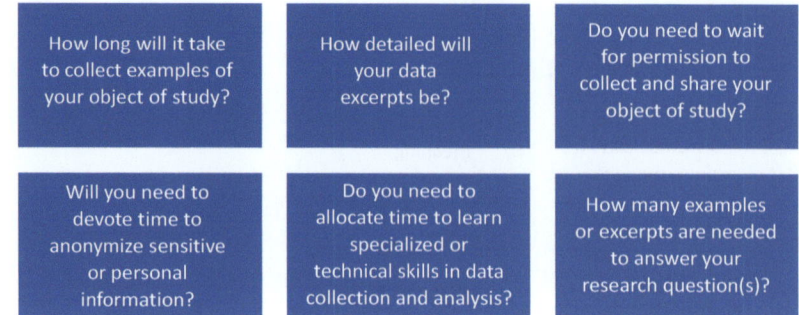

FIGURE 7.4
Planning your analysis

how time shapes a spectrum of data types. To this end, Figure 7.5 offers a simple way of visualizing how time may shape what object of study you select for your analysis.

Less time commitment				More time commitment
Picture (e.g., road signs, screenshots, still photographs)	**Text** (e.g., business reports, email exchanges)	**Speech** (e.g., radio talk, phone calls, voice messages)	**Visual** (e.g., embodied talk, sign language, gestures)	**Multimodal** (i.e., any combination in the spectrum)

FIGURE 7.5
Time commitment

The time commitment involved in using pictures for your research is very low in comparison to other data types. Pictures are often taken by the researcher or are publicly available, reducing the time that it may take to get permission to use an object of study for research purposes and gain any potential ethical approval. Pictures do not typically require time to edit or transcribe: once captured, they are largely ready to present in a report. In some situations, when for example researching sensitive or confidential issues, pictures must be anonymized. Anonymizing pictures requires the use of specialized software, which takes time to learn and to develop into a competent user (for a more nuanced and theoretical account of how to plan an analysis around picture data, see Norris, 2019).

Text data involves more time commitment than pictures, as they require basic editing before they can be shared, analyzed, and disseminated. For example, a student essay that is used as an object of study must be broken into smaller excerpts or segments of data. This editing process may entail copying and pasting, changing the font type and size, adjusting the line spacing, and anonymizing sensitive information, to name a few. Unlike speech data, however, transcribing objects of study that are textual is not a lengthy and complex process. Aside from several basic editing and planning tasks, text data are generally ready to use for an analysis (for a more nuanced and theoretical account of how to plan an analysis around text data, see Jenks, 2011).

The time commitment involved in planning an analysis based on speech data is significantly more than pictures and texts. Although current speech recognition technology is capable of automating the transcription process for basic data types (David et al., 2009), such as monologues that are spoken clearly, slowly, and without any background noise, most speech data are far too nuanced and complex for automation technology. It is advised, therefore, to temper any urge to use technology to transcribe speech data with the reality that most speech recognition tools were, as recently as the early 2020s, not ready for discourse analytic purposes. Furthermore, manual transcription work is an integral part of the analysis process, creating a more intimate and nuanced understanding of an object of study. The upshot is that speech data must be transcribed from voice to text, so that an analysis can be easily presented and shared (for a more nuanced and theoretical account of how to plan an analysis around speech data, see Jenks, 2011). This transcription process is incredibly time intensive.

Visual data are one of the most time-consuming data types to use for a discourse analysis project. Planning an analysis around visual data consumes a significant amount of time, as they are captured as dynamic video recordings of complex movements and meaning-making actions, but must be transformed into a static transcription or excerpt of still pictures and possible textual data. Visual data may also be multimodal, as many discourse analysis projects are based on face-to-face or online video interactions that are often made up of long stretches of verbal communication that must be transcribed (for a more nuanced and theoretical account of how to plan an analysis around visual data, see Mondada, 2018).

On the far end of the spectrum are objects of study that are multimodal in nature, meaning that they combine any combination of data types (e.g., analytic observations that are based on text and speech data). Multimodal data combine the planning considerations of each data type used, making them potentially the most challenging to manage. In addition to reflecting on the planning implications of each data type, dealing with multimodal data demands advanced presentation skills, as they require transforming two or more types of data into one coherent analytic presentation (for a more nuanced and theoretical account of how to plan an analysis around multimodal data, see Mondada, 2018; Norris, 2019).

As noted earlier, selecting an object of study is an iterative process that entails considering a range of planning issues for different possible data types until a final decision is made. The research competences required to engage in a particular type of analysis, such as knowledge of transcribing multimodal data, will partly determine what object of study you select. Other important factors in selecting an object of study are time and resources. That is, do you have the time and resources to analyze a particular object of study? Considering these planning issues is a prerequisite to analyzing an object of study.

7.2.2 Analyzing Your Object of Study

A practical model for discourse analysis presents discourse and analysis as separate (though interconnected) steps. Although discourse and analysis are inextricably connected throughout the research process, each dimension is based on a complex set of theories and practices that necessitate a bifurcated view of doing discourse analysis. A bifurcated view of discourse analysis means first understanding what discourse is, knowing how data types possess different planning implications, and selecting an object of study that is both feasible and interesting.

Selecting an object of study that is feasible to investigate is foundational to a successful discourse analysis project. After selecting a feasible object of study, it is time to move on to the analysis in discourse analysis. Analyzing an object of study is a multifaceted endeavor, though the process begins with two ostensibly simple questions. What do you see? What do you want to say? (See Figure 7.6.)

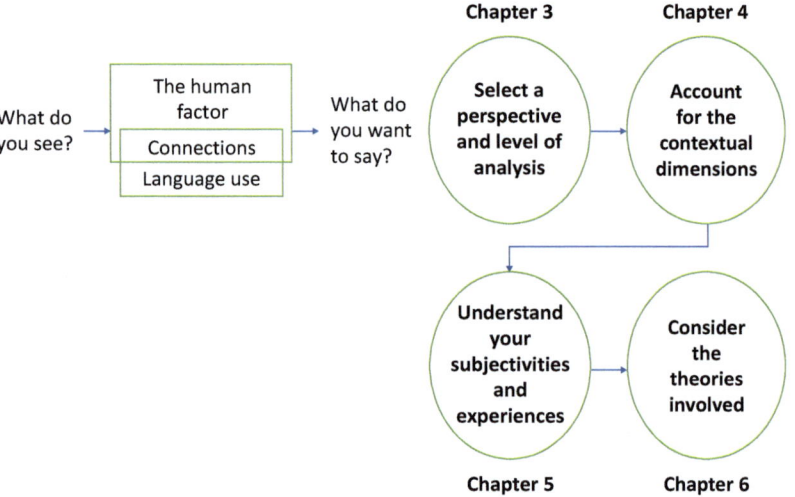

FIGURE 7.6
Analyzing your object of study

A practical model for discourse analysis views analysis as four interrelated analytic categories: (1) selecting a perspective and level of analysis; (2) accounting for the contextual dimensions of your object of study; (3) understanding how your subjectivities and experiences shape your understanding of the object of study; (4) considering the theories that are involved in all aspects of your research. These four categories are presented in this order because they are designed to answer the "see" and "say" questions. In other words, addressing the four analytic categories sequentially from one to four establishes a bottom-up approach that allows you to focus on what is best for your research interests rather than following what a theory dictates.

It is, of course, possible to select a theory first and then answer the "see" and "say" questions. Yet, this approach of first reading Chapter 6 means that the "see" and "say" questions are not strictly answered by you, but are rather addressed by a theory. This theory-first approach is widely accepted and practiced, and you may indeed begin with a theory after you have completed your first discourse analysis project given that you have already developed some level of competence in a set of theories. The theory-first approach will, however, ultimately leave you with a more superficial understanding of discourse analysis, as it dictates the perspective and level of analysis that you adopt, the contextual dimensions that you consider, and the extent to which your subjectivities and experiences shape your understanding of the object of study.

A practical model for discourse analysis, conversely, offers readers a practice-first approach that reflects the core themes and issues underpinning most discourse analytic observations. In so doing, a practical model privileges a broad foundation of knowledge that simultaneously attends to personal and academic interests. This practice-first approach is illustrated in Figure 7.7, which offers an alternative way of visually depicting the practical model for discourse analysis introduced earlier in this section. Special attention should be placed on Chapter 3 when considering Figure 7.7.

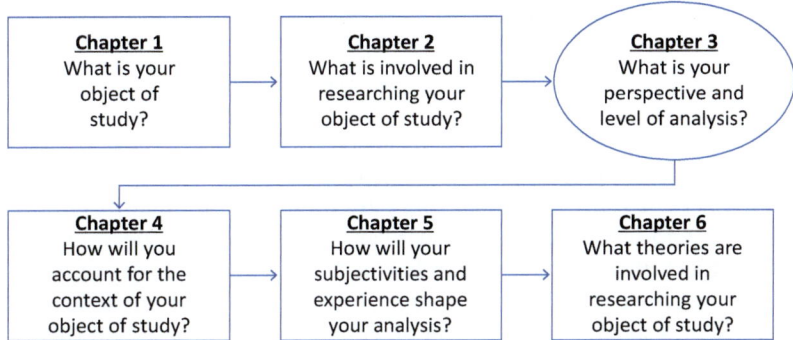

FIGURE 7.7
A practice-first approach

A practice-first approach uses Chapter 3 as the transition point for moving from selecting an object of study to analyzing it. That is, the transition from selecting an object of study to analyzing it occurs when the perspective and level of analysis are considered. Numerous discourse analysis topics and themes must be considered when analyzing an object of study, including reflecting on what it means to describe, interpret, evaluate, or transform language use and the human factor. Figure 7.8 offers a simplified overview that highlights some of the key points to consider for each perspective and level of analysis.

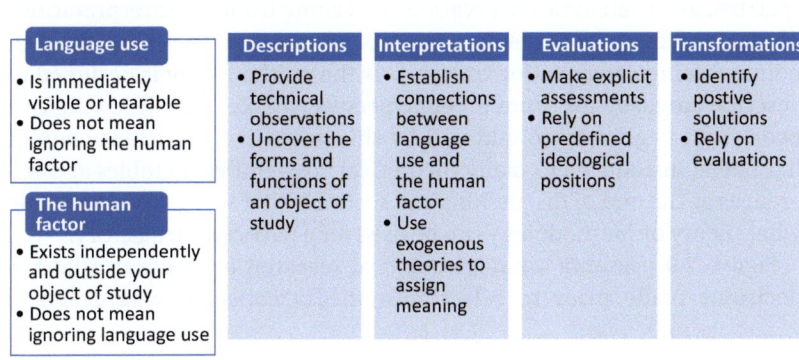

FIGURE 7.8
Perspectives and levels of analysis

This transition that occurs when selecting a perspective and level of analysis is pivotal when doing discourse analysis, as it largely determines how a researcher considers subsequent analytic issues such as context, subjectivities, and theory. For example, in the example research trajectory depicted in Figure 7.9, describing an aspect of language use has consequences for subsequent steps in the analytic process.

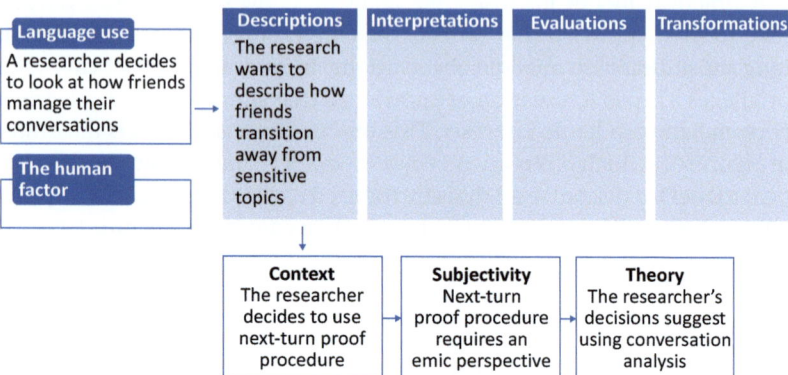

FIGURE 7.9
Example trajectory

The trajectory begins with the researcher selecting a conversation as an object of study. Although there are multiple combinations of perspectives and levels of analysis that can be adopted to understand any given object of study, the researcher in this example decides to examine a conversation from a language use perspective and at the level of description – again, this selection process need not be based on theory, but can rather come from personal interests in a particular aspect of discourse. The researcher should now consider what conditions of the object of study will be examined (i.e., the context), having determined the perspective and level of analysis that will be adopted. Like all objects of study, numerous conditions may potentially shape a conversation, which can in turn be accounted for in numerous ways. The researcher in this example is interested in turn-taking practices, so ultimately decides to use next-turn proof procedure to understand how friends transition away from sensitive topics. Using next-turn proof procedure means that the issue of subjectivity should be addressed by adopting an emic perspective, as the analytic observations will come from the interpretations of the participants (or friends) as they communicate. These decisions all point to using conversation analysis, as the methodology is designed to describe language use from an emic perspective. Readers following this book from beginning to end will by this point in the current chapter have been introduced to many theoretical possibilities (in tables and references at the end of discussions and sections) that will help in knowing what theory or methodology can be used for a particular trajectory.

Figure 7.9 presents a straightforward research example in that the decisions made prior to selecting a theory collectively represent a methodology. In contrast, the decisions made during the analytic process for most discourse analysis research do not fit within a coherent applied framework or methodology. Rather, researchers often pick and choose theories that reflect their interests or research questions. Understanding how theory shapes the analytic process can be done by acquainting yourself with some of the more common theories that are used in the literature. Chapter 6 offers an excellent starting point for this acquainting process. In practice, however, considering analytic issues, such as context and researcher subjectivities, is a theory-laden process. That is, theories are inextricably connected to perspectives and levels of analysis, context, and research subjectivities. Therefore, reaching the end of the practical model for doing discourse analysis does not mean that it is time to identify a theory. Rather, reaching the end of the practical model for doing discourse analysis means reflecting on how the theories that may be selected will shape the analytic process.

Readers who are interested in identifying theories that fit within a coherent analytic system should consider beginning their research (before selecting an object of study) with an applied framework or methodology. It must be noted, however, that placing theory at the beginning of the research process is more challenging. A theory-first approach is challenging for novice discourse analysts, as it entails reading an introduction to a methodology or theoretical framework, which often relies heavily on technical jargon and specialized background knowledge, making the learning curve very steep for someone encountering discourse analysis for the first time.

Conversely, a practical model for doing discourse analysis places an explicit discussion of theory at the end of the research process. In so doing, the core principles of doing discourse analysis establish a practical foundation from which theory can be considered. This practical approach is preferred for introductory purposes, as it is often easier to understand the core principles that underpin discourse analysis than attempting to learn a new methodology or theoretical framework from scratch.

Summary 7.2

1. A practical model for doing discourse analysis begins with an object of study.
2. A practical model for doing discourse analysis ends with theoretical considerations.
3. A practical model views doing discourse analysis as a series of interrelated steps.
4. A practical model for doing discourse analysis is a practice-first approach to research.
5. A practical model for doing discourse analysis is one of several ways of doing research.

7.3 Some Practical Tips for Doing Discourse Analysis

A practical model for doing discourse analysis maps out a trajectory that can be followed when selecting and analyzing an object of study. This roadmap is established by identifying generic themes and issues that are central to doing discourse analysis.

In addition to following this roadmap, readers should consider the following practical tips for completing a successful discourse analysis project. A successful discourse analysis project addresses its research objectives, offers interesting analytic observations that are based on theory, and is completed in a timely manner. These practical tips expand on previous discussions, as well as offer new principles to consider. These practical tips are (1) create a plan, (2) know your object of study, (3) know the literature, (4) have a research question, (5) let the data speak for itself, (6) ask for help, (7) avoid making generalizations, (8) connect with society, (9) leave time to edit and revise, and (10) avoid playing the numbers game.

1. **Create a plan**. Developing a research plan is necessary for a successful discourse analysis project. When using the themes and issues covered in the practical model for doing discourse analysis, readers should establish a plan that includes (1) a research question, (2) the logistics of obtaining and analyzing an object of study, (3) milestones and deadlines, (4) relevant literature, and (5) the decisions that will be made during the analytic process. These five components of planning a discourse analysis project should also include, or be presented as, a timeline. PERT charts, Gantt charts, and work breakdown structures are timelines commonly used for research purposes.

2. **Know your object of study**. The chances of completing a successful discourse analysis project are much higher when the researcher has a substantial degree of cultural knowledge of the object of study. This principle includes avoiding objects of study in which you (or your team members) are not highly proficient. Furthermore, it is important to have an intimate understanding of the setting and context in which your object of study exists or occurs. Understanding the setting and context will help you make deeper, more nuanced analytic observations. For example, if your object of study is lexical choice in student essays, then you should be not only highly proficient in the language of the students' writing, but also knowledgeable of the classroom and teaching context.

3. **Know the literature**. Most objects of study have been investigated by scholars before you. It is often useful to draw inspiration from such people, as planning and carrying out a successful discourse analysis project is much easier to accomplish when there is a literature to which you can refer. An established literature will

help you formulate research questions, select the appropriate perspective and level of analysis, and understand the significance of your discourse analysis project, to name a few. For novice discourse analysts, it is therefore advisable to select an object of study that has already been investigated. A quick search on most academic or scholarly databases will reveal whether this is the case.

4. **Have a research question**. All successful discourse analysis projects possess a research question (or thesis statement). A research question identifies your empirical aim for you and your audience. A research question is a waypoint for your discourse analysis project, pointing you in the right direction when important decisions are made when selecting and analyzing an object of study. For your audience, a research question represents a critical reference point from which evaluations regarding the quality of your discourse analysis project are made. In other words, without a research question, your audience (e.g., your instructor) will struggle to understand the reasons for, and quality of, your discourse analysis project. The subsequent section offers a more extensive discussion of research questions.

5. **Let the data speak for itself**. A successful discourse analysis project lets the data speak for itself. In other words, a successful discourse analysis project is data-driven or data-first. This statement means that the entire analytic process is based on your object of study. Letting the data speak for itself means analytic observations are based on both the explicit and implicit meaning related to, and stemming from, an object of study. Put differently, analytic observations should be neither detached from the object of study nor simply based on a researcher's intuition. Letting the data speak for itself means forming analytic observations that your peers or audience would recognize as being valid, which is related to the next practical tip.

6. **Ask for help**. The chances of completing a successful discourse analysis project are much higher when you have at least one person offering their opinions about your object of study. Even the most experienced discourse analysts benefit from asking for help from their colleagues during the analytic process. Help comes in many forms during the analytic process, including asking a colleague to validate a transcript, presenting your preliminary data to a group of peers, and requesting a more experienced researcher to read your analytic observations before submission. In short, asking for help is not a sign of incompetence and is indeed a practice that is followed by most successful discourse analysts.

7. **Avoid making generalizations**. A successful discourse analysis project is not only data-first, but it is also data-restricted. What this statement means in practice is ostensibly simple. Do not generalize your analytic observations beyond the object of study. For example, if you are investigating lexical choice in student essays, then do not

suggest that your findings are applicable to classrooms that were not included in your discourse analysis project. Put differently, a successful discourse analysis project is not dependent on making larger generalizations beyond your object of study.

8. **Connect with society**. Connecting with society is necessary for a successful discourse analysis project. This practice means analyzing an object of study that has some degree of social significance. An object of study has social significance if it is important to a particular community, or is integral to how people behave. Objects of study possess social significance when they are timely, meaning that they are a topic of discussion or a source of debate within societies. Analyzing an object of study that has social significance makes it easier to establish a rationale for your discourse analysis project, which is important for all studies, and will help your audience understand the importance of your analytic observations.

9. **Leave time to edit and revise**. A successful discourse analysis project will incorporate sufficient time for the researcher to edit and revise any necessary changes that must be made. This principle ties back to creating a plan and asking for help. A plan should identify editing and revising as a milestone to achieve near the end of the research process. Asking for help will lead to feedback and suggestions from your peers, which will require additional time to make further changes.

10. **Avoid playing the numbers game**. A successful discourse analysis project is not dependent on asking many research questions, collecting a large corpus of data, or presenting numerous data excerpts to analyze an object of study. In other words, a successful discourse analysis project does not subscribe to a "the more the merrier" approach to conducting research. For example, novice discourse analysts often assume that it is necessary to ask many research questions for their project to be successful. Although it is not a problem to ask more than one research question, doing so requires more work and does not always lead to better results. More importantly, a successful discourse analysis project can be achieved by asking one research question and using small data sets if the goal is to offer a detailed account of an object of study.

Many of the practical tips identified in this section reference, or are centrally related to, research questions. The importance of research questions to a successful discourse analysis project cannot be overstated, and is therefore the topic of discussion in Section 7.4.

Summary 7.3 1. Practical tips are specific to doing discourse analysis research.
2. Practical tips are also based on general research practices.
3. Practical tips must be considered early in the research process.
4. Practical tips do not favor particular approaches or theories.

7.4 Making Sense of Research Questions

A research question establishes an aim for your discourse analysis project to achieve. A good research question is concise, using keywords that allow your audience to recognize the aim of the project. Research questions should also be narrowly focused. These characteristics of a good research question will be returned to later in this section (see also Sunderland, 2010).

A research question is needed early in the research process, as it establishes the aim of your discourse analysis project. It is thus exceptionally difficult to complete a successful discourse analysis project without identifying a research question early in the research process. As noted in Chapter 6, a research question should be identified either before or immediately after selecting an object of study. Figure 7.10 illustrates where in the research process a research question should be formulated.

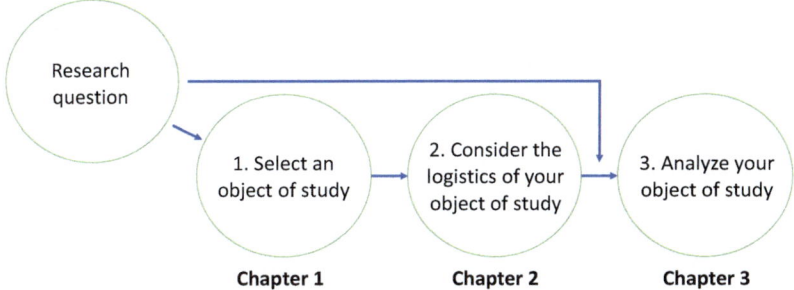

FIGURE 7.10
Research question
sequence

It is common to begin the research process with a research question by modifying or using a question formulated in a published discourse analysis project. Modifying or using a research question from a published discourse analysis project limits the possibilities for selecting an object of study, but the approach will offer an analytic template that will likely represent good practice. This approach will also select your perspective and level of analysis for you, which is compelling for some readers wanting more structure at the beginning of the research process. It is also possible to select an object of study and then formulate a research question, but this approach requires knowing what approach best addresses the aim of your discourse analysis project. Both approaches require formulating a research question before analyzing your object of study, as all successful discourse analysis projects are based on a clear relationship between their aims and findings.

As noted in the third practical tip in Section 7.3, a successful discourse analysis project is more attainable when it is based on established research topics. Similarly, knowing the literature will help you formulate a research question. It is advisable to refer to the literature when considering research questions and an object of study. Searching academic and scholarly databases with keywords that represent your discourse analysis project is the best approach to take when formulating research questions (for a similar but different overview of research questions, see Chapter 10 of Paltridge, 2021).

As discourse analysis is data-driven (let the data speak for itself), you may find yourself in a situation where your research question may need to be revised after moving on to the analysis stages. In such situations, it is often advisable to revise your research question according to what you are analyzing, as the alternative requires time that most researchers do not have. That is, the alternative is to collect new data, or to select a new object of study, if the analysis reveals that your analytic observations are not addressing your research question. In this sense, formulating a research question is potentially a cyclical process. Furthermore, research questions are never completely finalized or set in stone, and should always be evaluated throughout the research process to ensure that what you are analyzing refers back to what you are asking.

Constructing a good research question requires knowing its essential components. Consider the following research question and the keywords that are used in a published journal article. Think about how the research question indicates a particular empirical focus. It is useful to reflect on how each recognizable keyword communicates what will be accomplished in the analysis.

1.   *Topic maintenance in video-mediated virtual exchanges: Rolling the ball back in L2 interactions* (Çimenli, Sert, & Jenks, 2022)

1a. **Research question**: How are RBBs designed and organized sequentially in video-mediated virtual exchanges?

1b. **Keywords**: A good research question includes common keywords that reveal the aim of a discourse analysis project. The first keyword in this research question is *RBB*, which stands for "rolling the ball back." Uncommon keywords, such as *RBB*, must be defined before presenting the research question. Common keywords, such as *designed* and *organized sequentially*, can but need not be defined before presenting the research question. However, keywords that represent the analytic focus, such as *designed* and *organized sequentially*, must be operationalized in the methods/methodology section. Operationalizing means defining, but more importantly explaining, how you will investigate a particular keyword.

1c. **Object of study**: Research questions should explicitly or implicitly reveal what the object of study is. In this example, the object of study is RBB. RBBs are utterances that individuals use to maintain a topic of discussion. The design and sequential organization keywords in the research question are two aspects of this object of study that will be investigated.

1d. **Setting or context**: All good research questions identify the setting or context (or both) in which an object of study is situated. In this research question, the setting is video-mediated virtual exchanges. The context is topic maintenance, as the definition of RBB reveals.

1e. **Perspective of analysis**: The perspective of analysis taken in this example is language use. Design, organize, sequence, and related lexical derivations (e.g., sequence organization) are keywords that suggest a focus on how language is used, and the ways in which communication is organized.

1f. **Level of analysis**: The level of analysis taken in this example is description. Descriptions are the most common level of analysis when a research question aims to understand language use.

Although there is great variation in how research questions are formulated, there are several basic components that should be included, such as keywords, context, and object of study. A second and final research question example is provided below to demonstrate this point. Again, please reflect on how each recognizable keyword communicates what will be accomplished in the analysis.

2. *Critical talk moves in critical conversations: Examining power and privilege in an English Language Arts classroom* (Vetter, Schieble, & Martin, 2021)

2a. **Research question**: What talk moves did Carlson use to foster critical conversations in his classroom?

2b. **Keywords**: The research question includes two keywords that suggest how the discourse analysis project will be conducted. The first keyword in this research question is *talk moves*, which the authors define before the research question as interactional patterns, such as questions, that promote critical conversations. The second keyword is *critical conversations*, which the authors define as the topics and means of communication that promote a heightened awareness of important social topics, such as power and self-reflection, respectively. The authors also define this keyword before the research question. The word *foster*, while not strictly a keyword, ties talk moves and critical conversations together by demonstrating that the researchers will look at how one facilitates the other. The researchers discuss who Carlson is immediately after presenting the research question.

2c. **Object of study**: Again, research questions should explicitly or implicitly reveal what the object of study is. In this example, the object of study is talk moves. Although not the primary focus of analysis, critical conversations are also an object of study in that the researchers show how talk moves lead to certain types of dialogue.

2d. **Setting or context**: This research question example reveals the context (critical conversations) and the setting (Carlson's classroom).

2e. **Perspective of analysis**: The perspective of analysis taken in this example is language use, though the word *critical* often suggests making connections to the human factor. In this example, the authors focus on language use, but are also concerned with the human factor.

2f. **Level of analysis**: The level of analysis taken in this example is description and interpretation. The authors use descriptions to discuss talk moves. The critical conversations are used to make connections between language use and the human factor (i.e., making interpretations).

The two examples show how keywords used in research questions indicate a particular focus and type of analysis. It is also useful to think about how the types of question lead to a certain discourse analysis project. Research questions in discourse analysis projects typically come in the form of interrogatives (*do*, *what*, *how*, and *why*). Although *do* and *why* questions can be found in the literature, there are other question types that better represent what discourse analysis does. That is to say, *how* and *what* questions are more compatible with analyzing how discourse is organized and what it does. Conversely, *do* questions lead to yes/no answers, which do not capture the spirit of discourse analysis. Furthermore, *why* questions seek to explain discourse rather than describe, interpret, evaluate, or transform it.

Although *how* and *what* questions are preferred in discourse analysis projects, they indicate different research foci. Two sets of research questions with the same keywords are provided in the following learning activity to demonstrate this point.

Learning Activity 7.1 Reflecting on *How* and *What* Questions

In this exercise, the learning objective is to reflect on how the wording of a research question changes the way readers interpret it.

Two sets of research questions with the same keywords are presented below. For the first set of research questions, please think about the ways in which the "how" and the "what" change the analytic focus.

1a. How do news media organizations use metaphors to portray migrant workers in the United States?
1b. What metaphors are used by media organizations to portray migrant workers in the United States?

While the word order in both questions is different, the same keywords are used. For the *how* question, the research focuses on the manner or condition of metaphors. For the *what* question, the research focuses on identifying the types of metaphors used. The *what* question can be answered by listing metaphors and connecting them with portrayals of migrant workers, whereas the *how* question should be answered by uncovering the metaphors' features that lead to certain portrayals.

For the second set of research questions, please think about the ways in which the "how" and the "what" change the analytic focus. Answers will not be provided this time for these questions.

2a. How are images used by Dutch teenagers to construct their language ideologies and identities?
2b. What images are used by Dutch teenagers to construct their language ideologies and identities?

Are your observations similar to the ones provided for the first set of research questions? What would happen to these research questions if you changed the first word to do or why? Is it possible to conduct the same type of analysis with both research questions?

In addition to needing to know how the types of question lead to different empirical goals, readers must consider the number of research questions that they wish to answer. Although answering one research question is often sufficient for a successful discourse analytic project, it is not uncommon to have a main research question followed by additional sub-research questions. For example, many discourse analysis projects will have a main research question that begins with a *how*, and then ask a sub-research question that starts with a *what*. The answer for the sub-research question is often dependent on answering the main research question. The following research question examples demonstrate this point.

1. *Main research question*: How is translanguaging between English and Spanish used in school playgrounds in Austin, Texas?
2. *Sub-research question*: What are the social and political implications of English–Spanish translanguaging practices?

The order in which research questions are presented should reflect the steps taken during the analytic process. The answer to the main research question demonstrates how language is used, which is needed to answer the sub-research question. In addition, sub-research questions may require a different set of analytic tools and theories. For example, the main research question is based on the language use of translanguaging, which requires a different approach from what is needed for the subsequent question. The sub-research question is based on the human factor of translanguaging. The main research question should be conducted at the level of description, while the sub-research question should be carried out at the level of interpretation.

When formulating research questions, it is also important to reflect on their logistical implications. For instance, answering two or more research questions for your discourse analysis project will be conceptually more demanding than addressing one research question. Additional time is also needed to answer two or more research questions. For many discourse analysis projects, possessing two or more research questions means using multiple methodologies or theoretical frameworks for which the time needed to learn such approaches must be accounted. Consequently, like the planning that goes into selecting an object of study, the logistics of research questions must be considered early in the research process.

When formulating a research question, it is essential to be concise and focused. It should be possible to formulate a research question in one sentence or fewer than approximately fifty words. Longer research questions are more likely to be convoluted, leading to confusion and misinterpretation.

The location of your research question(s) is also important. In many discourse analysis projects, research questions are placed at the very end of the introduction (see the research question example for Çimenli, Sert, & Jenks, 2022). This location allows your audience to understand how your discourse analysis project is related to the rationale for your investigation. Other researchers prefer to place their research questions before the data analysis or what is typically referred to as the methodology section (see the research question example for Vetter, Schieble, & Martin, 2021).

Although formulating research questions is a common practice in discourse analysis, researchers do not typically engage in hypothesis testing. In other words, you will not need to generate hypotheses for your discourse analysis project. Discourse analysis is an exploratory approach to understanding language and communication, and therefore hypotheses add little value to an investigation.

Summary 7.4

1. Research questions must be concise.
2. Research questions must be narrowly focused.
3. Research questions must include familiar keywords.
4. Research questions must identify your object of study.
5. Research questions must identify aspects of your analysis.

7.5 Two Case Studies

The final section will use two case studies to review the main themes and topics of this book. The two case studies that will be used have already been introduced in Section 7.4, so the present discussion will not focus on research questions. Rather, general reflection questions that help readers more thoroughly conceptualize and carry out their own discourse analysis study will be included.

7.5.1 Case Study 1: Topic Maintenance Study

The case study presented in this section is based on the work published by Çimenli, Sert, & Jenks (2022). The title of the publication is "Topic maintenance in video-mediated virtual exchanges: Rolling the ball back in L2 interactions."

In this discourse analysis study, the researchers examine how conversational topics are organized and co-constructed by university students in Turkey and Kazakhstan when conversing online during pair work activities. The study looks specifically at a discourse feature that the researchers call "rolling the ball back," which refers to moments when students use language to maintain a topic that was introduced earlier or is currently being discussed.

The object of study is rolling the ball back, which is simply the language used by students in classrooms. The focus of analysis is how these devices are used by students to manage their conversational topics. Putting yourself in the shoes of these researchers, please think of how you would move from identifying the object of study to planning the analysis. Please use the following questions to guide your reflection.

1. How will you collect examples of your object of study?
2. How many examples are needed?

3. Do you need permission to collect data?
4. Do you need time to learn any skills to collect or analyze this data?
5. Are there any special tools or technology needed to collect data?

The researchers adopted conversation analysis to investigate their object of study. The adoption of conversation analysis means that the researchers are primarily concerned with describing the language use of students. In other words, the perspective of analysis is language use, and the level of analysis is description.

Using the perspective-level figure, which is re-presented here, please consider the following questions that will help you understand what can be done differently analytically for this object of study.

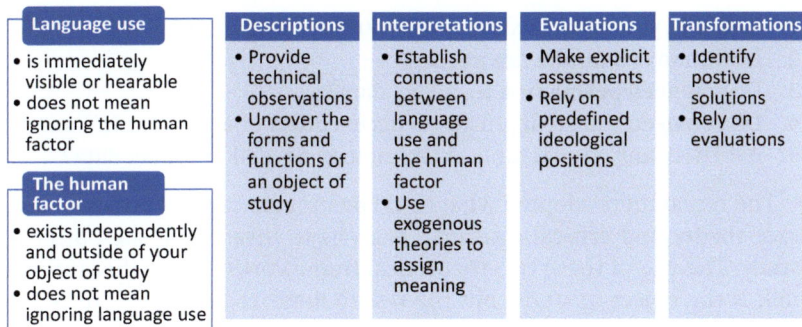

Language use	Descriptions	Interpretations	Evaluations	Transformations
• is immediately visible or hearable • does not mean ignoring the human factor	• Provide technical observations • Uncover the forms and functions of an object of study	• Establish connections between language use and the human factor • Use exogenous theories to assign meaning	• Make explicit assessments • Rely on predefined ideological positions	• Identify postive solutions • Rely on evaluations
The human factor				
• exists independently and outside of your object of study • does not mean ignoring language use				

1. What perspective of analysis would you adopt if investigating rolling the ball back?
2. What reasons motivated you to select this perspective?
3. What level of analysis would you adopt if investigating rolling the ball back?
4. What reasons motivated you to select this level?
5. How would you use your own experiences with student talk to shape your analysis?
6. What pair work activities would allow you to investigate rolling the ball back?
7. Are there any theories that could help you investigate rolling the ball back?
8. What level of analysis is best suited to investigating how students communicate?
9. Can you combine multiple perspectives and levels in your analysis?
10. Is there a particular methodology that you would use in your analysis?

A second case study is introduced to offer additional opportunities to reflect on the themes and topics of this book.

7.5.2 Case Study 2: Critical Talk Study

The case study presented in this section is based on the work published by Vetter, Schieble, & Martin (2021). The title of the publication is "Critical talk moves in critical conversations: Examining power and privilege in an English Language Arts classroom." In this discourse analysis study, the researchers investigate how a teacher manages conversations with students on critical issues such as racism, classism, and sexism. The study looks specifically at a discourse feature that the researchers call "talk moves," which refers to instances when a teacher attempts to facilitate a discussion on critical issues by asking questions to students, providing examples, and sharing personal experiences, to name a few.

The object of study is talk moves, which are examples of the teacher using language. The focus of analysis is talk moves within critical conversations. Putting yourself in the shoes of these researchers, please think of how you would move from identifying the object of study to planning the analysis. Please use the following questions to guide your reflection.

1. How will you collect examples of your object of study?
2. How many examples are needed?
3. Do you need permission to collect data?
4. Do you need time to learn any skills to collect or analyze this data?
5. Are there any special tools or technology needed to collect data?

The researchers adopted what could be broadly categorized as critical race theory and critical discourse analysis to investigate the object of study. The use of these two theoretical frameworks means that teacher talk is the object of study, but the researchers are largely interested in how these examples of "language use" feed into an understanding of "the human factor" (i.e., the importance of, and conversations based on, racism, classism, and sexism).

Using the perspective-level figure, which is re-presented here, please consider the following questions that will help you understand what can be done differently analytically for this object of study.

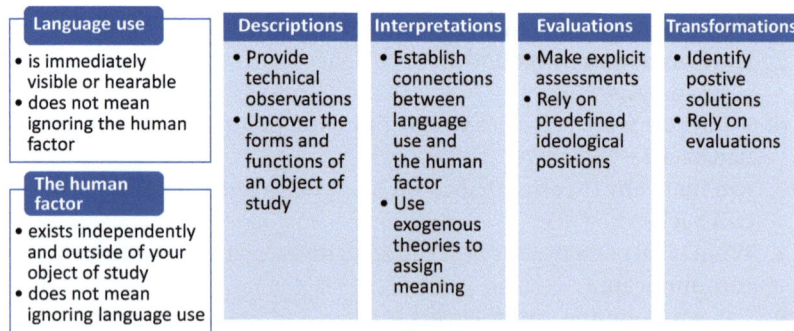

1. What perspective of analysis would you adopt if investigating talk moves?
2. What reasons motivated you to select this perspective?
3. What level of analysis would you adopt if investigating talk moves?
4. What reasons motivated you to select this level?
5. How would you use your own experiences with classrooms to shape your analysis?
6. What classroom contexts would allow you to investigate talk moves?

7. Are there any theories that could help you investigate talk moves?
8. What level of analysis is best suited to investigate how teachers communicate?
9. Can you combine multiple perspectives and levels in your analysis?
10. Is there a particular methodology that you would use in your analysis?

Your answers to these questions should help you understand what is involved in planning an analysis based on an object of study (as well as a research question). Readers interested in reflecting on additional studies can apply these questions to any published discourse analysis paper, including the references included in this book.

Learning Accomplishments

The chapter has summarized the main points established in this book and reviewed how research questions factor into doing discourse analysis. The aim of the chapter was to help you synthesize the different aspects of conducting discourse analysis research into a coherent set of principles. This was done by introducing a practical model for doing discourse analysis.

This section identifies how each learning outcome has been addressed in this chapter.

1. You will be able to recall the mains points of doing discourse analysis;

The chapter established that doing analysis can be broken into two main stages of research: selecting and analyzing an object of study. Selecting an object of study requires knowing what discourse is. Discourse has different meanings and can be found in all domains of life. Selecting an object of study also requires knowing how to collect, organize, and disseminate data, which is a process that is based on a range of practical and theoretical issues. Analyzing an object of study is based on dimensions of research, including perspectives and levels of analysis, setting and context, researcher subjectivities, and applied theories.

2. You will be able to use a model for doing discourse analysis to conduct research;

A practical model for doing discourse analysis views the research process as a series of interrelated steps starting from the selection of an object of study and ending with a consideration of theory. The contents of this book are presented in the order of this practice model for doing discourse analysis.

3. You will know a number of practical tips for doing discourse analysis;

Many practical tips were given to readers planning to conduct research using discourse analysis. This chapter offered ten practical tips, including creating a plan, knowing your object of study, searching the literature, having a research question, letting the data speak for itself, asking for help, avoiding generalizations, connecting with society, leaving time to edit and revise, and dismissing "the more the merrier" approach.

4. You will be able to construct research questions that are relevant to discourse analysis research.

The chapter established that research questions must be concise, focused, and use familiar keywords. Research questions should also reveal your setting or context, perspective and level of analysis, and object of study. It was also established that the wording of research questions, the number of questions asked, and their placement in a report all have implications for how a discourse analysis project is completed and interpreted.

Key Themes

Book Summary

1. Chapters 1 and 2 are devoted to selecting an object of study.
2. Chapters 3 through 6 are devoted to analyzing an object of study.
3. Chapter 7 presents a practical model for doing discourse analysis.
4. Chapter 7 offers ten practical tips for doing discourse analysis.
5. Chapter 7 reviews the importance of research questions in discourse analysis research.

Practical Model for Doing Discourse Analysis

1. A practical model for doing discourse analysis begins with an object of study.
2. A practical model for doing discourse analysis ends with theoretical considerations.
3. A practical model views doing discourse analysis as a series of interrelated steps.
4. A practical model for doing discourse analysis is a practice-first approach to research.
5. A practical model for doing discourse analysis is one of several ways of doing research.

Practical Tips

1. Practical tips are specific to doing discourse analysis research.
2. Practical tips are also based on general research practices.
3. Practical tips must be considered early in the research process.
4. Practical tips do not favor particular approaches or theories.

Research Questions

1. Research questions must be concise.
2. Research questions must be narrowly focused.
3. Research questions must include familiar keywords.
4. Research questions must identify your object of study.
5. Research questions must identify aspects of your analysis.

Reading List

Hesse-Biber (2016) The author provides an extensive and practical overview of doing qualitative research. Although the book is not focused on discourse analysis, many of the tools and methods discussed by the author will be of interest to readers. For example, the author discusses the practices related to conducting interviews and ethnographies. The author also explores the practices of writing qualitative research, which share many practical tips offered in this chapter.

Wetherell, Taylor, & Yates (2001) The authors offer a broad overview of the theory and practice of discourse analysis. The book is organized around research themes, such as cultural and social relations, with each chapter presenting a unique look at a specific example of doing discourse analysis. Chapters require more discourse analysis background knowledge than is required of the next suggested book.

Woods (2006) The book also takes a practice-first approach, privileging practical accounts over theoretical discussions. The chapters are based on different research topics, and thus provide an excellent overview of the practical aspects of doing discourse analysis research. The example topics presented in each chapter guide readers through the research process.

References

Anderson, B. 2016. *Taking-Place: Non-Representational Theories and Geography*. London: Routledge.

Anderson, K. T. 2009. Applying positioning theory to the analysis of classroom interactions: Mediating micro-identities, macro-kinds, and ideologies of knowing. *Linguistics and Education*, 20, 4: 291–310.

Anderson, L. 2006. Analytic autoethnography. *Journal of Contemporary Ethnography*, 35, 4: 373–95.

Antaki, C., Billig, M., Edwards, D, & Potter, J. 2003. Discourse analysis means doing analysis: A critique of six analytic shortcomings. *Discourse Analysis Online*, 1, 1–9.

Appleby, R. 2013. Desire in translation: White masculinity and TESOL. *TESOL Quarterly*, 47, 122–47.

Baker, P., & Ellece, S. 2011. *Key Terms in Discourse Analysis*. London: Continuum.

Bakhtin, M. M. 1981. *The Dialogic Imagination: Four Essays by MM Bakhtin*. University of Texas Press.

Bamberg, M., & Georgakopoulou, A. 2008. Small stories as a new perspective in narrative and identity analysis. *Text & Talk*, 28, 3: 377–96.

Barkhuizen, G. 2014. Revisiting narrative frames: An instrument for investigating language teaching and learning. *System*, 47, 12–27.

Bateson, G. 1972. *Steps to an Ecology of Mind*. New York: Chandler Publishing Company.

Benson, P. 2014. Narrative inquiry in applied linguistics research. *Annual Review of Applied Linguistics*, 34, 154–70

Benwell, B., & Stokoe, E. 2006. *Discourse and Identity*. Edinburgh University Press.

Bhabha, H. K. 2004. *The Location of Culture*. London: Routledge.

Bhatia, A., & Jenks, C. J. 2018. Fabricating the American dream in US media portrayals of Syrian refugees: A discourse analytical study. *Discourse & Communication*, 12, 3: 221–39.

Bhattacharya, U., Jiang, L., & Canagarajah, S. 2020. Race, representation, and diversity in the American Association for Applied Linguistics. *Applied Linguistics*, 41, 6: 999–1004.

Block, D. 2017. Political economy in applied linguistics research. *Language Teaching*, 50, 32–64.

Blommaert, J. 2017. Commentary: Mobility, contexts, and the chronotope. *Language in Society*, 46, 1: 95–9.

Brown, G. & Yule, G. 1983. *Discourse Analysis*. Cambridge University Press.

Chang, H. 2016. *Autoethnography as Method*. London: Routledge.

Chomsky, N. 1999. *Profit over People: Neoliberalism and Global Order*. New York: Seven Stories Press.

Chomsky, N. 2021. Linguistics then and now: Some personal reflections. *Annual Review of Linguistics*, 7, 1–11.

Cicourel, A. V. 1987. The interpenetration of communicative contexts: Examples from medical encounters. *Social Psychology Quarterly*, 50, 2: 217–26.

Çimenli, B., Sert, O., & Jenks, C. 2022. Topic maintenance in video-mediated virtual exchanges: Rolling the ball back in L2 interactions. *System*, 108, 102834.

Collier, J., & Collier, M. 1986. *Visual Anthropology: Photography as a Research Method*. University of New Mexico Press.

Consoli, S., & Ganassin, S. 2023. *Reflexivity in Applied Linguistics: Opportunities, Challenges, and Suggestions*. London: Routledge.

Coupland, N. 2003. Sociolinguistic authenticities. *Journal of Sociolinguistics*, 7, 3: 417–31.

David, G. C., Garcia, A. C., Rawls, A. W., & Chand, D. 2009. Listening to what is said–transcribing what is heard: The impact of speech recognition technology (SRT) on the practice of medical transcription (MT). *Sociology of Health and Illness*, 31, 6: 924–38.

Day, D., & Kjærbeck, S. 2019. Membership categorization and storytelling: The cake story. *Pragmatics and Society*, 10, 3: 359–74.

De Fina, A., & Georgakopoulou, A. 2019. *The Handbook of Narrative Analysis*. Malden, MA: Wiley-Blackwell.

De Fina, A., & Georgakopoulou, A. 2020. *The Cambridge Handbook of Discourse Studies*. Cambridge University Press.

Dong, J., & Blommaert, J. 2009. Space, scale and accents: Constructing migrant identity in Beijing. *Multilingua*, 28, 1–24.

Dunn, K. C., & Neumann, I. B. 2016. *Undertaking Discourse Analysis for Social Research*. University of Michigan Press.

Duranti, A., & Goodwin, C. 1992. (eds.) *Rethinking Context: Language as an Interactive Phenomenon*. Cambridge University Press.

Engward, H., & Goldspink, S. 2020. Lodgers in the house: Living with the data in interpretive phenomenological analysis research. *Reflective Practice*, 21, 1: 41–53.

Fairclough, N. 1989. *Language and Power*. London: Longman.

Fairclough, N. 2010. *Critical Discourse Analysis: The Critical Study of Language*. London: Routledge.

Finlay, L. 2002. "Outing" the research: The provenance, process, and practice of reflexivity. *Qualitative Health Research*, 12, 4: 531–45.

Firth, J. R. 1957. *Papers in Linguistics 1934–1951*. Oxford University Press.

Fitzgerald, R., & Housley, W. 2015. *Advances in Membership Categorization Analysis*. London: SAGE.

Flowerdew, J. 2014. *Discourse in Context*. London: Bloomsbury.

Flyvbjerg, B. 2002. Bringing power to planning research: One researcher's praxis story. *Journal of Planning Education and Research*, 21, 4: 353–66.

Forchtner, B. 2011. Critique, the discourse-historical approach, and the Frankfurt School, *Critical Discourse Studies*, 8, 1: 1–14

Gandhi, L. 2019. *Postcolonial Theory: A Critical Introduction*. New York: Columbia University Press.

Gee, J. P. 2011. *An Introduction to Discourse Analysis: Theory and Method* (3rd edition). London: Routledge.

Gee, J. P. 2014. *How to Do Discourse Analysis: A Toolkit*. New York: Routledge.

Gee, J. P. 2018. *Introducing Discourse Analysis: From Grammar to Society*. New York: Routledge.

Geertz, C. 1973. *The Interpretation of Cultures*. New York: Basic Books.

Giles, H. 2016. *Communication Accommodation Theory: Negotiating Personal Relationships and Social Identities across Contexts*. Cambridge University Press.

Goffman, E. 1981. *Forms of Talk*. University of Philadelphia Press.

Goffman, E. 1986. *Frame Analysis: An Essay on the Organization of Experience*. Northeastern University Press.

Goodwin, C. 1994. Professional vision. *American Anthropologist*, 96, 3: 606–33.

Grice, P. 1991. *Studies in the Way of Words*. Harvard University Press.

Gumperz, J. J. 1982. *Discourse Strategies*. Cambridge University Press.

Gumperz, J. J. 1992. Contextualization and Understanding. In A. Duranti and C. Goodwin (eds.), *Rethinking Context: Language as an Interactive Phenomenon*, 229–52. Cambridge University Press.

Halliday, M. A. K. 1994. *Introduction to Functional Grammar*. London: Arnold.

Halliday, M. A. K., & Hasan, R. 1976. *Cohesion in English*. London: Longman.

Halliday, M. A. K., & Hasan, R. 1989. (eds.), *Language, Context, and Text: Aspects of Language in a Social-Semiotic Perspective*. Oxford University Press.

Halliday, M. A. K., & Matthiessen, C. 2014. *Halliday's Introduction to Functional Grammar*. London: Routledge.

Hammersley, M. 2003. Conversation analysis and discourse analysis: Methods or paradigms? *Discourse and Society*, 14, 6: 751–81.

Hart, C. 2014. *Discourse, Grammar and Ideology: Functional and Cognitive Perspectives*. London: Bloomsbury.

Hart, C. 2020. *Researching Discourse: A Student Guide*. London: Routledge.

Hasan, R. 1989. The Texture of a Text. In M. A. K. Halliday & R. Hasan (eds.), *Language, Context, and Text: Aspects of Language in a Social-Semiotic Perspective*, 70–96. Oxford University Press.

Hellawell, D. 2006. Inside-out: Analysis of the insider-outsider concept as a heuristic device to develop reflexivity in students doing qualitative research. *Teaching in Higher Education*, 11, 4: 483–94.

Henwood, K. 2007. Beyond hypercriticality: Taking forward methodological inquiry and debate in discursive and qualitative social psychology. *Discourse Studies*, 9, 2: 270–5.

Herzog, B. 2018. Marx's critique of ideology for discourse analysis: From analysis of ideologies to social critique. *Critical Discourse Studies*, 15, 4: 402–13.

Hesse-Biber, S. N. 2016. *The Practice of Qualitative Research: Engaging Students in the Research Process*. London: SAGE.

Holt, E. 2007. "I'm eyeing your chop up mind": Reporting and enacting. In E. Holt & R. Clift (eds.), *Reporting Talk: Reported Speech in Interaction*, 47–80. Cambridge University Press.

Hyland, K., & Paltridge, B. 2011. *Continuum Companion to Discourse Analysis*. London: Continuum.

Hymes, D. 1972. Models of the interaction of language and social life. In J. J. Gumperz & D. Hymes (eds.), *Directions in Sociolinguistics: The Ethnography of Communication*, 35–71. New York: Holt, Rinehart and Winston.

Jaworski, A. 2014. Metrolingual art: Multilingualism and heteroglossia. *International Journal of Bilingualism*, 18, 2: 134–58.

Jaworski, A., & Coupland, N. 2014. *The Discourse Reader*. London: Routledge.

Jenks, C. J. 2011. *Transcribing Talk and Interaction: Issues in the Representation of Communication Data*. Amsterdam: John Benjamins.

Jenks, C. J. 2013. Working with transcripts: An abridged review of issues in transcription. *Language and Linguistics Compass*, 7, 4: 251–61.

Jenks, C. J. 2017. *Race and Ethnicity in English Language Teaching: Korea in Focus*. Bristol: Multilingual Matters.

Jenks, C. J., & Lee, J. W. 2016. Heteroglossic ideologies in world Englishes: An examination of the Hong Kong context. *International Journal of Applied Linguistics*, 26, 3: 384–402.

Jenks, C. J., & Lee, J. 2020. Native speaker saviorism: A racialized teaching ideology. *Critical Inquiry in Language Studies*, 17, 3: 186–205.

Jones, S. H., Adams, T. E., & Ellis, C. 2013. *Handbook of Autoethnography*. London: Routledge.

Johnstone, B. 2018. *Discourse Analysis*. Malden, MA: Wiley-Blackwell.

Keller, R. 2011. The sociology of knowledge approach to discourse. *Human Studies*, 34, 43–65.

Kern, F. 2007. Prosody as a resource in children's game explanations: Some aspects of turn construction and recipiency. *Journal of Pragmatics*, 39, 1: 111–33.

Kress, G., & van Leeuwen, T. 2001. *Multimodal Discourse: The Modes and Media of Contemporary Communication*. London: Arnold.

Kroskrity, P. V. 2018. On recognizing persistence in the indigenous language ideologies of multilingualism in two Native American Communities. *Language and Communication*, 62, B: 133–44.

Kubota, R. 2020. Confronting epistemological racism, decolonizing scholarly knowledge: Race and gender in applied linguistics. *Applied Linguistics*, 41, 5: 712–32.

Ladyman, J. 2002. *Understanding Philosophy of Science*. London: Routledge.

Lazar, M. M. 2005. *Feminist Critical Discourse Analysis: Gender, Power and Ideology in Discourse*. Basingstoke: Palgrave Macmillan.

Lee, J. W. 2014. Transnational linguistic landscapes and the transgression of metadiscursive regimes of language. *Critical Inquiry in Language Studies*, 11, 1: 50–74.

Lempert, M., & Summerson Carr, E. 2016. *Scale: Discourse and Dimensions of Social Life*. University of California Press.

Liddicoat, A. J. 2007. *An Introduction to Conversation Analysis*. London: Continuum.

Lynch, M. 2000. The ethnomethodological foundations of conversation analysis. *Text and Talk*, 20, 4: 517–32.

Lynch, M. 2016. Social constructivism in science and technology studies. *Human Studies*, 101–12.

Malinowski, B. 1923. The Problem of Meaning in Primitive Languages. In C. K. Ogden & I. A. Richards (eds.), *The Meaning of Meaning*, 296–336. London: Harcourt-Brace.

Maynard, D. W., & Clayman, S. E. 1991. The diversity of ethnomethodology. *Annual Review of Sociology*, 17, 385–418.

McCarthy, M. 1991. *Discourse Analysis for Language Teachers*. Cambridge University Press.

McGee, R. J., & Warms, R. L. 2013. *Theory in Social and Cultural Anthropology: An Encyclopedia*. London: SAGE.

Moerman, M. 1988. *Talking Culture: Ethnography and Conversation Analysis*. University of Pennsylvania Press.

Mondada, L. 2018. Multiple temporalities of language and body in interaction: Challenges for transcribing multimodality. *Research on Language and Social Interaction*, 51, 1: 85–106.

Moore, E. 2006. "You tell all the stories": Using narrative to explore hierarchy within a Community of Practice. *Journal of Sociolinguistics*, 10, 5: 611–40.

Moore, R. 2020. Registers, styles, indexicality. In A. de Fina & A. Georgakopoulou (eds.), *The Cambridge Handbook of Discourse Studies*, 9–31. Cambridge University Press.

Morrow, R. A., & Torres, C. A. 2002. *Reading Freire and Habermas: Critical Pedagogy and Transformative Social Change*. New York: Teachers College Press.

Nikander, P. 2008. Constructionism and discourse analysis. In J. A. Holstein & J. F. Gubrium (eds.), *Handbook of Constructionist Research*, 413–28. New York: The Guilford Press.

Norris. S. 2019. *Systematically Working with Multimodal Data*. Malden, MA: Wiley-Blackwell.

Norris, S., & Jones, R. H. 2005. *Discourse in Action: Introducing Mediated Discourse Analysis*. London: Routledge.

O'Halloran, K. L. 2004. *Multimodal Discourse Analysis: Systemic-Functional Perspectives*. London: Continuum.

O'Keeffe, A., & McCarthy, M. 2010. *The Routledge Handbook of Corpus Linguistics*. London: Routledge.

Paltridge, B. 2021. *Discourse Analysis: An Introduction*. London: Bloomsbury.

Park, Y. S., Konge, L., & Artino, A. R. 2020. The positivism paradigm of research. *Academic Medicine*, 95, 5: 690–694.

Pavlenko, A. 2007. Autobiographic narratives as data in applied linguistics. *Applied Linguistics*, 28, 163–188.

Pellegrini, A. D., Brody, G. H., & Stoneman, Z. 1987. Children's conversational competence with their parents. *Discourse Processes*, 10, 1: 93–106.

Pike, K. L. 1967. *Language in Relation to a Unified Theory of the Structure of Human Behavior*. The Hague: Mouton.

Pike, K. L. 1990. On the Emics and Etics of Pike and Harris. In T. N. Headland, K. L. Pike, & M. Harris (eds.), *Emics and Etics: The Insider/Outsider Debate*, 28–47. London: SAGE.

Pink, S. 2006. *The Future of Visual Anthropology: Engaging the Senses*. London: Routledge.

Rafalovich, A. 2006. Making sociology relevant: The assignment and application of breaching experiments. *Teaching Sociology*, 34, 2: 156–63.

Sacks, H. 1992. *Lectures on Conversation*. Volumes 1 and 2. Oxford: Basil Blackwell.

Schegloff, E. A. 2007. *Sequence Organization in Interaction: A Primer in Conversation Analysis*. Cambridge University Press.

Scollon, R. 2001. *Mediated Discourse: The Nexus of Practice*. London: Routledge.

Scollon, R., & Scollon, S. W. 2003. *Discourse Places: Language in the Material World*. London: Routledge.

Searle, J. R. 1976. A classification of illocutionary acts. *Language in Society*, 5, 1: 1–23.

Silva, D. N., & Lee, J. W. 2021. "Marielle, presente": Metaleptic temporality and the enregisterment of hope in Rio de Janeiro. *Journal of Sociolinguistics*, 25, 2: 179–97.

Spencer, S. 2006. *Race and Ethnicity: Culture, Identity and Representation*. London: Routledge.

Stryker, S., & Serpe, R. T. 1982. Commitment, Identity Salience, and Role Behavior: Theory and Research Example. In W. Ickes & E. Knowles (eds.), *Personality, Roles, and Social Behavior*, 199–218. New York: Springer.

Sunderland, J. 2010. Research Questions in Linguistics. In L. Litosseliti (ed.), *Research Methods in Linguistics*, 9–28. London: Continuum.

Swales, J. M. 1990. *Genre Analysis*. Cambridge University Press.

ten Have, P. 2005. The notion of member is the heart of the matter: On the role of membership knowledge in ethnomethodological inquiry. *Historical Social Research*, 30, 1: 28–53.

Thurlow, C., & Jaworski, A. 2006. The alchemy of the upwardly mobile: Symbolic capital and the stylization of elites in frequent-flyer programmes. *Discourse and Society*, 17, 1: 99–135.

van Dijk, T. A. 1993. Principles of critical discourse analysis. *Discourse and Society*, 4, 2: 249–83.

van Dijk, T. A. 2006. Ideology and discourse analysis. *Journal of Political Ideologies*, 11, 2: 115–40.

van Dijk, T. A. 2009. *Society and Discourse: How Social Contexts Influence Text and Talk*. Cambridge University Press.

Vetter, A., Schieble, M., & Martin, K. M. 2021. Critical talk moves in critical conversations: examining power and privilege in an English

Language Arts classroom. *English in Education*, 55, 4: 313–36.

Waring, H. Z. 2007. The multi-functionality of accounts in advice giving. *Journal of Sociolinguistics*, 11, 3: 367–91.

Waring, H. Z. 2017. *Discourse Analysis: The Questions Discourse Analysts Ask and How They Answer Them* (1st edition). London: Routledge.

Wenger, E. 1998. *Communities of Practice: Learning, Meaning, and Identity*. Cambridge University Press.

Wetherell, M., Taylor, S., & Yates, S. J. 2001. *Discourse Theory and Practice: A Reader*. London: SAGE and Milton Keynes: The Open University.

Williams, G. 2014. *French Discourse Analysis: The Method of Post-Structuralism*. London: Routledge.

Wodak, R. 1989. *Language, Power and Ideology: Studies in Political Discourse*. Amsterdam: John Benjamins.

Wodak, R., & Chilton, P. 2005. *A New Agenda in (Critical) Discourse Analysis*. Amsterdam: John Benjamins.

Woods, N. 2006. *Describing Discourse: A Practical Guide to Discourse Analysis*. London: Routledge.

Wooffitt, R. 2005. *Conversation Analysis and Discourse Analysis*. London: SAGE.

Yang, G., & Ryser, T. A. 2008. Whiting up and Blacking out: White privilege, race, and White chicks. *African American Review*, 42, 3/4: 731–46.

Żuk, P., & Żuk, P. 2020. 'Murderers of the unborn' and 'sexual degenerates': Analysis of the 'anti-gender' discourse of the Catholic Church and the nationalist right in Poland. *Critical Discourse Studies*, 17, 5: 566–88.

Index